D0532137

American
Attitudes

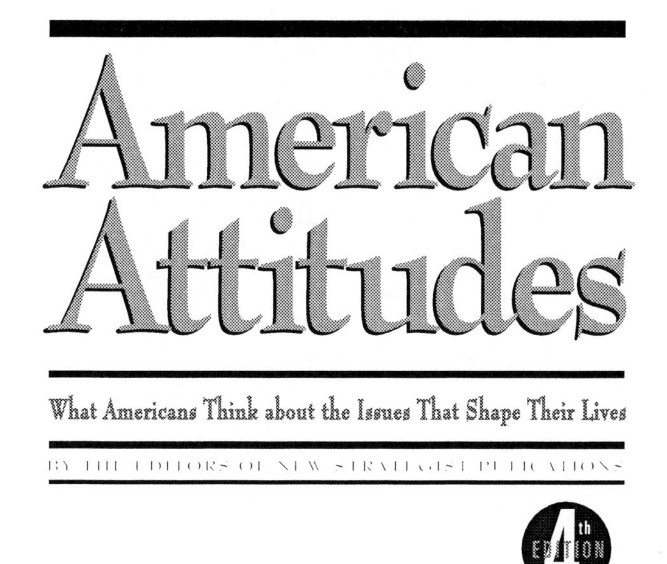

New Strategist Publications, Inc.
Ithaca, New York

New Strategist Publications, Inc.
P.O. Box 242, Ithaca, New York 14851
800/848-0842; 607/273-0913
www.newstrategist.com

ISBN 1-885070-43-8

Printed in the United States of America

Table of Contents

List of Tables

Chapter 1. General Social Survey Core Questions

Abortion

Confidence in Institutions

Family Type and Mobility

Funding to Solve Problems

Women and Work

Introduction

Change has been a constant in the United States for more than two-hundred years. New technologies have radically altered the way we live and work. The traditional household of the 1950s has fractured into dual-income families, single parents, and single persons. We are more racially and ethnically diverse than ever before.

It is no surprise, then, that over the past thirty years Americans have changed their minds about many issues. Some of the biggest changes pertain to opinions about race and the roles of women. Thirty years ago, far more Americans believed in separate societies for blacks and whites and separate spheres for men and women. Since then, many people have changed their minds about these issues. Generational replacement has also resulted in changing attitudes as younger generations with different attitudes have replaced older generations with more traditional perspectives toward race, women's roles, homosexuality, and other issues.

While the public has changed its mind about some things, there has been remarkably little change on many other issues. Most Americans still say they are at least "pretty happy," most of the married say their marriage is "very happy," most rate their health as "good" or "excellent." Religion remains highly important to the majority, although religious diversity has increased. Most people still support the death penalty, and most support abortion in some—but not all—circumstances.

The fourth edition of *American Attitudes: What Americans Think about the Issues That Shape Their Lives* is a unique reference book, chronicling the changes and consistencies in the attitudes of the public over the past thirty years. The source of the data presented in *American Attitudes* is the nation's premier attitudinal survey—the General Social Survey of the University of Chicago's National Opinion Research Center. NORC is the oldest non-profit, university affiliated national survey research facility in the nation. It conducts the GSS through face-to-face interviews with an independently drawn, representative sample of 1,500 to 3,000 noninstitutionalized English-speaking people aged 18 or older living in the United States. NORC fielded the first GSS in 1972, conducted it annually through 1994 (except for the years 1979, 1981, and 1992), and now conducts the survey every two years.

The GSS data presented in *American Attitudes* are not readily available to the public. While the GSS is frequently used by social scientists to study trends, the results are not published comprehensively or regularly. Most GSS analysis appears in academic papers and journals not accessible to the general public. *American Attitudes* brings the results of the General Social Survey, its historical trends and 2002 data, into the hands of the public, giving students, reporters, marketers, policymakers, and other researchers a chance to explore its findings.

The fourth edition of *American Attitudes* is organized into two sections: historical and topical. The historical section (General Social Survey Core Questions) reveals public opinion on most of the questions that have been asked by the survey repeatedly over the past thirty years and were also included in the 2002 survey. Some of the questions in the historical section were first asked in 1972, while others were introduced in later years. Within this section, questions are organized alphabetically by broad topical area such as abortion, the role of government, and sexual attitudes and behavior.

The topical section presents responses to most of the questions included in the topical modules of the 2002 GSS. Again, the tables are organized alphabetically by topic, from altruism to quality of working life. The 2002 GSS also included two International Social Survey Program modules, and responses to those questions appear in this section as well (social relations; women and work).

The exact wording of each GSS question, as presented to respondents by survey interviewers, is shown at the top of each table. Tables also show the size of the sample being asked each question and the percentage distribution of responses. The historical tables show responses for each year a question was asked, from 1972 at the earliest through 2002. The topical section shows responses to the 2002 topical modules. A few topical tables include data from earlier years if the same question was asked before.

For more information about the General Social Survey, contact the National Opinion Research Center at the University of Chicago; telephone (773) 753-7500; or Internet http://www.norc.uchicago.edu. The Roper Center for Public Opinion Research in Storrs, Connecticut, distributes GSS data; Internet site http://www.ropercenter.uconn.edu/.

About the General Social Survey

by Tom W. Smith
Director of the General Social Survey
National Opinion Research Center
University of Chicago

The National Data Program for the Social Sciences of the National Opinion Research Center (NORC) at the University of Chicago is a social indicators and data diffusion program. Its basic purposes are 1) to gather and disseminate data on contemporary American society in order to monitor and explain social trends and constants in attitudes, behaviors, and attributes, and to examine the structure and functioning of society in general as well as the role of various subgroups; 2) to compare the United States to other societies in order to place American society in comparative perspective, and to develop cross-national models of human society; and 3) to make high-quality data easily and quickly available to scholars, students, policy makers, and others.

These purposes are accomplished by the regular collection and distribution of the NORC General Social Survey (GSS) and its allied surveys in the International Social Survey Program (ISSP).

Origins of the General Social Survey

James A. Davis, then at Dartmouth College, drew on two intellectual currents of the 1960s to conceive the GSS. First, the social indicators movement was stressing the importance of measuring trends and adding noneconomic measures to the large repertoire of national accounts indices. Second, scholarly egalitarianism was advocating that data be available to scientists at all universities and not restricted to an elite of senior investigators at large research centers and laboratories. In 1971 Davis put these ideas together in a modest proposal to the National Science Foundation (NSF) for "twentysome questions" that called for the periodic asking of a number of social indicators on national samples with these data immediately distributed to the social science community for analysis and teaching. Approval from NSF plus supplemental funding from the Russell Sage Foundation spawned the first GSS in 1972.

Growth of the General Social Survey

Since 1972 the GSS has conducted twenty-four independent, cross-sectional, in-person surveys of adults living in households in the United States and in 1982 and 1987 carried out oversamples of black Americans. A total of 42,991 respondents have been interviewed in the cross-sections and 707 black respondents in the oversamples. During most years there have been annual surveys of about 1,500 respondents. Currently 3,000 cases are collected in a biennial, double-sample GSS.

In addition, since 1982 the GSS has expanded internationally. A growing number of countries have established GSS-like programs, and we have formed ties to these counterparts. The cross-national research also started modestly with a bilateral collaboration between the GSS and the Allbus of the Zentrum für Umfragen, Methoden, und Analysen in Germany in 1982 and 1984. Then in 1984 the GSS and the Allbus joined with the British Social Attitudes Survey of the National Centre for Social Research in London and the National Social Science Survey at Australian National University to form the ISSP. Along with Eurisko in Italy and the University of Graz in Austria, the founding four fielded the first ISSP in 1985. An ISSP survey has collected data annually since then, and there are now thirty-nine member countries (the founding four plus Austria, Brazil, Bulgaria, Canada, Chile, the Czech Republic, Cyprus, Denmark, Finland, Flanders, France, Hungary, Ireland, Israel, Italy, Japan, Korea (South), Latvia, Mexico, the Netherlands, New Zealand, Norway, the Philippines, Poland, Portugal, Russia, Slovakia, Slovenia, South Africa, Spain, Sweden, Switzerland, Taiwan, Uruguay, and Venezuela).

Content of the General Social Survey

The GSS lives up to its first name of being general. The 4,220 variables in the 1972–2002 cumulative file run from legal abortion if a woman wants one for any reason to behavioral medication for children and have major core batteries on such topics as civil liberties, confidence in institutions, crime and violence, feminism, governmental spending priorities, psychological wellbeing, race relations, and work.

While the balance of components has changed over the years, currently half of the GSS is a replicating core, one sixth cross-national (i.e., the ISSP questions), and one-third in-depth topical modules. Recent ISSP modules include the environment, gender and work, national identity, and the role of government (social welfare, economic regulation, civil liberties). Recent topical modules include work organizations, culture, multiculturalism, emotions, gender, mental health, market exchanges, giving and volunteering, altruism, Internet use, and genetics.

Research Opportunities

The GSS's design greatly facilitates several important types of research. First, the replication of items allows the study of social change. Moreover, since all surveys and all variables are organized in one cumulative file, one does not have to patch together time series from numerous different and often incompatible data sets. One merely asks for cross-tabulations or correlations and over 1,400 trends can be tracked.

Second, replication also means that subgroups can be pooled across surveys to aggregate an adequate sample for analysis. For example, blacks at about 12 percent of the population account for about 175 respondents in a 1,500-case GSS—too few for detailed analysis. But in the 1972–2002 surveys there are 6,017 blacks—more than enough for analysis.

Third, one can both track trends and pool cases. For example, blacks from the 1970s, 1980s, 1990s, and 2000s can be combined to have four time points and still have between 834 and 2,208 black respondents in each subsample.

Fourth, the seventeen ISSP studies (1985–2004) offer the largest and most readily accessible body of cross-national social science data available. Moreover, keeping with the GSS's core interest in social trends the ISSP's also have an across-time component. For example, the first module on role of government from 1985 was repeated in 1990 and 1996; the 1987 social inequality bloc was refielded in 1992 and 1999; the women-and-work module has been asked in 1988, 1994, and 2002. Thus, the GSS / ISSP has both a cross-national and a cross-time perspective.

Finally, because the GSS employs a detailed and extensive set of demographics, in-depth analysis of background influences is possible. For example, the GSS doesn't just have a measure of education, but eight standard measures—the exact number of years of schooling completed and the highest degree obtained for respondents, their mothers, their fathers, and spouses. For occupation, the GSS has three-digit Census codes, International Standard Classification of Occupation codes, NORC-GSS prestige scores, and Duncan SEI values for respondents, parents, and spouses.

Impact on the Social Sciences

As the largest and longest-running project funded by the Sociology Program of NSF, the GSS has had a tremendous impact on social science research in the United States. The 2004 bibliography documents over 8,500 uses of the GSS and new usages are accumulating at over 600 per year. Among the top sociology journals (*American Journal of Sociology, American Sociological Review, Social Forces*), the GSS is second only to the Census / Current Population Survey in frequency of use.

The GSS has also had a large influence on college teaching. Hundreds of thousands have learned about American society and / or research methodology in courses built around the GSS. For example, MicroCase has developed more than a dozen textbooks in sociology, criminology, political science, and statistics built around the GSS and texts by Earl Babbie (*Adventure in Social Research, The Practice of Social Research*) include diskettes with GSS subsets.These GSS-centric courses have allowed students to learn about society through hands-on analysis of fresh, high-quality, relevant data.

Conclusion

The National Academy of Science has aptly described the GSS as a "national resource." The NSF has called it a "public utility for the community at large," and the American Sociology Association has labeled it as "rigorous and exceptionally useful."

The GSS is grounded in the past, but growing to the future. It joins together replication and innovation, incorporates both the social change and comparative perspectives, and combines patrician quality standards with plebeian dissemination. Through these synergies it has and will continue to serve the social science communities and others.

CHAPTER

1

General Social Survey Core Questions

The General Social Survey consists of three types of questions: core questions asked in most surveys, topical modules with questions that probe certain subjects and change from survey to survey, and cross-national questions that are included in surveys in dozens of other countries—allowing for international comparison.

The replicating core questions comprise about half the GSS questions in any given year. Their topics range from abortion to the death penalty, from race relations to the government's role in providing help for the sick. The American public has been asked the same questions in the same way year after year, with many questions dating back to the early 1970s. The resulting responses track both change and stability in public opinion over the decades.

Abortion

Most Americans favor a woman's right to obtain an abortion under certain circumstances, and opinions regarding abortion have changed surprisingly little over the past few decades. Americans have always been least likely to support abortion for "any reason." In 2002, 56 percent opposed it and 42 percent favored it. These figures have not changed much over the past two decades.

Americans are most likely to support abortion if a woman's health is seriously endangered by a pregnancy. In this situation, 90 percent of the public supports a woman's right to an abortion. Only 8 percent oppose it. Again, these figures have changed little over the past three decades.

The majority of the public also supports abortion if there is a chance of serious defect in the baby (76 percent) and in the case of rape (78 percent). The majority opposes abortion if a married woman wants no more children (54 percent), if a low-income woman cannot support more children (54 percent), and if a pregnant woman is unmarried (56 percent).

The only significant shift in public opinion toward abortion over the past three decades is greater opposition to allowing abortion for low-income women who cannot afford more children. In 2002, the 54 percent majority of the public was against abortion in this circumstance while 43 percent supported it. In 1974, the figures were 43 percent against and 52 percent in favor.

Table 1.1 Abortion for Any Reason, 1977 to 2002

Do you think it should be possible for a pregnant woman to obtain a legal abortion if the woman wants it for any reason?

(number of respondents aged 18 or older, and percent distribution by response, 1977–2002)

	number of respondents	total	yes	no	don't know
2002	923	100.0%	41.9%	55.6%	2.5%
2000	1,855	100.0	38.0	57.3	4.7
1998	1,876	100.0	38.8	56.0	5.2
1996	1,915	100.0	42.8	52.3	4.9
1994	1,990	100.0	45.0	52.2	2.8
1993	1,069	100.0	42.8	51.6	5.5
1991	986	100.0	41.1	55.4	3.5
1990	913	100.0	41.7	54.3	3.9
1989	1,028	100.0	38.8	57.4	3.8
1988	973	100.0	34.7	61.5	3.8
1987	1,807	100.0	38.6	57.2	4.2
1985	1,529	100.0	35.8	61.1	3.1
1984	1,462	100.0	37.5	59.6	2.9
1983	1,565	100.0	33.2	63.6	3.2
1982	1,852	100.0	38.9	56.8	4.3
1980	1,465	100.0	39.5	56.5	4.0
1978	1,527	100.0	32.4	64.8	2.8
1977	1,523	100.0	36.6	60.5	2.9

Source: General Social Surveys, National Opinion Research Center, University of Chicago; calculations by New Strategist

Table 1.2 Abortion If Chance of Serious Defect in Baby, 1972 to 2002

Do you think it should be possible for a pregnant woman to obtain a legal abortion if there is a strong chance of serious defect in the baby?

(number of respondents aged 18 or older, and percent distribution by response, 1972–2002)

	number of respondents	total	yes	no	don't know
2002	920	100.0%	76.4%	21.0%	2.6%
2000	1,857	100.0	75.2	20.3	4.5
1998	1,879	100.0	75.3	20.5	4.2
1996	1,916	100.0	79.0	17.5	3.4
1994	1,994	100.0	79.5	17.1	3.4
1993	1,070	100.0	78.5	18.0	3.5
1991	985	100.0	80.0	15.8	4.2
1990	915	100.0	78.1	18.0	3.8
1989	1,029	100.0	78.6	18.1	3.3
1988	975	100.0	76.3	20.5	3.2
1987	1,811	100.0	77.3	19.4	3.3
1985	1,531	100.0	76.2	20.8	2.9
1984	1,465	100.0	77.8	19.2	3.0
1983	1,567	100.0	76.2	20.4	3.4
1982	1,855	100.0	81.6	14.6	3.8
1980	1,467	100.0	80.4	16.4	3.3
1978	1,528	100.0	80.3	17.7	2.0
1977	1,524	100.0	83.4	14.2	2.4
1976	1,495	100.0	81.8	15.7	2.5
1975	1,487	100.0	80.4	16.3	3.3
1974	1,484	100.0	82.6	14.4	3.0
1973	1,500	100.0	82.5	15.1	2.4
1972	1,607	100.0	74.6	20.3	5.0

Source: General Social Surveys, National Opinion Research Center, University of Chicago; calculations by New Strategist

Table 1.3 Abortion If Woman's Health Is Seriously Endangered, 1972 to 2002

Do you think it should be possible for a pregnant woman to obtain a legal abortion if the woman's own health is seriously endangered by the pregnancy?

(number of respondents aged 18 or older, and percent distribution by response, 1972–2002)

	number of respondents	total	yes	no	don't know
2002	922	100.0%	89.5%	8.2%	2.3%
2000	1,857	100.0	85.1	11.0	3.9
1998	1,879	100.0	84.0	11.6	4.4
1996	1,915	100.0	88.5	8.1	3.4
1994	1,993	100.0	88.0	9.1	3.0
1993	1,071	100.0	86.2	9.8	4.0
1991	986	100.0	88.6	8.2	3.1
1990	914	100.0	89.1	8.0	3.0
1989	1,027	100.0	88.0	9.6	2.3
1988	974	100.0	85.8	10.9	3.3
1987	1,814	100.0	85.6	11.2	3.3
1985	1,531	100.0	87.0	10.4	2.6
1984	1,462	100.0	87.6	10.3	2.1
1983	1,567	100.0	87.0	10.0	3.0
1982	1,855	100.0	89.2	8.2	2.6
1980	1,466	100.0	87.9	9.6	2.5
1978	1,528	100.0	88.5	9.2	2.4
1977	1,522	100.0	88.5	9.3	2.2
1976	1,492	100.0	89.1	9.0	1.9
1975	1,487	100.0	88.4	9.1	2.6
1974	1,484	100.0	90.4	7.4	2.2
1973	1,502	100.0	90.7	7.6	1.7
1972	1,605	100.0	83.4	12.5	4.1

Source: General Social Surveys, National Opinion Research Center, University of Chicago; calculations by New Strategist

Table 1.4 Abortion If Married Woman Wants No More Children, 1972 to 2002

Do you think it should be possible for a pregnant woman to obtain a legal abortion if she is married and does not want any more children?

(number of respondents aged 18 or older, and percent distribution by response, 1972–2002)

	number of respondents	total	yes	no	don't know
2002	922	100.0%	43.4%	53.5%	3.1%
2000	1,855	100.0	38.8	56.6	4.6
1998	1,877	100.0	40.4	55.0	4.6
1996	1,916	100.0	44.5	50.7	4.7
1994	1,990	100.0	46.7	50.0	3.3
1993	1,070	100.0	44.9	50.4	4.8
1991	986	100.0	43.0	53.3	3.7
1990	912	100.0	43.4	53.0	3.6
1989	1,028	100.0	42.9	53.5	3.6
1988	975	100.0	38.9	58.5	2.7
1987	1,811	100.0	41.1	55.5	3.4
1985	1,529	100.0	39.2	58.1	2.7
1984	1,463	100.0	41.4	55.6	2.9
1983	1,569	100.0	37.7	59.1	3.1
1982	1,855	100.0	45.8	49.4	4.8
1980	1,465	100.0	45.3	50.8	4.0
1978	1,529	100.0	39.1	57.9	3.0
1977	1,523	100.0	44.6	51.3	4.0
1976	1,493	100.0	44.7	52.2	3.1
1975	1,488	100.0	43.8	52.0	4.2
1974	1,484	100.0	44.6	50.5	4.9
1973	1,502	100.0	46.1	50.6	3.3
1972	1,608	100.0	37.7	57.3	5.0

Source: General Social Surveys, National Opinion Research Center, University of Chicago; calculations by New Strategist

Table 1.5 Abortion If Low-Income Woman Cannot Afford More Children, 1972 to 2002

Do you think it should be possible for a pregnant woman to obtain a legal abortion if the family has a very low income and cannot afford any more children?

(number of respondents aged 18 or older, and percent distribution by response, 1972–2002)

	number of respondents	total	yes	no	don't know
2002	921	100.0%	43.0%	53.9%	3.1%
2000	1,854	100.0	40.4	55.2	4.4
1998	1,878	100.0	42.0	52.9	5.1
1996	1,916	100.0	44.5	51.0	4.5
1994	1,993	100.0	48.7	47.9	3.4
1993	1,070	100.0	47.5	47.8	4.8
1991	985	100.0	46.5	49.4	4.1
1990	912	100.0	45.6	49.2	5.2
1989	1,028	100.0	46.0	50.5	3.5
1988	975	100.0	40.5	56.0	3.5
1987	1,813	100.0	44.3	52.1	3.5
1985	1,530	100.0	42.5	54.8	2.7
1984	1,459	100.0	44.8	52.1	3.1
1983	1,568	100.0	42.0	54.1	3.9
1982	1,852	100.0	48.7	47.2	4.2
1980	1,466	100.0	49.7	46.4	4.0
1978	1,528	100.0	45.5	50.6	3.9
1977	1,522	100.0	51.8	45.3	2.9
1976	1,491	100.0	51.0	45.1	3.8
1975	1,485	100.0	50.7	44.6	4.6
1974	1,482	100.0	52.4	43.3	4.4
1973	1,502	100.0	51.8	45.1	3.1
1972	1,605	100.0	45.8	48.1	6.1

Source: General Social Surveys, National Opinion Research Center, University of Chicago; calculations by New Strategist

Table 1.6 Abortion in Case of Rape, 1972 to 2002

Do you think it should be possible for a pregnant woman to obtain a legal abortion if she became pregnant as a result of rape?

(number of respondents aged 18 or older, and percent distribution by response, 1972–2002)

	number of respondents	total	yes	no	don't know
2002	924	100.0%	78.0%	19.9%	2.1%
2000	1,855	100.0	76.0	18.3	5.7
1998	1,879	100.0	76.6	19.0	4.4
1996	1,916	100.0	80.9	15.1	4.0
1994	1,994	100.0	81.0	15.9	3.0
1993	1,071	100.0	79.4	16.3	4.3
1991	986	100.0	82.9	13.0	4.2
1990	912	100.0	81.1	14.6	4.3
1989	1,028	100.0	80.3	16.1	3.6
1988	974	100.0	76.9	18.0	5.1
1987	1,811	100.0	77.3	18.6	4.1
1985	1,531	100.0	78.2	18.1	3.7
1984	1,463	100.0	77.2	18.9	3.9
1983	1,567	100.0	79.5	16.5	4.0
1982	1,852	100.0	83.0	12.9	4.1
1980	1,465	100.0	80.3	16.0	3.7
1978	1,526	100.0	80.7	16.3	2.9
1977	1,521	100.0	80.9	15.6	3.4
1976	1,492	100.0	80.8	15.8	3.5
1975	1,487	100.0	80.0	15.6	4.4
1974	1,482	100.0	82.9	13.0	4.2
1973	1,501	100.0	80.7	15.9	3.3
1972	1,604	100.0	74.6	19.7	5.7

Source: General Social Surveys, National Opinion Research Center, University of Chicago; calculations by New Strategist

Table 1.7 Abortion If a Woman Is Unmarried, 1972 to 2002

Do you think it should be possible for a pregnant woman to obtain a legal abortion if she is not married and does not want to marry the man?

(number of respondents aged 18 or older, and percent distribution by response, 1972–2002)

	number of respondents	total	yes	no	don't know
2002	922	100.0%	40.8%	56.3%	2.9%
2000	1,855	100.0	37.3	58.0	4.7
1998	1,877	100.0	40.3	55.0	4.6
1996	1,912	100.0	43.0	52.8	4.2
1994	1,990	100.0	46.4	51.0	2.6
1993	1,070	100.0	45.6	49.2	5.2
1991	986	100.0	43.2	53.1	3.7
1990	913	100.0	43.3	52.2	4.5
1989	1,028	100.0	43.5	52.3	4.2
1988	973	100.0	37.7	58.1	4.2
1987	1,812	100.0	40.8	55.6	3.6
1985	1,529	100.0	40.0	57.2	2.8
1984	1,462	100.0	43.0	54.2	2.9
1983	1,566	100.0	37.5	57.8	4.7
1982	1,854	100.0	46.2	49.0	4.7
1980	1,466	100.0	46.4	49.4	4.2
1978	1,528	100.0	39.7	56.7	3.6
1977	1,523	100.0	47.7	48.1	4.2
1976	1,494	100.0	48.4	47.9	3.7
1975	1,485	100.0	45.9	49.3	4.8
1974	1,484	100.0	47.9	47.8	4.3
1973	1,499	100.0	47.5	49.2	3.3
1972	1,605	100.0	40.7	52.8	6.4

Source: General Social Surveys, National Opinion Research Center, University of Chicago; calculations by New Strategist

Confidence in Institutions

Americans' confidence in most public institutions has fallen over the past few decades, rocked by scandals in the oval office, in corporate boardrooms, and in the church. Confidence in the leaders of organized religion has fallen to a historic low. Only 19 percent of the public said they had a "great deal of confidence" in organized religion in 2002, down from a high of 44 percent who felt that way in 1974. Twenty-four percent of the public say they have "hardly any confidence" in organized religion.

Confidence in the people running major companies has also plummeted, thanks to the collapse of Enron and other corporate scandals. In 2002, just 17 percent of the public said they had a great deal of confidence in corporations, down from a high of 31 percent in 1974.

Other institutions that have experienced a decline in confidence over the past few decades include financial institutions, education, medicine, television, and the press. In 2002, only 9.5 percent of the public said they had a great deal of confidence in television and only 10 percent had a great deal of confidence in the press.

Only one institution is enjoying greater public confidence: the military. In 2002, the 54 percent majority of the public expressed a great deal of confidence in the military, up from a low of just 28 percent in 1980. Confidence in the military has been higher in the past, however. It peaked at 60 percent in 1991.

Table 1.8 Confidence in Banks and Financial Institutions, 1975 to 2002

As far as the people running these institutions are concerned, would you say you have a great deal of confidence, only some, or hardly any confidence at all in banks and financial institutions?

(number of respondents aged 18 or older, and percent distribution by response, 1975–2002)

	number of respondents	total	a great deal	only some	hardly any	don't know
2002	912	100.0%	22.0%	58.2%	18.3%	1.4%
2000	1,887	100.0	29.2	54.3	14.1	2.4
1998	1,907	100.0	25.7	56.0	16.0	2.3
1996	1,920	100.0	24.8	56.3	16.5	2.4
1994	2,002	100.0	17.8	60.8	20.1	1.2
1993	1,054	100.0	15.0	56.7	26.1	2.2
1991	1,014	100.0	12.3	51.7	33.9	2.1
1990	899	100.0	17.8	57.8	22.0	2.3
1989	1,032	100.0	18.7	58.6	19.3	3.4
1988	995	100.0	26.7	57.6	13.3	2.4
1987	1,816	100.0	27.4	56.6	14.1	2.0
1986	1,466	100.0	21.0	59.7	17.5	1.8
1984	976	100.0	31.8	55.1	10.8	2.4
1983	1,597	100.0	23.5	58.4	15.8	2.3
1982	1,853	100.0	26.7	55.6	15.8	1.9
1980	1,463	100.0	31.6	50.4	15.2	2.7
1978	1,528	100.0	32.9	54.0	11.7	1.4
1977	1,526	100.0	41.9	47.4	8.8	1.8
1976	1,492	100.0	39.5	48.1	10.0	2.4
1975	1,488	100.0	31.9	54.0	11.1	3.0

Source: General Social Surveys, National Opinion Research Center, University of Chicago; calculations by New Strategist

Table 1.9 Confidence in Major Companies, 1973 to 2002

As far as the people running these institutions are concerned, would you say you have a great deal of confidence, only some, or hardly any confidence at all in major companies?

(number of respondents aged 18 or older, and percent distribution by response, 1973–2002)

	number of respondents	total	a great deal	only some	hardly any	don't know
2002	911	100.0%	17.3%	62.8%	17.9%	2.0%
2000	1,889	100.0	28.0	57.0	11.0	4.1
1998	1,908	100.0	26.2	56.5	12.7	4.6
1996	1,924	100.0	23.2	59.1	13.5	4.2
1994	2,005	100.0	25.4	61.4	9.9	3.2
1993	1,055	100.0	20.9	62.7	12.3	4.1
1991	1,016	100.0	20.2	61.9	13.0	4.9
1990	897	100.0	24.9	60.6	10.8	3.7
1989	1,032	100.0	23.6	60.4	10.3	5.7
1988	993	100.0	24.7	60.2	10.6	4.5
1987	1,815	100.0	30.1	56.9	8.6	4.5
1986	1,466	100.0	24.1	61.9	10.2	3.8
1984	981	100.0	30.7	57.2	8.7	3.5
1983	1,595	100.0	23.8	58.7	13.4	4.1
1982	1,853	100.0	23.3	58.4	13.4	5.0
1980	1,466	100.0	27.2	53.1	14.2	5.5
1978	1,529	100.0	21.6	57.9	16.0	4.4
1977	1,526	100.0	27.2	56.5	12.3	4.0
1976	1,491	100.0	22.0	51.2	21.7	5.0
1975	1,483	100.0	19.3	54.0	21.2	5.5
1974	1,483	100.0	31.4	50.6	14.5	3.6
1973	1,500	100.0	29.3	53.3	10.8	6.7

Source: General Social Surveys, National Opinion Research Center, University of Chicago; calculations by New Strategist

Table 1.10 Confidence in Education, 1973 to 2002

As far as the people running these institutions are concerned, would you say you have a great deal of confidence, only some, or hardly any confidence at all in the leaders of education?

(number of respondents aged 18 or older, and percent distribution by response, 1973–2002)

	number of respondents	total	a great deal	only some	hardly any	don't know
2002	912	100.0%	24.9%	58.9%	15.6%	0.7%
2000	1,889	100.0	26.8	56.5	15.6	1.1
1998	1,904	100.0	26.8	55.4	16.5	1.2
1996	1,923	100.0	22.9	57.7	18.2	1.2
1994	2,005	100.0	24.9	56.6	17.4	1.1
1993	1,052	100.0	22.2	57.9	18.3	1.6
1991	1,016	100.0	30.1	54.8	13.4	1.7
1990	895	100.0	26.9	59.1	12.3	1.7
1989	1,031	100.0	30.4	57.6	10.5	1.6
1988	994	100.0	29.5	60.1	8.7	1.8
1987	1,815	100.0	34.3	55.4	8.9	1.4
1986	1,465	100.0	27.6	60.3	10.6	1.4
1984	976	100.0	28.2	59.3	10.5	2.0
1983	1,594	100.0	28.7	56.5	13.1	1.8
1982	1,851	100.0	33.7	51.6	13.1	1.5
1980	1,466	100.0	29.9	55.6	12.5	2.0
1978	1,528	100.0	28.5	55.0	15.1	1.4
1977	1,526	100.0	40.6	49.6	8.8	0.9
1976	1,489	100.0	37.5	45.1	15.4	2.0
1975	1,488	100.0	30.9	54.6	12.8	1.7
1974	1,480	100.0	49.1	41.4	8.2	1.4
1973	1,495	100.0	37.0	53.4	8.2	1.4

Source: General Social Surveys, National Opinion Research Center, University of Chicago; calculations by New Strategist

Table 1.11 Confidence in the Executive Branch of Government, 1973 to 2002

As far as the people running these institutions are concerned, would you say you have a great deal of confidence, only some, or hardly any confidence at all in the executive branch of government?

(number of respondents aged 18 or older, and percent distribution by response, 1973–2002)

	number of respondents	total	a great deal	only some	hardly any	don't know
2002	910	100.0%	26.7%	50.0%	21.2%	2.1%
2000	1,887	100.0	13.2	49.0	33.5	4.3
1998	1,905	100.0	13.9	47.7	35.2	3.1
1996	1,924	100.0	10.1	44.8	41.6	3.5
1994	2,003	100.0	11.3	51.6	35.0	2.1
1993	1,052	100.0	11.8	52.9	32.3	3.0
1991	1,014	100.0	25.9	50.8	20.9	2.4
1990	899	100.0	23.4	50.2	23.1	3.3
1989	1,031	100.0	19.6	54.0	21.8	4.6
1988	994	100.0	16.5	53.3	26.8	3.4
1987	1,816	100.0	18.7	51.2	27.1	3.0
1986	1,468	100.0	20.6	53.1	23.6	2.8
1984	977	100.0	18.5	50.5	28.7	2.4
1983	1,597	100.0	12.9	54.4	29.5	3.3
1982	1,853	100.0	19.4	54.0	24.1	2.5
1980	1,465	100.0	12.1	50.3	34.3	3.3
1978	1,528	100.0	12.5	59.4	24.9	3.2
1977	1,525	100.0	27.9	54.4	14.5	3.1
1976	1,494	100.0	13.5	58.5	25.0	3.0
1975	1,488	100.0	13.3	54.6	29.5	2.6
1974	1,482	100.0	13.6	42.5	41.7	2.2
1973	1,498	100.0	29.3	50.4	18.4	1.9

Source: General Social Surveys, National Opinion Research Center, University of Chicago; calculations by New Strategist

Table 1.12 Confidence in Medicine, 1973 to 2002

As far as the people running these institutions are concerned, would you say you have a great deal of confidence, only some, or hardly any confidence at all in the medical community?

(number of respondents aged 18 or older, and percent distribution by response, 1973–2002)

	number of respondents	total	a great deal	only some	hardly any	don't know
2002	912	100.0%	37.0%	51.3%	11.2%	0.5%
2000	1,887	100.0	43.7	45.4	9.5	1.4
1998	1,905	100.0	44.3	45.4	8.8	1.6
1996	1,924	100.0	44.5	45.3	8.9	1.3
1994	2,003	100.0	41.5	48.0	9.8	0.7
1993	1,052	100.0	39.1	51.2	8.5	1.2
1991	1,013	100.0	47.5	43.6	7.6	1.3
1990	898	100.0	45.7	46.5	6.8	1.0
1989	1,030	100.0	46.3	45.4	6.8	1.5
1988	993	100.0	51.3	41.9	5.9	0.9
1987	1,813	100.0	51.7	41.9	5.2	1.2
1986	1,466	100.0	45.9	45.3	7.5	1.3
1984	977	100.0	51.1	41.7	6.3	0.9
1983	1,596	100.0	51.6	41.0	6.0	1.4
1982	1,854	100.0	45.3	46.4	7.3	1.1
1980	1,467	100.0	52.4	38.7	7.4	1.5
1978	1,527	100.0	46.0	44.0	9.2	0.8
1977	1,526	100.0	51.5	41.2	6.2	1.1
1976	1,492	100.0	54.1	35.3	9.2	1.3
1975	1,487	100.0	50.5	40.1	7.9	1.5
1974	1,482	100.0	60.4	33.7	4.5	1.5
1973	1,496	100.0	54.1	39.2	5.7	0.9

Source: General Social Surveys, National Opinion Research Center, University of Chicago; calculations by New Strategist

Table 1.13 Confidence in the Military, 1973 to 2002

As far as the people running these institutions are concerned, would you say you have a great deal of confidence, only some, or hardly any confidence at all in the military?

(number of respondents aged 18 or older, and percent distribution by response, 1973–2002)

	number of respondents	total	a great deal	only some	hardly any	don't know
2002	912	100.0%	53.9%	37.6%	6.9%	1.5%
2000	1,886	100.0	38.5	48.1	9.8	3.6
1998	1,906	100.0	36.1	48.6	12.4	2.8
1996	1,923	100.0	37.2	48.5	11.1	3.2
1994	2,000	100.0	36.9	48.6	12.3	2.3
1993	1,052	100.0	41.9	45.3	11.0	1.7
1991	1,014	100.0	59.7	32.6	5.9	1.8
1990	899	100.0	32.6	51.1	13.5	2.9
1989	1,032	100.0	32.5	50.0	13.5	4.1
1988	995	100.0	34.0	49.3	13.5	3.2
1987	1,814	100.0	34.6	49.8	12.7	2.9
1986	1,466	100.0	31.4	52.4	13.6	2.5
1984	977	100.0	36.0	48.4	12.8	2.8
1983	1,596	100.0	29.3	54.7	13.0	3.0
1982	1,854	100.0	30.6	52.4	14.6	2.3
1980	1,467	100.0	27.6	52.1	16.2	4.2
1978	1,528	100.0	29.5	54.0	12.8	3.7
1977	1,526	100.0	36.3	50.3	10.3	3.1
1976	1,491	100.0	39.2	41.3	13.3	6.2
1975	1,487	100.0	35.2	45.8	14.3	4.6
1974	1,483	100.0	39.6	44.4	13.4	2.6
1973	1,498	100.0	31.7	49.5	16.1	2.7

Source: General Social Surveys, National Opinion Research Center, University of Chicago; calculations by New Strategist

Table 1.14 Confidence in the Press, 1973 to 2002

As far as the people running these institutions are concerned, would you say you have a great deal of confidence, only some, or hardly any confidence at all in the press?

(number of respondents aged 18 or older, and percent distribution by response, 1973–2002)

	number of respondents	total	a great deal	only some	hardly any	don't know
2002	912	100.0%	10.1%	46.6%	41.9%	1.4%
2000	1,885	100.0	10.1	46.6	40.7	2.5
1998	1,908	100.0	9.2	46.0	42.3	2.4
1996	1,921	100.0	10.7	47.8	38.7	2.8
1994	2,001	100.0	9.7	49.6	39.1	1.5
1993	1,053	100.0	10.8	48.6	38.6	2.0
1991	1,014	100.0	16.4	53.7	27.8	2.1
1990	898	100.0	14.7	57.5	24.4	3.5
1989	1,031	100.0	16.6	53.9	26.7	2.8
1988	990	100.0	18.4	53.4	25.3	2.9
1987	1,816	100.0	18.4	55.7	23.9	2.0
1986	1,465	100.0	18.3	54.4	25.5	1.8
1984	978	100.0	17.0	58.7	22.4	1.9
1983	1,595	100.0	13.5	61.1	23.5	1.9
1982	1,854	100.0	17.8	59.8	20.4	2.0
1980	1,467	100.0	21.9	57.9	17.2	2.9
1978	1,528	100.0	20.1	58.4	19.7	1.8
1977	1,526	100.0	25.1	57.3	15.5	2.2
1976	1,490	100.0	28.5	52.1	17.7	1.8
1975	1,484	100.0	23.9	55.5	17.9	2.8
1974	1,481	100.0	25.9	55.4	17.5	1.2
1973	1,500	100.0	23.1	60.7	14.7	1.5

Source: General Social Surveys, National Opinion Research Center, University of Chicago; calculations by New Strategist

Table 1.15 Confidence in the Scientific Community, 1973 to 2002

As far as the people running these institutions are concerned, would you say you have a great deal of confidence, only some, or hardly any confidence at all in the scientific community?

(number of respondents aged 18 or older, and percent distribution by response, 1973–2002)

	number of respondents	total	a great deal	only some	hardly any	don't know
2002	912	100.0%	36.8%	48.2%	8.9%	6.0%
2000	1,888	100.0	41.3	43.4	7.5	7.9
1998	1,905	100.0	39.7	44.9	7.8	7.6
1996	1,918	100.0	39.2	45.2	7.5	8.1
1994	2,001	100.0	38.4	49.3	7.0	5.2
1993	1,052	100.0	37.5	47.1	6.7	8.6
1991	1,014	100.0	40.5	46.1	6.2	7.2
1990	898	100.0	37.3	47.3	6.6	8.8
1989	1,030	100.0	40.2	44.7	6.1	9.0
1988	992	100.0	38.8	47.7	5.6	7.9
1987	1,811	100.0	44.3	42.7	6.3	6.6
1986	1,463	100.0	38.9	47.6	7.7	5.7
1984	976	100.0	44.7	44.1	5.5	5.7
1983	1,593	100.0	41.6	46.8	5.3	6.3
1982	1,847	100.0	38.3	46.5	5.9	9.3
1980	1,462	100.0	41.5	42.5	6.4	9.6
1978	1,527	100.0	36.2	48.3	7.3	8.3
1977	1,522	100.0	41.0	45.7	5.5	7.8
1976	1,486	100.0	42.9	38.0	7.5	11.6
1975	1,487	100.0	37.7	45.2	6.5	10.7
1974	1,481	100.0	45.0	37.7	6.7	10.6
1973	1,495	100.0	36.9	47.1	6.5	9.5

Source: General Social Surveys, National Opinion Research Center, University of Chicago; calculations by New Strategist

Table 1.16 Confidence in Television, 1973 to 2002

As far as the people running these institutions are concerned, would you say you have a great deal of confidence, only some, or hardly any confidence at all in television?

(number of respondents aged 18 or older, and percent distribution by response, 1973–2002)

	number of respondents	total	a great deal	only some	hardly any	don't know
2002	912	100.0%	9.5%	47.0%	42.5%	0.9%
2000	1,885	100.0	9.8	46.7	41.8	1.6
1998	1,907	100.0	10.3	49.1	39.0	1.6
1996	1,920	100.0	10.2	46.2	41.6	2.0
1994	2,000	100.0	9.5	49.8	39.8	0.9
1993	1,054	100.0	11.6	50.5	36.8	1.1
1991	1,013	100.0	14.4	54.6	30.2	0.8
1990	899	100.0	13.7	58.1	26.8	1.4
1989	1,031	100.0	14.0	55.0	28.8	2.2
1988	988	100.0	14.3	58.3	26.4	1.0
1987	1,814	100.0	11.9	58.2	28.4	1.5
1986	1,464	100.0	14.9	55.6	27.7	1.8
1984	978	100.0	13.2	57.1	28.4	1.3
1983	1,596	100.0	12.5	57.5	28.1	1.9
1982	1,852	100.0	14.0	58.0	26.8	1.1
1980	1,467	100.0	16.0	54.6	27.7	1.7
1978	1,526	100.0	13.8	53.4	31.0	1.8
1977	1,525	100.0	17.4	55.9	25.1	1.5
1976	1,490	100.0	18.7	52.3	27.2	1.7
1975	1,486	100.0	17.8	57.4	22.4	2.4
1974	1,481	100.0	23.4	58.1	17.3	1.1
1973	1,497	100.0	18.6	58.5	21.8	1.1

Source: General Social Surveys, National Opinion Research Center, University of Chicago; calculations by New Strategist

Table 1.17 Confidence in the United States Supreme Court, 1973 to 2002

As far as the people running these institutions are concerned, would you say you have a great deal of confidence, only some, or hardly any confidence at all in the U.S. Supreme Court?

(number of respondents aged 18 or older, and percent distribution by response, 1973–2002)

	number of respondents	total	a great deal	only some	hardly any	don't know
2002	911	100.0%	35.2%	49.8%	11.4%	3.5%
2000	1,888	100.0	31.8	49.4	12.7	6.1
1998	1,905	100.0	31.1	49.9	14.0	5.0
1996	1,921	100.0	28.3	49.9	16.6	5.3
1994	2,004	100.0	30.1	50.0	16.4	3.4
1993	1,054	100.0	30.6	51.8	13.4	4.3
1991	1,012	100.0	36.9	46.4	12.3	4.4
1990	899	100.0	35.0	47.9	12.7	4.3
1989	1,033	100.0	34.5	50.0	10.7	4.7
1988	992	100.0	34.7	50.3	10.6	4.4
1987	1,813	100.0	36.5	48.8	10.8	3.9
1986	1,460	100.0	29.7	52.4	14.1	3.8
1984	978	100.0	33.2	50.8	12.4	3.6
1983	1,595	100.0	27.2	54.9	14.1	3.8
1982	1,852	100.0	30.2	53.7	12.5	3.6
1980	1,468	100.0	24.6	50.0	19.5	5.9
1978	1,527	100.0	28.1	52.8	14.6	4.5
1977	1,522	100.0	35.7	49.4	10.8	4.1
1976	1,491	100.0	35.4	43.6	15.4	5.6
1975	1,485	100.0	30.8	46.3	18.6	4.3
1974	1,482	100.0	33.2	47.9	14.4	4.5
1973	1,497	100.0	31.5	49.8	15.4	3.3

Source: General Social Surveys, National Opinion Research Center, University of Chicago; calculations by New Strategist

Table 1.18 Confidence in Organized Labor, 1973 to 2002

As far as the people running these institutions are concerned, would you say you have a great deal of confidence, only some, or hardly any confidence at all in organized labor?

(number of respondents aged 18 or older, and percent distribution by response, 1973–2002)

	number of respondents	total	a great deal	only some	hardly any	don't know
2002	911	100.0%	11.1%	60.4%	23.1%	5.5%
2000	1,886	100.0	12.7	51.0	26.5	9.8
1998	1,907	100.0	11.0	51.7	29.2	8.1
1996	1,923	100.0	11.2	50.9	29.5	8.4
1994	2,002	100.0	9.9	52.2	32.4	5.5
1993	1,053	100.0	8.3	52.5	32.3	6.9
1991	1,015	100.0	11.0	48.4	34.0	6.6
1990	898	100.0	10.7	53.0	31.1	5.2
1989	1,032	100.0	9.4	50.8	33.4	6.4
1988	993	100.0	10.0	50.2	34.6	5.2
1987	1,813	100.0	10.4	50.9	33.4	5.4
1986	1,465	100.0	8.0	47.3	39.3	5.4
1984	978	100.0	8.6	52.9	36.1	2.5
1983	1,597	100.0	8.0	48.5	39.4	4.1
1982	1,850	100.0	12.5	53.0	30.1	4.4
1980	1,466	100.0	15.0	49.6	29.6	5.8
1978	1,528	100.0	11.0	46.3	37.6	5.1
1977	1,524	100.0	14.8	49.7	31.7	3.9
1976	1,494	100.0	11.6	47.5	33.0	7.9
1975	1,488	100.0	10.1	54.2	29.3	6.4
1974	1,481	100.0	18.2	53.5	25.5	2.8
1973	1,495	100.0	15.5	54.6	25.7	4.1

Source: General Social Surveys, National Opinion Research Center, University of Chicago; calculations by New Strategist

Table 1.19 Confidence in Organized Religion, 1973 to 2002

As far as the people running these institutions are concerned, would you say you have a great deal of confidence, only some, or hardly any confidence at all in organized religion?

(number of respondents aged 18 or older, and percent distribution by response, 1973–2002)

	number of respondents	total	a great deal	only some	hardly any	don't know
2002	910	100.0%	18.5%	56.2%	23.8%	1.5%
2000	1,890	100.0	27.5	49.4	18.8	4.3
1998	1,905	100.0	26.9	51.1	18.8	3.2
1996	1,922	100.0	25.1	51.2	19.0	4.7
1994	2,002	100.0	24.3	51.7	21.8	2.2
1993	1,051	100.0	22.8	49.6	24.5	3.1
1991	1,015	100.0	25.2	51.5	20.8	2.5
1990	898	100.0	22.6	49.2	23.6	4.6
1989	1,031	100.0	21.6	44.5	30.4	3.5
1988	995	100.0	20.0	46.2	31.0	2.8
1987	1,813	100.0	29.1	48.7	19.1	3.0
1986	1,467	100.0	25.2	50.4	21.0	3.4
1984	979	100.0	31.1	46.7	18.8	3.5
1983	1,593	100.0	28.2	50.5	17.4	3.8
1982	1,855	100.0	32.6	49.4	14.8	3.2
1980	1,465	100.0	35.3	43.1	17.8	3.8
1978	1,526	100.0	30.7	47.3	18.2	3.8
1977	1,526	100.0	40.0	45.1	11.6	3.3
1976	1,491	100.0	30.7	44.7	18.3	6.3
1975	1,485	100.0	24.4	47.9	21.3	6.4
1974	1,481	100.0	44.3	42.8	10.8	2.1
1973	1,495	100.0	34.8	45.8	15.9	3.5

Source: General Social Surveys, National Opinion Research Center, University of Chicago; calculations by New Strategist

Family Type and Mobility

Family life has changed in the United States over the past three decades as divorce and out-of-wedlock births have become more common. The General Social Survey has documented these changes.

When asked in 2002 about their family status at age 16, only 67 percent of Americans (a record low) said they lived with both their mother and father at that age. Three decades ago, three-quarters of the public said they lived with both parents at age 16 .

In another lifestyle shift, fewer people are growing up in a rural environment. In 1974, more than 30 percent of the public said they had grown up in the country or on a farm. In 2002, the figure had fallen to 23 percent. The proportion of Americans who say they grew up in a small town has barely budged over the past 30 years, hovering at about 30 percent. The share of Americns growing up in a city (or suburb) with a population of 50,000 or more has grown from 39 percent in 1973 to 47 percent in 2002.

While we think of America as a nation of movers, people's actual experience contradicts that notion. In 2002, only 33 percent of the population lived in a different state than they did at age 16—a percentage that has not changed during the past three decades. The percentage who say they still live in the same city as they did at age 16 has fluctuated around the 40 percent mark during all those years as well.

Table 1.20 Living with Both Parents at Age 16, 1972 to 2002

Were you living with both your own mother and father around the time you were 16?

(number of respondents aged 18 or older, and percent distribution by response, 1972–2002)

	number of respondents	total	mother and father	mother only	mother and stepfather	father only	father and stepmother	male and female relatives	female relatives	male relatives	other
2002	2,762	100.0%	67.4%	14.1%	6.5%	2.8%	1.8%	2.1%	2.0%	0.5%	2.9%
2000	2,817	100.0	68.7	14.8	5.4	2.2	2.2	2.1	1.5	0.3	2.8
1998	2,832	100.0	69.2	13.6	5.6	1.9	3.2	1.8	1.6	0.2	3.0
1996	2,901	100.0	69.4	14.0	4.7	2.4	2.7	2.4	1.4	0.1	2.8
1994	2,992	100.0	70.2	13.5	5.4	2.4	2.5	2.1	1.2	0.4	2.3
1993	1,606	100.0	74.2	10.3	4.5	2.1	2.1	2.4	1.9	0.4	2.1
1991	1,517	100.0	72.6	11.6	4.5	2.4	2.4	1.5	1.9	0.5	2.5
1990	1,371	100.0	72.4	12.4	5.4	1.8	1.5	2.1	1.5	0.5	2.4
1989	1,536	100.0	75.1	11.2	3.9	2.5	1.1	1.5	1.6	0.2	2.9
1988	1,481	100.0	72.4	11.5	6.2	2.4	1.8	2.4	1.2	0.1	1.9
1987	1,816	100.0	76.4	10.4	3.5	2.1	2.1	2.2	1.8	0.2	1.2
1986	1,470	100.0	73.6	12.2	4.9	1.7	1.3	2.4	1.3	0.3	2.3
1985	1,534	100.0	75.6	10.0	3.3	2.4	2.2	2.7	1.2	0.5	2.2
1984	1,472	100.0	74.7	10.3	5.0	2.2	1.5	2.1	1.6	0.4	2.2
1983	1,599	100.0	76.6	10.6	3.7	2.2	1.8	2.1	1.5	0.1	1.4
1982	1,856	100.0	75.6	10.7	3.6	2.6	1.8	2.1	1.4	0.3	1.9
1980	1,468	100.0	72.9	12.2	4.7	2.0	1.7	1.5	1.6	0.5	2.9
1978	1,531	100.0	75.6	11.2	3.7	2.2	1.4	2.4	1.4	0.3	1.8
1977	1,528	100.0	74.1	11.3	5.0	2.9	1.8	2.3	0.9	0.3	1.4
1976	1,496	100.0	76.1	10.8	3.0	2.7	1.9	2.2	1.1	0.2	1.9
1975	1,490	100.0	76.5	8.3	5.5	1.6	2.3	2.4	1.4	0.3	1.7
1974	1,484	100.0	75.9	10.2	3.2	2.4	1.7	2.0	1.3	0.6	2.6
1973	1,502	100.0	78.2	8.2	2.9	3.1	2.1	2.7	0.9	0.4	1.6
1972	1,613	100.0	74.3	10.7	3.2	2.2	1.7	5.8	1.5	0.6	–

Source: General Social Surveys, National Opinion Research Center, University of Chicago; calculations by New Strategist

Table 1.21 Type of Place Lived in at Age 16, 1972 to 2002

Which comes closest to the type of place you were living in when you were 16 years old?

(number of respondents aged 18 or older, and percent distribution by response, 1972–2002)

	number of respondents	total	country, nonfarm	farm	town, less than 50,000	city, 50,000 to 250,000	big-city suburb	city greater than 250,000	don't know
2002	2,764	100.0%	11.8%	11.4%	30.1%	15.9%	14.1%	16.6%	0.1%
2000	2,811	100.0	11.1	13.7	31.0	16.4	11.8	16.0	0.0
1998	2,830	100.0	11.6	13.1	30.3	15.9	12.8	16.3	0.1
1996	2,901	100.0	11.5	12.9	31.8	17.0	12.3	14.4	0.1
1994	2,988	100.0	11.9	13.6	31.2	15.7	12.3	15.3	0.1
1993	1,604	100.0	11.7	18.0	29.1	13.7	12.8	14.7	0.1
1991	1,515	100.0	11.6	16.6	33.1	14.0	10.4	14.2	0.1
1990	1,371	100.0	9.8	17.2	31.9	14.3	10.1	16.6	0.1
1989	1,534	100.0	11.0	16.8	32.3	15.6	11.0	13.2	0.1
1988	1,479	100.0	11.6	17.0	32.3	14.7	9.6	14.8	–
1987	1,814	100.0	11.8	19.4	27.9	15.3	10.7	14.8	0.1
1986	1,470	100.0	9.5	18.2	30.5	16.8	9.3	15.6	–
1985	1,529	100.0	9.5	18.4	34.2	15.4	10.1	12.4	0.1
1984	1,469	100.0	9.8	21.6	31.7	13.6	9.1	14.0	0.1
1983	1,599	100.0	10.6	15.8	33.5	15.3	9.8	15.1	–
1982	1,849	100.0	10.3	20.2	33.0	12.4	9.5	14.7	–
1980	1,467	100.0	9.9	21.1	31.7	13.9	8.0	15.3	–
1978	1,531	100.0	11.4	21.8	30.8	13.5	8.5	14.0	0.1
1977	1,526	100.0	11.1	22.5	34.3	12.3	5.8	13.8	0.1
1976	1,498	100.0	10.7	22.8	29.9	12.4	8.0	16.2	0.1
1975	1,490	100.0	12.9	22.6	28.9	12.0	6.8	16.8	–
1974	1,481	100.0	9.7	24.4	29.6	13.0	8.3	15.0	–
1973	1,503	100.0	9.0	22.8	31.9	12.5	7.1	16.6	0.1
1972	1,611	100.0	9.1	21.1	31.0	12.3	5.6	20.7	0.1

Source: General Social Surveys, National Opinion Research Center, University of Chicago; calculations by New Strategist

Table 1.22 Living in Same Place at Age 16, 1972 to 2002

When you were 16 years old, were you living in this same (city/town/county)?

(number of respondents aged 18 or older, and percent distribution by response, 1972–2002)

	number of respondents	total	same city	same state different city	different state	don't know
2002	2,763	100.0%	41.7%	25.3%	33.0%	–
2000	2,802	100.0	39.3	26.1	34.6	0.0%
1998	2,817	100.0	39.1	25.8	35.1	–
1996	2,890	100.0	37.8	24.4	37.9	–
1994	2,985	100.0	39.5	25.3	35.2	–
1993	1,603	100.0	41.3	26.6	32.1	–
1991	1,510	100.0	40.8	26.6	32.6	–
1990	1,360	100.0	39.8	28.8	31.5	–
1989	1,528	100.0	40.7	26.4	32.9	–
1988	1,466	100.0	40.7	25.4	33.9	0.1
1987	1,797	100.0	41.8	24.8	33.4	–
1986	1,449	100.0	42.9	25.1	32.0	–
1985	1,527	100.0	40.1	27.8	32.0	–
1984	1,464	100.0	40.0	27.1	32.9	–
1983	1,578	100.0	45.2	24.0	30.7	–
1982	1,851	100.0	45.8	26.0	28.2	–
1980	1,462	100.0	43.1	26.4	30.5	–
1978	1,522	100.0	40.7	28.5	30.7	0.1
1977	1,457	100.0	43.1	25.4	31.5	–
1976	1,462	100.0	43.4	25.6	31.1	–
1975	1,426	100.0	43.5	25.0	31.5	–
1974	1,438	100.0	42.8	27.4	29.8	–
1973	1,473	100.0	41.1	23.7	35.2	–
1972	1,562	100.0	46.4	20.2	33.4	–

Source: General Social Surveys, National Opinion Research Center, University of Chicago; calculations by New Strategist

Funding to Solve Problems

Many Americans want the government to spend more to solve the nation's problems. The majority thinks the United States spends too little on education, the environment, fighting drug addiction and crime, health, and Social Security. The percentage of Americans who think we don't spend enough on education, health, and Social Security has been growing. In 2002, 74 percent of Americans said we don't spend enough on improving and protecting the nation's health, up from a low of 55 percent who felt that way in 1980. Seventy-three percent said we don't spend enough on education, up from only 48 percent in 1977. The percentage of those who think we don't spend enough on Social Security stood at 59 percent in 2002, up from a low of 44 percent in 1993.

The largest share of the public thinks we spend the right amount of money on highways, mass transportation, space exploration, the condition of blacks, and the military. The majority thinks we spend the right amount on parks and recreation. Over the past three decades, the only significant shift in opinion regarding these issues is growing support for space exploration. In 1973, the majority of American thought we spent too much on space exploration. By 2002, only 35 percent felt that way, while 47 percent said we spent the right amount and 11 percent said we spent too little on space exploration.

The largest share of the public thought we spent too much on welfare in 2002, but this figure is down considerably from the majority who felt that way at various times during the past three decades. Spending on foreign aid gets the least public support. The majority of Americans think we spend too much on foreign aid.

Table 1.23 Spending on Education, 1973 to 2002

We are faced with many problems in this country, none of which can be solved easily or inexpensively. Are we spending too much, too little money, or about the right amount on improving the nation's education system?

(number of respondents aged 18 or older, and percent distribution by response, 1973–2002)

	number of respondents	total	too little	about right	too much	don't know
2002	1,356	100.0%	73.2%	20.5%	5.4%	1.0%
2000	1,407	100.0	70.6	22.8	4.7	1.8
1998	1,380	100.0	69.7	22.2	6.3	1.8
1996	1,439	100.0	68.4	22.9	6.2	2.6
1994	1,503	100.0	70.8	21.6	5.9	1.8
1993	794	100.0	67.0	24.7	5.8	2.5
1991	746	100.0	67.4	24.8	5.2	2.5
1990	671	100.0	71.2	23.2	3.0	2.5
1989	765	100.0	67.2	26.8	2.9	3.1
1988	711	100.0	63.9	29.3	3.7	3.2
1987	598	100.0	62.0	29.3	5.7	3.0
1986	726	100.0	60.5	32.5	4.1	2.9
1985	746	100.0	60.5	31.4	5.2	2.9
1984	483	100.0	63.6	31.5	3.3	1.7
1983	1,593	100.0	60.0	31.1	5.8	3.1
1982	1,857	100.0	56.0	31.8	8.3	3.9
1980	1,463	100.0	52.7	33.1	10.2	4.0
1978	1,530	100.0	51.6	33.7	10.9	3.8
1977	1,527	100.0	47.6	38.9	9.7	3.8
1976	1,495	100.0	50.2	37.3	9.4	3.1
1975	1,487	100.0	49.0	35.3	11.2	4.5
1974	1,474	100.0	50.7	37.0	8.5	3.8
1973	1,499	100.0	49.0	37.7	9.0	4.3

Source: General Social Surveys, National Opinion Research Center, University of Chicago; calculations by New Strategist

Table 1.24 Spending on the Environment, 1973 to 2002

We are faced with many problems in this country, none of which can be solved easily or inexpensively. Are we spending too much, too little money, or about the right amount on improving and protecting the environment?

(number of respondents aged 18 or older, and percent distribution by response, 1973–2002)

	number of respondents	total	too little	about right	too much	don't know
2002	1,355	100.0%	58.5%	32.4%	6.6%	2.4%
2000	1,407	100.0	61.0	27.4	8.0	3.7
1998	1,377	100.0	60.0	28.0	7.7	4.3
1996	1,440	100.0	58.1	27.2	10.6	4.2
1994	1,506	100.0	58.8	29.4	8.4	3.4
1993	794	100.0	56.0	30.1	9.3	4.5
1991	751	100.0	68.0	24.0	4.9	3.1
1990	669	100.0	71.2	19.0	4.6	5.2
1989	763	100.0	71.8	20.3	3.7	4.2
1988	714	100.0	65.0	26.3	4.6	4.1
1987	597	100.0	65.2	24.8	4.9	5.2
1986	725	100.0	59.4	29.4	5.2	5.9
1985	747	100.0	56.4	31.6	8.0	4.0
1984	485	100.0	59.0	32.8	4.3	3.9
1983	1,592	100.0	54.3	31.3	8.2	6.2
1982	1,857	100.0	49.7	32.1	11.5	6.6
1980	1,465	100.0	47.9	31.0	15.4	5.7
1978	1,528	100.0	52.4	32.8	9.6	5.2
1977	1,524	100.0	47.5	34.3	11.0	7.2
1976	1,494	100.0	54.8	31.3	9.3	4.6
1975	1,490	100.0	53.4	30.8	9.7	6.2
1974	1,476	100.0	59.0	26.6	7.7	6.6
1973	1,498	100.0	61.1	25.8	7.4	5.7

Source: General Social Surveys, National Opinion Research Center, University of Chicago; calculations by New Strategist

Table 1.25 Spending on Drug Addiction, 1973 to 2002

We are faced with many problems in this country, none of which can be solved easily or inexpensively. Are we spending too much, too little money, or about the right amount on dealing with drug addiction?

(number of respondents aged 18 or older, and percent distribution by response, 1973–2002)

	number of respondents	total	too little	about right	too much	don't know
2002	1,354	100.0%	57.2%	30.2%	9.4%	3.2%
2000	1,402	100.0	58.6	27.8	8.3	5.3
1998	1,376	100.0	58.4	28.1	9.4	4.2
1996	1,435	100.0	58.4	26.6	11.1	3.9
1994	1,503	100.0	59.8	26.4	8.6	5.1
1993	792	100.0	60.1	27.4	8.0	4.5
1991	749	100.0	57.5	31.6	7.3	3.5
1990	669	100.0	64.1	26.0	6.6	3.3
1989	764	100.0	70.8	19.2	6.3	3.7
1988	713	100.0	68.4	24.4	4.1	3.1
1987	597	100.0	66.2	27.5	4.0	2.3
1986	726	100.0	58.1	31.5	6.1	4.3
1985	748	100.0	61.8	28.3	5.5	4.4
1984	485	100.0	63.1	27.4	5.8	3.7
1983	1,591	100.0	59.5	29.8	5.4	5.3
1982	1,854	100.0	56.6	27.3	8.3	7.8
1980	1,460	100.0	59.8	25.1	7.7	7.3
1978	1,527	100.0	55.3	31.0	8.8	4.9
1977	1,520	100.0	55.2	29.0	8.6	7.2
1976	1,493	100.0	58.7	26.9	7.6	6.9
1975	1,482	100.0	55.1	28.9	8.4	7.6
1974	1,478	100.0	60.0	27.9	6.5	5.5
1973	1,493	100.0	65.9	21.8	6.0	6.3

Source: General Social Surveys, National Opinion Research Center, University of Chicago; calculations by New Strategist

Table 1.26 Spending on Halting Crime, 1973 to 2002

We are faced with many problems in this country, none of which can be solved easily or inexpensively. Are we spending too much, too little money, or about the right amount on halting the rising crime rate?

(number of respondents aged 18 or older, and percent distribution by response, 1973–2002)

	number of respondents	total	too little	about right	too much	don't know
2002	1,356	100.0%	55.9%	34.9%	6.6%	2.6%
2000	1,401	100.0	59.0	32.4	5.4	3.1
1998	1,377	100.0	61.1	28.5	7.0	3.4
1996	1,437	100.0	67.2	23.0	6.8	3.1
1994	1,504	100.0	75.2	16.0	6.2	2.6
1993	794	100.0	70.9	20.5	4.9	3.7
1991	748	100.0	64.7	27.1	4.8	3.3
1990	671	100.0	69.7	21.9	4.0	4.3
1989	763	100.0	72.5	19.7	4.7	3.1
1988	712	100.0	68.3	23.2	3.9	4.6
1987	591	100.0	69.0	23.4	4.2	3.4
1986	725	100.0	63.9	27.0	4.7	4.4
1985	747	100.0	62.9	27.7	5.5	3.9
1984	484	100.0	67.8	24.6	4.5	3.1
1983	1,591	100.0	66.6	24.2	4.8	4.4
1982	1,846	100.0	71.8	18.4	5.3	4.5
1980	1,463	100.0	68.9	20.8	6.0	4.3
1978	1,526	100.0	64.4	25.2	6.1	4.3
1977	1,524	100.0	65.7	22.2	5.9	6.1
1976	1,489	100.0	65.7	21.2	7.9	5.1
1975	1,484	100.0	65.6	23.2	5.5	5.7
1974	1,481	100.0	66.6	23.4	4.9	5.1
1973	1,497	100.0	64.6	24.6	4.7	6.1

Source: General Social Surveys, National Opinion Research Center, University of Chicago; calculations by New Strategist

Table 1.27 Spending on Solving the Problems of Big Cities, 1973 to 2002

We are faced with many problems in this country, none of which can be solved easily or inexpensively. Are we spending too much, too little money, or about the right amount on solving the problems of big cities?

(number of respondents aged 18 or older, and percent distribution by response, 1973–2002)

	number of respondents	total	too little	about right	too much	don't know
2002	1,355	100.0%	41.5%	36.5%	13.5%	8.6%
2000	1,402	100.0	44.7	31.3	10.4	13.6
1998	1,378	100.0	45.6	29.9	12.1	12.3
1996	1,437	100.0	52.3	23.4	12.9	11.3
1994	1,504	100.0	56.1	22.8	13.1	8.0
1993	792	100.0	54.2	22.1	11.6	12.1
1991	749	100.0	46.5	30.8	11.3	11.3
1990	669	100.0	50.4	26.6	10.0	13.0
1989	764	100.0	46.3	29.1	10.9	13.7
1988	713	100.0	45.9	29.3	10.1	14.7
1987	596	100.0	37.8	32.7	13.4	16.1
1986	720	100.0	43.6	30.7	16.1	9.6
1985	747	100.0	39.4	32.7	16.5	11.5
1984	485	100.0	44.1	30.5	12.4	13.0
1983	1,591	100.0	41.4	29.4	15.5	13.7
1982	1,855	100.0	42.9	23.5	19.5	14.2
1980	1,464	100.0	40.0	26.0	21.3	12.7
1978	1,531	100.0	38.7	29.5	18.9	12.9
1977	1,525	100.0	40.3	26.2	19.4	14.0
1976	1,492	100.0	42.6	26.2	19.5	11.7
1975	1,479	100.0	47.1	24.9	11.8	16.1
1974	1,474	100.0	49.9	24.4	11.0	14.7
1973	1,499	100.0	48.2	27.5	12.3	12.0

Source: General Social Surveys, National Opinion Research Center, University of Chicago; calculations by New Strategist

Table 1.28 Spending on Improving the Nation's Health, 1973 to 2002

We are faced with many problems in this country, none of which can be solved easily or inexpensively. Are we spending too much, too little money, or about the right amount on improving and protecting the nation's health?

(number of respondents aged 18 or older, and percent distribution by response, 1973–2002)

	number of respondents	total	too little	about right	too much	don't know
2002	1,357	100.0%	73.7%	20.9%	3.8%	1.5%
2000	1,406	100.0	71.8	22.7	3.6	1.9
1998	1,379	100.0	66.9	25.0	5.7	2.5
1996	1,436	100.0	66.2	23.1	7.9	2.9
1994	1,502	100.0	64.2	23.2	8.5	4.1
1993	794	100.0	71.9	17.3	7.6	3.3
1991	749	100.0	69.2	25.5	2.7	2.7
1990	670	100.0	72.2	22.5	2.7	2.5
1989	766	100.0	68.0	25.3	3.0	3.7
1988	714	100.0	66.0	27.7	3.2	3.1
1987	594	100.0	68.9	25.1	4.0	2.0
1986	726	100.0	58.7	34.0	4.0	3.3
1985	749	100.0	57.7	33.1	6.3	2.9
1984	486	100.0	57.6	31.5	6.6	4.3
1983	1,591	100.0	57.4	33.7	5.2	3.8
1982	1,855	100.0	56.0	32.3	6.5	5.1
1980	1,467	100.0	54.7	33.5	7.6	4.1
1978	1,532	100.0	55.4	33.7	6.9	4.0
1977	1,526	100.0	55.8	32.6	6.9	4.7
1976	1,491	100.0	60.5	31.2	5.0	3.4
1975	1,485	100.0	62.6	28.4	5.1	4.0
1974	1,477	100.0	63.9	28.1	4.5	3.5
1973	1,497	100.0	60.8	31.1	4.7	3.5

Source: General Social Surveys, National Opinion Research Center, University of Chicago; calculations by New Strategist

Table 1.29 Spending on Improving the Condition of Blacks, 1973 to 2002

We are faced with many problems in this country, none of which can be solved easily or inexpensively. Are we spending too much, too little money, or about the right amount on improving the condition of blacks?

(number of respondents aged 18 or older, and percent distribution by response, 1973–2002)

	number of respondents	total	too little	about right	too much	don't know
2002	1,346	100.0%	30.6%	45.8%	17.1%	6.5%
2000	1,399	100.0	33.5	40.2	14.6	11.7
1998	1,375	100.0	34.1	40.4	16.4	9.2
1996	1,437	100.0	31.8	38.8	19.3	10.1
1994	1,502	100.0	30.8	40.3	20.3	8.7
1993	793	100.0	35.8	39.7	15.3	9.2
1991	749	100.0	34.2	42.9	14.4	8.5
1990	670	100.0	36.9	40.4	14.9	7.8
1989	765	100.0	32.3	41.4	15.9	10.3
1988	714	100.0	34.7	41.0	16.0	8.3
1987	594	100.0	35.9	42.4	14.5	7.2
1986	724	100.0	33.6	42.5	15.9	8.0
1985	749	100.0	30.7	42.6	20.0	6.7
1984	485	100.0	35.1	42.9	15.9	6.2
1983	1,592	100.0	29.3	43.5	18.2	9.1
1982	1,851	100.0	27.9	43.7	20.2	8.2
1980	1,462	100.0	24.1	44.1	23.9	7.9
1978	1,529	100.0	24.3	43.2	25.2	7.3
1977	1,525	100.0	25.1	42.2	24.6	8.1
1976	1,491	100.0	27.4	40.5	25.4	6.6
1975	1,486	100.0	26.9	41.5	24.0	7.7
1974	1,477	100.0	30.9	41.7	20.7	6.6
1973	1,499	100.0	32.6	39.4	21.6	6.5

Source: General Social Surveys, National Opinion Research Center, University of Chicago; calculations by New Strategist

Table 1.30 Spending on the Military, 1973 to 2002

We are faced with many problems in this country, none of which can be solved easily or inexpensively. Are we spending too much, too little money, or about the right amount on military, armaments, and defense?

(number of respondents aged 18 or older, and percent distribution by response, 1973–2002)

	number of respondents	total	too little	about right	too much	don't know
2002	1,357	100.0%	30.5%	45.3%	21.7%	2.4%
2000	1,403	100.0	23.0	45.7	24.4	6.8
1998	1,373	100.0	17.6	46.6	30.4	5.4
1996	1,440	100.0	16.9	46.1	30.9	6.0
1994	1,501	100.0	15.9	47.3	32.8	3.9
1993	795	100.0	10.3	44.4	41.5	3.8
1991	750	100.0	14.1	56.3	27.3	2.3
1990	670	100.0	10.3	42.5	41.8	5.4
1989	764	100.0	14.5	40.7	39.1	5.6
1988	712	100.0	15.9	40.0	38.5	5.6
1987	594	100.0	15.7	39.7	40.4	4.2
1986	726	100.0	16.3	38.4	40.5	4.8
1985	747	100.0	14.3	42.2	40.2	3.3
1984	486	100.0	17.3	41.2	38.1	3.5
1983	1,595	100.0	24.1	37.8	32.5	5.6
1982	1,848	100.0	29.3	35.2	30.1	5.4
1980	1,465	100.0	56.3	25.7	11.5	6.5
1978	1,529	100.0	27.0	43.6	21.8	7.6
1977	1,527	100.0	23.6	45.4	22.9	8.1
1976	1,492	100.0	24.1	42.1	27.3	6.5
1975	1,484	100.0	16.6	45.8	31.1	6.5
1974	1,479	100.0	16.9	45.4	31.0	6.7
1973	1,496	100.0	11.2	45.0	37.9	5.9

Source: General Social Surveys, National Opinion Research Center, University of Chicago; calculations by New Strategist

Table 1.31 Spending on Foreign Aid, 1973 to 2002

We are faced with many problems in this country, none of which can be solved easily or inexpensively. Are we spending too much, too little money, or about the right amount on foreign aid?

(number of respondents aged 18 or older, and percent distribution by response, 1973–2002)

	number of respondents	total	too little	about right	too much	don't know
2002	1,355	100.0%	6.5%	26.9%	63.5%	3.1%
2000	1,405	100.0	8.1	28.3	56.9	6.7
1998	1,378	100.0	6.7	27.0	60.4	5.9
1996	1,438	100.0	4.2	21.5	68.4	5.9
1994	1,503	100.0	4.3	20.2	71.7	3.9
1993	795	100.0	4.9	20.8	69.8	4.5
1991	747	100.0	4.0	19.1	72.8	4.0
1990	671	100.0	5.4	23.5	66.5	4.6
1989	762	100.0	4.5	21.5	67.8	6.2
1988	715	100.0	5.0	22.1	67.8	5.0
1987	596	100.0	7.2	19.3	69.5	4.0
1986	726	100.0	6.2	19.3	70.7	3.9
1985	745	100.0	6.6	24.4	65.4	3.6
1984	486	100.0	4.3	20.6	70.2	4.9
1983	1,595	100.0	3.9	17.1	73.7	5.4
1982	1,854	100.0	5.2	17.9	72.1	4.9
1980	1,466	100.0	5.1	19.8	69.8	5.3
1978	1,532	100.0	3.9	23.9	66.5	5.7
1977	1,527	100.0	3.4	23.5	66.1	6.9
1976	1,494	100.0	2.9	17.9	75.4	3.7
1975	1,489	100.0	5.4	16.6	73.1	4.9
1974	1,481	100.0	3.0	17.4	75.6	4.0
1973	1,503	100.0	4.2	20.1	70.3	5.5

Source: General Social Surveys, National Opinion Research Center, University of Chicago; calculations by New Strategist

Table 1.32 Spending on Welfare, 1973 to 2002

We are faced with many problems in this country, none of which can be solved easily or inexpensively. Are we spending too much, too little money, or about the right amount on welfare?

(number of respondents aged 18 or older, and percent distribution by response, 1973–2002)

	number of respondents	total	too little	about right	too much	don't know
2002	1,355	100.0%	20.6%	37.0%	39.3%	3.0%
2000	1,403	100.0	20.1	37.8	36.9	5.1
1998	1,379	100.0	16.0	36.1	43.4	4.5
1996	1,439	100.0	15.1	25.9	55.9	3.1
1994	1,502	100.0	12.6	23.9	59.9	3.6
1993	796	100.0	16.3	24.9	53.8	5.0
1991	746	100.0	22.3	35.0	37.5	5.2
1990	670	100.0	22.1	34.6	38.1	5.2
1989	762	100.0	22.8	29.9	41.7	5.5
1988	709	100.0	22.8	31.9	41.9	3.4
1987	596	100.0	22.1	29.5	43.8	4.5
1986	726	100.0	22.3	33.6	40.5	3.6
1985	749	100.0	18.6	32.8	44.6	4.0
1984	484	100.0	24.0	33.5	39.9	2.7
1983	1,594	100.0	21.4	28.0	46.6	4.0
1982	1,858	100.0	20.2	27.6	47.8	4.4
1980	1,463	100.0	13.4	25.8	56.5	4.2
1978	1,529	100.0	13.0	25.0	58.3	3.7
1977	1,524	100.0	12.3	23.0	59.7	4.9
1976	1,493	100.0	13.3	22.4	59.9	4.3
1975	1,484	100.0	23.4	28.5	42.8	5.3
1974	1,481	100.0	22.1	31.8	42.1	4.0
1973	1,497	100.0	19.8	24.4	51.4	4.3

Source: General Social Surveys, National Opinion Research Center, University of Chicago; calculations by New Strategist

Table 133 Spending on the Space Program, 1973 to 2002

We are faced with many problems in this country, none of which can be solved easily or inexpensively. Are we spending too much, too little money, or about the right amount on space exploration?

(number of respondents aged 18 or older, and percent distribution by response, 1973–2002)

	number of respondents	total	too little	about right	too much	don't know
2002	1,356	100.0%	11.1%	47.2%	35.3%	6.4%
2000	1,407	100.0	13.9	37.6	41.1	7.5
1998	1,379	100.0	10.1	43.9	39.4	6.7
1996	1,439	100.0	11.0	40.1	41.8	7.2
1994	1,507	100.0	9.0	37.3	48.2	5.4
1993	796	100.0	8.4	37.1	47.7	6.8
1991	750	100.0	11.7	42.8	38.0	7.5
1990	671	100.0	11.2	43.8	39.2	5.8
1989	766	100.0	14.8	44.1	34.7	6.4
1988	714	100.0	17.8	42.0	34.5	5.7
1987	599	100.0	16.0	37.6	40.6	5.8
1986	727	100.0	11.3	43.5	41.1	4.1
1985	748	100.0	11.5	44.3	40.6	3.6
1984	487	100.0	11.9	43.1	39.4	5.5
1983	1,598	100.0	13.8	40.5	39.7	6.0
1982	1,860	100.0	12.4	40.9	40.3	6.3
1980	1,466	100.0	18.0	34.5	39.2	8.3
1978	1,532	100.0	11.6	35.0	47.2	6.3
1977	1,530	100.0	10.1	34.4	49.6	5.9
1976	1,496	100.0	9.2	28.0	60.4	2.5
1975	1,490	100.0	7.4	30.1	58.1	4.4
1974	1,480	100.0	7.7	27.6	61.1	3.6
1973	1,503	100.0	7.5	29.3	58.5	4.7

Source: General Social Surveys, National Opinion Research Center, University of Chicago; calculations by New Strategist

Table 1.34 Spending on Mass Transportation, 1984 to 2002

We are faced with many problems in this country, none of which can be solved easily or inexpensively. Are we spending too much, too little money, or about the right amount on mass transportation?

(number of respondents aged 18 or older, and percent distribution by response, 1984–2002)

	number of respondents	total	too little	about right	too much	don't know
2002	2,756	100.0%	34.8%	49.4%	10.1%	5.7%
2000	2,810	100.0	35.4	46.4	7.7	10.4
1998	2,817	100.0	31.9	47.6	9.5	11.0
1996	2,844	100.0	32.2	46.9	9.8	11.0
1994	2,948	100.0	35.1	48.3	8.0	8.6
1993	1,590	100.0	34.8	44.2	9.6	11.4
1991	1,495	100.0	33.4	47.6	9.0	10.0
1990	1,352	100.0	33.7	46.5	8.3	11.5
1989	1,526	100.0	29.0	49.1	8.4	13.6
1988	1,459	100.0	28.2	49.4	9.9	12.5
1987	1,802	100.0	29.7	46.4	13.3	10.6
1986	1,457	100.0	28.5	50.0	12.4	9.1
1985	1,528	100.0	30.0	47.7	12.1	10.2
1984	972	100.0	33.5	45.8	11.3	9.4

Source: General Social Surveys, National Opinion Research Center, University of Chicago; calculations by New Strategist

Table 1.35 Spending on Highways and Bridges, 1984 to 2002

We are faced with many problems in this country, none of which can be solved easily or inexpensively. Are we spending too much, too little money, or about the right amount on highways and bridges?

(number of respondents aged 18 or older, and percent distribution by response, 1984–2002)

	number of respondents	total	too little	about right	too much	don't know
2002	2,762	100.0%	34.4%	49.9%	12.2%	3.5%
2000	2,805	100.0	34.0	49.8	11.6	4.6
1998	2,818	100.0	38.4	47.3	9.7	4.6
1996	2,841	100.0	35.8	49.2	9.0	5.9
1994	2,943	100.0	38.8	49.3	7.5	4.3
1993	1,591	100.0	37.9	48.0	9.1	5.0
1991	1,497	100.0	34.1	50.0	10.4	5.5
1990	1,351	100.0	43.8	43.4	6.4	6.4
1989	1,524	100.0	38.3	48.5	7.0	6.3
1988	1,459	100.0	36.1	52.0	7.6	4.3
1987	1,801	100.0	34.1	51.9	8.7	5.3
1986	1,459	100.0	35.0	52.1	8.4	4.5
1985	1,524	100.0	41.1	46.3	7.6	5.0
1984	973	100.0	46.5	43.1	6.7	3.8

Source: General Social Surveys, National Opinion Research Center, University of Chicago; calculations by New Strategist

Table 1.36 Spending on Social Security, 1984 to 2002

We are faced with many problems in this country, none of which can be solved easily or inexpensively. Are we spending too much, too little money, or about the right amount on Social Security?

(number of respondents aged 18 or older, and percent distribution by response, 1984–2002)

	number of respondents	total	too little	about right	too much	don't know
2002	2,760	100.0%	58.6%	33.3%	4.5%	3.6%
2000	2,811	100.0	57.8	31.9	4.7	5.6
1998	2,819	100.0	56.0	32.0	6.3	5.7
1996	2,841	100.0	48.9	37.5	7.9	5.7
1994	2,948	100.0	46.5	41.4	7.0	5.1
1993	1,591	100.0	43.6	43.1	7.1	6.2
1991	1,495	100.0	51.8	38.8	4.0	5.4
1990	1,351	100.0	49.4	39.8	5.6	5.2
1989	1,527	100.0	54.1	36.8	4.3	4.8
1988	1,467	100.0	52.6	37.7	5.5	4.2
1987	1,801	100.0	54.9	34.6	6.7	3.8
1986	1,456	100.0	55.6	35.6	6.2	2.5
1985	1,527	100.0	52.0	38.4	6.6	3.0
1984	968	100.0	50.9	35.5	8.8	4.8

Source: General Social Surveys, National Opinion Research Center, University of Chicago; calculations by New Strategist

Table 1.37 Spending on Parks and Recreation, 1984 to 2002

We are faced with many problems in this country, none of which can be solved easily or inexpensively. Are we spending too much, too little money, or about the right amount on parks and recreation?

(number of respondents aged 18 or older, and percent distribution by response, 1984–2002)

	number of respondents	total	too little	about right	too much	don't know
2002	2,761	100.0%	34.0%	57.9%	5.3%	2.8%
2000	2,809	100.0	35.3	55.1	5.5	4.1
1998	2,824	100.0	34.1	55.4	6.1	4.4
1996	2,843	100.0	32.4	56.8	5.9	4.9
1994	2,947	100.0	29.7	60.0	6.4	3.9
1993	1,591	100.0	30.2	57.8	6.3	5.7
1991	1,496	100.0	30.1	60.2	5.0	4.7
1990	1,353	100.0	30.5	57.9	5.6	6.1
1989	1,528	100.0	32.5	56.2	5.1	6.2
1988	1,468	100.0	28.7	60.9	5.5	4.9
1987	1,804	100.0	29.9	59.9	6.2	4.0
1986	1,459	100.0	29.4	59.9	6.1	4.6
1985	1,530	100.0	30.6	58.1	7.1	4.2
1984	974	100.0	32.1	58.4	6.0	3.5

Source: General Social Surveys, National Opinion Research Center, University of Chicago; calculations by New Strategist

The Government's Role

There is a great debate in the United States over the proper role of the federal government. The consequences of this debate can be seen in the General Social Survey's measures of public opinion on this issue, which reveal that Americans are of two minds about the role of the federal government.

When asked whether it is the responsibility of government to help improve people's standard of living or whether people should help themselves, the proportion of those who agree with both positions (in other words, that the government should have at least some responsibility for helping poor Americans improve their standard of living) has grown from 35 percent in 1975 to 46 percent in 2002.

When asked whether government should help reduce income differences between rich and poor, a larger share of people come down on the side of government intervention. In 2002, 46 percent placed themselves on the "should" side versus 33 percent who believed it "should not." These figures have not changed much over the years.

When asked whether the government in Washington is trying to do too many things that should be left to individuals and private businesses, the 47 percent plurality of the public chose the middle position in 2002, up from only 29 percent who felt that way in 1975. Even as many politicians and voters profess free-market principles, only 25 percent of Americans in 2002 thought the government did too much, while 24 percent thought the government should do more.

On one issue there is less debate: The majority of Americans believe government should help people pay their medical bills. In 2002, 51 percent of Americans chose this position, while 34 percent agreed with both positions (government should help and people should help themselves). Only 14 percent of the public thinks paying for health care should be an individual responsibility.

Table 1.38 Should Government Improve the Standard of Living, 1975 to 2002

Some people think that the government in Washington should do everything possible to improve the standard of living of all poor Americans. Other people think it is not the government's responsibility, and that each person should take care of himself. Where would you place yourself on this scale?

(number of respondents aged 18 or older, and percent distribution by response, 1975–2002)

	number of respondents	total	1 government should act	2	3 agree with both	4	5 people should help themselves	don't know
2002	911	100.0%	16.9%	10.4%	46.1%	12.6%	11.4%	2.5%
2000	1,887	100.0	13.9	12.6	41.7	16.4	12.0	3.4
1998	1,905	100.0	12.5	12.6	42.9	16.6	12.1	3.3
1996	1,918	100.0	12.9	12.0	45.4	15.5	10.6	3.5
1994	1,998	100.0	12.6	13.4	43.5	15.9	11.6	2.9
1993	1,053	100.0	12.4	13.5	47.6	13.8	10.4	2.4
1991	1,013	100.0	16.9	16.2	42.9	13.0	8.1	2.9
1990	898	100.0	18.7	14.9	43.1	12.4	8.4	2.6
1989	1,033	100.0	16.5	14.9	43.1	13.6	8.6	3.3
1988	995	100.0	17.2	12.8	44.3	11.9	11.5	2.4
1987	1,810	100.0	17.4	11.9	44.3	13.2	10.7	2.6
1986	1,466	100.0	18.2	12.3	44.8	11.5	10.7	2.5
1984	1,462	100.0	17.3	10.9	45.6	14.2	8.4	3.6
1983	1,593	100.0	16.8	14.8	39.6	13.5	11.3	4.0
1975	1,490	100.0	29.1	9.9	34.8	10.4	13.0	2.8

Source: General Social Surveys, National Opinion Research Center, University of Chicago; calculations by New Strategist

Table 1.39 Should Government Do More or Less, 1975 to 2002

Some people think that the government in Washington is trying to do too many things that should be left to individuals and private businesses. Others disagree and think that the government should do even more to solve our country's problems. Still others have opinions somewhere in between. Where would you place yourself on this scale?

(number of respondents aged 18 or older, and percent distribution by response, 1975–2002)

	number of respondents	total	1 government should do more	2	3 agree with both	4	5 government does too much	don't know
2002	911	100.0%	14.2%	10.2%	47.3%	13.5%	11.9%	3.0%
2000	1,887	100.0	11.3	12.0	37.6	17.5	16.6	5.0
1998	1,908	100.0	10.6	12.1	39.3	17.8	14.8	5.5
1996	1,918	100.0	11.9	12.5	37.6	16.9	15.8	5.2
1994	1,996	100.0	11.8	13.6	35.5	17.9	16.3	4.9
1993	1,051	100.0	13.1	14.8	38.2	15.4	14.7	3.7
1991	1,012	100.0	13.7	14.7	39.0	14.6	11.0	6.9
1990	899	100.0	13.1	15.0	40.5	14.8	10.6	6.0
1989	1,033	100.0	13.0	14.2	37.8	15.4	12.7	7.0
1988	996	100.0	13.8	13.9	39.4	14.2	12.9	6.0
1987	1,811	100.0	14.5	14.0	37.7	14.8	13.6	5.4
1986	1,467	100.0	12.3	12.6	41.2	15.5	12.9	5.5
1984	1,449	100.0	14.1	12.7	37.1	16.6	14.1	5.5
1983	1,595	100.0	12.4	11.0	36.0	17.6	16.2	6.9
1975	1,487	100.0	24.9	10.8	29.1	11.6	16.5	7.0

Source: General Social Surveys, National Opinion Research Center, University of Chicago; calculations by New Strategist

Table 1.40 Should Government Reduce Income Differences, 1978 to 2002

Some people think that the government in Washington ought to reduce the income differences between the rich and the poor, perhaps by raising the taxes of wealthy families or by giving income assistance to the poor. Others think that the government should not concern itself with reducing this income difference between the rich and the poor. Think of a score of 1 as meaning that the government ought to reduce the income differences between rich and poor, and a score of 7 meaning that the government should not concern itself with reducing income differences. What score between 1 and 7 comes closest to the way you feel?

(number of respondents aged 18 or older, and percent distribution by response, 1978–2002)

	number of respondents	total	1 government should	2	3	4	5	6	7 government should not	don't know
2002	911	100.0%	19.2%	9.2%	18.0%	19.4%	13.7%	7.2%	12.0%	1.2%
2000	1,887	100.0	16.0	11.5	15.6	19.8	13.7	8.5	13.0	2.0
1998	1,904	100.0	14.8	9.5	17.4	21.1	11.2	8.2	15.9	1.8
1996	1,917	100.0	17.3	10.4	15.8	21.3	12.4	8.2	12.2	2.3
1994	2,003	100.0	14.4	9.1	16.1	21.0	14.6	8.3	15.1	1.3
1993	1,053	100.0	17.5	11.6	19.1	17.8	12.3	7.7	12.3	1.7
1991	1,014	100.0	19.8	12.4	17.1	19.7	12.1	7.4	8.8	2.7
1990	896	100.0	21.0	11.9	17.5	21.2	8.9	6.3	10.4	2.8
1989	1,033	100.0	17.6	12.8	19.3	19.9	11.2	7.0	10.5	1.7
1988	994	100.0	19.4	9.6	18.1	19.8	12.2	7.5	11.3	2.1
1987	1,811	100.0	22.5	8.8	17.0	20.4	12.0	5.7	12.2	1.4
1986	1,467	100.0	23.0	8.9	16.8	20.6	10.9	6.1	12.4	1.3
1984	1,462	100.0	20.9	12.2	15.3	17.2	13.1	8.0	11.7	1.6
1983	1,596	100.0	19.7	10.7	16.0	17.4	11.1	8.2	14.4	2.4
1980	1,463	100.0	16.8	9.3	16.3	19.8	12.3	7.2	15.5	2.7
1978	758	100.0	19.3	10.8	17.2	20.7	10.7	7.5	12.4	1.5

Source: General Social Surveys, National Opinion Research Center, University of Chicago; calculations by New Strategist

Table 1.41 Should Government Help the Sick, 1975 to 2002

In general, some people think that it is the responsibility of the government in Washington to see to it that people have help in paying for doctors and hospital bills. Others think that these matters are not the responsibility of the federal government and that people should take care of these things themselves. Where would you place yourself on this scale?

(number of respondents aged 18 or older, and percent distribution by response, 1975–2002)

	number of respondents	total	1 government should help	2	3 agree with both	4	5 people should help themselves	don't know
2002	911	100.0%	31.5%	19.2%	33.8%	7.1%	6.9%	1.4%
2000	1,887	100.0	28.6	21.3	31.1	10.3	5.8	3.0
1998	1,905	100.0	24.8	22.2	32.0	9.7	8.3	2.9
1996	1,918	100.0	27.0	21.0	32.4	10.3	6.6	2.7
1994	1,998	100.0	25.2	21.0	31.0	10.9	9.3	2.7
1993	1,049	100.0	28.3	22.3	31.6	9.3	6.2	2.2
1991	1,013	100.0	31.7	24.7	26.8	9.2	5.7	2.0
1990	897	100.0	29.7	25.5	30.1	7.5	4.3	2.9
1989	1,031	100.0	30.5	22.4	30.1	7.6	7.5	2.0
1988	993	100.0	26.6	21.6	34.7	8.6	6.4	2.1
1987	1,813	100.0	26.4	20.1	35.2	8.4	7.6	2.2
1986	1,463	100.0	28.4	20.0	31.6	11.2	6.4	2.5
1984	1,449	100.0	23.9	18.6	34.9	12.1	7.7	2.8
1983	1,593	100.0	25.9	18.8	31.6	10.2	10.1	3.3
1975	1,484	100.0	35.8	12.7	28.5	7.7	13.1	2.1

Source: General Social Surveys, National Opinion Research Center, University of Chicago; calculations by New Strategist

Health Status

Despite many fundamental changes that have taken place in American society over the past three decades—including the aging of the population, the growing diversity of Americans, and more single-parent households—the public still rates its health pretty much as it did in the early 1970s. More than three-quarters of Americans describe their health as "good" or "excellent."

In 2002, 31 percent of Americans described their health as excellent, almost identical to the 30 percent of 1972. Forty-six percent of Americans rated their health as good in 2002, up slightly from the 45 percent of 1972. The proportion who say their health is only "fair" has fallen slightly from 20 to 17 percent over those years. And the 5.6 percent who say their health is "poor" is about the same as the 5.3 percent of 1972.

One factor that might explain the stability in the health status of the American population is its rising educational level. The more educated a person is, the better is his or her reported health, according to many studies. Although the American population is getting older, it is also much better educated than it was in the 1970s, resulting in health status stability.

Table 1.42 Health Status, 1972 to 2002

Would you say your own health, in general, is excellent, good, fair, or poor?

(number of respondents aged 18 or older, and percent distribution by self-reported health status, 1972–2002)

	number of respondents	total	excellent	good	fair	poor	don't know
2002	1,851	100.0%	30.7%	46.1%	17.4%	5.6%	0.2%
2000	2,326	100.0	30.2	47.4	16.9	5.4	0.1
1998	2,823	100.0	31.0	47.6	16.5	4.8	0.1
1996	2,421	100.0	30.9	49.0	16.0	3.9	0.1
1994	1,994	100.0	31.4	46.7	17.3	4.6	–
1993	1,072	100.0	31.6	45.4	16.6	6.3	0.1
1991	988	100.0	31.3	44.5	19.8	4.4	–
1990	916	100.0	31.1	45.7	17.7	5.2	0.2
1989	1,032	100.0	33.1	44.6	17.7	4.3	0.3
1988	976	100.0	30.7	45.1	17.8	6.4	–
1987	1,817	100.0	34.0	42.8	18.0	5.2	0.1
1985	1,531	100.0	33.5	42.3	17.6	6.6	0.1
1984	1,462	100.0	29.9	47.7	17.6	4.7	0.1
1982	1,859	100.0	31.8	42.0	18.9	7.3	–
1980	1,466	100.0	31.8	42.0	19.6	6.5	–
1977	1,527	100.0	31.8	40.9	20.5	6.9	–
1976	1,499	100.0	31.3	42.0	19.7	6.9	0.1
1975	1,489	100.0	32.4	39.8	21.4	6.4	–
1974	1,480	100.0	32.8	39.8	21.2	6.1	–
1973	1,501	100.0	31.9	39.9	21.0	7.1	0.1
1972	1,612	100.0	30.0	44.8	19.9	5.3	–

Source: General Social Surveys, National Opinion Research Center, University of Chicago; calculations by New Strategist

Personal Outlook

The personal outlook of Americans has remained remarkably stable over the past thirty years, despite wars, terrorist attacks, stock market ups and downs, recessions, and recoveries. The percentage of Americans who say they are "very happy," for example, has changed little since the early 1970s. In 2002, 30 percent said they were very happy while the 57 percent majority said they were "pretty happy."

Similarly, the percentage of the public that finds life "exciting" has not changed much despite good times and bad. In 2002, 51 percent of the public found life exciting. Although this is the highest percentage ever recorded by the GSS, the figure has waxed and waned over the years with little real trend in direction.

The public has become less trusting, however. In 1972, 46 percent of Americans agreed that "most people can be trusted." In 2002, only 34 percent felt that way. Similarly, there has been an upward trend in the percentage of the public believing "most people would try to take advantage of you if they got a chance," rising from 34 percent in 1972 to 40 percent in 2002. Fewer than half of Americans agree that "most of the time people try to be helpful," while a nearly equal proportion believe other people are "mostly looking out for themselves."

Marital happiness has also declined over the past three decades. In 1972, more than two-thirds of married people described their marriage as "very happy." By 2002 the figure had fallen to 61 percent.

Television viewing has remained pretty stable over the past thirty years, with about half the public watching two or fewer hours of TV a day and about half watching more than that. In contrast, newspaper readership has lost ground to other forms of news and entertainment. Only 41 percent of the public reads a newspaper every day, down from 69 percent in 1972.

Table 1.43 General Happiness, 1972 to 2002

Taken all together, how would you say things are these days—would you say that you are very happy, pretty happy, or not too happy?

(number of respondents aged 18 or older, and percent distribution by response, 1972–2002)

	number of respondents	total	very happy	pretty happy	not too happy	don't know
2002	1,370	100.0%	30.3%	57.2%	12.4%	0.1%
2000	2,778	100.0	31.7	57.7	10.5	0.0
1998	2,808	100.0	31.7	56.1	12.1	0.1
1996	2,886	100.0	30.4	57.5	12.1	0.0
1994	2,978	100.0	28.8	59.0	12.2	0.0
1993	1,601	100.0	31.6	57.3	11.1	–
1991	1,504	100.0	31.1	58.0	11.0	–
1990	1,361	100.0	33.4	57.6	9.0	–
1989	1,526	100.0	32.6	57.7	9.7	–
1988	1,466	100.0	34.0	56.8	9.3	–
1987	1,787	100.0	31.7	56.4	11.9	–
1986	1,449	100.0	32.3	56.3	11.4	–
1985	1,530	100.0	28.6	60.0	11.4	–
1984	1,446	100.0	34.7	52.3	12.9	0.1
1983	1,573	100.0	31.2	56.1	12.8	–
1982	1,857	100.0	33.0	54.1	12.9	–
1980	1,463	100.0	33.9	52.7	13.3	0.1
1978	1,517	100.0	34.3	56.1	9.6	–
1977	1,527	100.0	34.8	53.2	11.9	–
1976	1,499	100.0	34.1	53.4	12.5	–
1975	1,485	100.0	32.9	54.1	13.1	–
1974	1,480	100.0	37.9	49.0	13.1	–
1973	1,500	100.0	35.9	51.1	13.1	–
1972	1,606	100.0	30.3	53.2	16.5	–

Source: General Social Surveys, National Opinion Research Center, University of Chicago; calculations by New Strategist

Table 1.44 Is Life Exciting, 1973 to 2002

In general, do you find life exciting, pretty routine, or dull?

(number of respondents aged 18 or older, and percent distribution by response, 1973–2002)

	number of respondents	total	exciting	routine	dull	don't know
2002	924	100.0%	50.6%	43.0%	3.6%	2.8%
2000	1,854	100.0	46.0	48.3	4.9	0.9
1998	1,876	100.0	44.7	49.0	5.5	0.9
1996	1,918	100.0	49.6	45.5	4.2	0.7
1994	1,990	100.0	47.1	48.1	4.1	0.6
1993	1,071	100.0	46.3	46.9	6.4	0.4
1991	988	100.0	43.9	51.1	4.1	0.8
1990	912	100.0	44.7	49.8	4.9	0.5
1989	1,020	100.0	44.4	50.0	5.3	0.3
1988	957	100.0	44.7	49.6	4.9	0.7
1987	1,780	100.0	45.4	50.2	4.0	0.4
1985	1,530	100.0	47.5	45.2	6.4	0.8
1984	1,466	100.0	46.7	48.0	5.0	0.3
1982	1,853	100.0	44.7	48.8	6.0	0.5
1980	1,468	100.0	45.8	48.2	5.6	0.4
1977	1,503	100.0	44.2	48.6	6.7	0.5
1976	1,484	100.0	44.5	51.3	3.6	0.6
1974	1,450	100.0	43.2	51.5	4.7	0.6
1973	1,489	100.0	45.3	49.2	5.1	0.3

Source: General Social Surveys, National Opinion Research Center, University of Chicago; calculations by New Strategist

Table 1.45 Trusting in People, 1972 to 2002

Generally speaking, would you say that most people can be trusted or that you can't be too careful in life?

(number of respondents aged 18 or older, and percent distribution by response, 1972 to 2002)

	number of respondents	total	can trust	cannot trust	depends	don't know
2002	912	100.0%	34.0%	57.9%	7.9%	0.2%
2000	1,888	100.0	35.1	57.9	6.6	0.5
1998	2,353	100.0	37.5	56.4	5.8	0.3
1996	1,921	100.0	33.8	60.7	5.2	0.3
1994	2,002	100.0	34.0	61.4	4.2	0.3
1993	1,056	100.0	35.7	59.7	4.3	0.4
1991	1,015	100.0	38.4	56.5	4.9	0.2
1990	898	100.0	38.1	57.6	4.3	–
1989	1,033	100.0	40.9	55.1	3.8	0.3
1988	995	100.0	38.7	56.5	4.3	0.5
1987	1,813	100.0	43.8	52.0	4.0	0.1
1986	1,470	100.0	37.5	59.6	2.7	0.3
1984	1,465	100.0	47.8	49.4	2.5	0.3
1983	802	100.0	36.9	58.5	4.4	0.2
1980	1,466	100.0	45.4	50.5	3.8	0.3
1978	1,532	100.0	38.9	56.5	4.3	0.3
1976	1,497	100.0	44.4	51.8	3.7	0.1
1975	1,485	100.0	39.3	55.9	4.3	0.5
1973	1,502	100.0	45.9	50.9	2.9	0.2
1972	1,612	100.0	45.8	49.8	3.5	0.9

Source: General Social Surveys, National Opinion Research Center, University of Chicago; calculations by New Strategist

Table 1.46 Fairness of People, 1972 to 2002

Do you think most people would try to take advantage of you if they got a chance, or would they try to be fair?

(number of respondents aged 18 or older, and percent distribution by response, 1972–2002)

	number of respondents	total	take advantage	fair	depends	don't know
2002	912	100.0%	39.6%	49.5%	10.6%	0.3%
2000	1,887	100.0	38.0	51.6	9.1	1.3
1998	1,908	100.0	38.0	52.3	8.8	1.0
1996	1,912	100.0	42.1	49.9	6.9	1.2
1994	2,002	100.0	39.3	53.2	6.7	0.8
1993	1,055	100.0	36.4	55.8	7.0	0.8
1991	1,011	100.0	36.2	57.3	5.8	0.7
1990	899	100.0	36.2	57.3	5.9	0.7
1989	1,035	100.0	36.3	57.9	5.2	0.6
1988	996	100.0	33.6	60.0	5.1	1.2
1987	1,811	100.0	36.9	58.2	3.9	1.0
1986	1,465	100.0	33.4	62.2	3.8	0.6
1984	1,470	100.0	34.5	62.1	3.2	0.2
1983	1,599	100.0	34.6	59.4	5.1	0.9
1980	1,468	100.0	34.4	60.1	4.3	1.2
1978	1,525	100.0	29.8	64.5	5.1	0.7
1976	1,499	100.0	36.2	59.2	4.1	0.5
1975	1,488	100.0	30.5	61.6	7.1	0.8
1973	1,503	100.0	37.4	57.3	4.8	0.5
1972	1,611	100.0	33.6	59.2	6.0	1.2

Source: General Social Surveys, National Opinion Research Center, University of Chicago; calculations by New Strategist

Table 1.47 Helpfulness of People, 1972 to 2002

Would you say that most of the time people try to be helpful, or that they are mostly just looking out for themselves?

(number of respondents aged 18 or older, and percent distribution by response, 1972–2002)

	number of respondents	total	helpful	look out for self	depends	don't know
2002	912	100.0%	47.3%	42.9%	9.6%	0.2%
2000	1,893	100.0	45.7	45.0	8.8	0.5
1998	1,909	100.0	47.7	42.7	9.2	0.4
1996	1,921	100.0	43.4	48.9	7.2	0.5
1994	2,004	100.0	46.5	46.7	6.4	0.4
1993	1,056	100.0	52.2	40.8	5.7	1.3
1991	1,012	100.0	49.0	43.1	7.1	0.8
1990	898	100.0	51.7	41.4	6.1	0.8
1989	1,034	100.0	50.1	44.4	5.0	0.5
1988	994	100.0	49.7	45.1	4.6	0.6
1987	1,817	100.0	47.3	47.8	4.4	0.5
1986	1,465	100.0	55.8	38.6	5.2	0.5
1984	1,470	100.0	51.9	44.2	3.7	0.2
1983	1,599	100.0	57.3	37.7	4.3	0.7
1980	1,465	100.0	48.7	46.3	4.4	0.6
1978	1,527	100.0	59.4	35.1	5.2	0.3
1976	1,498	100.0	43.1	50.5	6.1	0.3
1975	1,488	100.0	56.2	36.6	6.7	0.5
1973	1,501	100.0	46.8	49.2	3.7	0.3
1972	1,612	100.0	46.5	45.9	6.2	1.4

Source: General Social Surveys, National Opinion Research Center, University of Chicago; calculations by New Strategist

Table 1.48 Happiness of Marriage, 1973 to 2002

Taking things all together, how would you describe your marriage? Would you say that your marriage is very happy, pretty happy, or not too happy?

(number of married respondents aged 18 or older, and percent distribution by response, 1973–2002)

	number of respondents	total	very happy	pretty happy	not too happy	don't know
2002	604	100.0%	61.3%	35.6%	3.0%	0.2%
2000	1270	100.0	62.1	34.2	3.2	0.5
1998	1338	100.0	63.9	33.3	2.8	0.1
1996	1383	100.0	61.7	35.8	2.2	0.3
1994	1533	100.0	60.5	36.2	3.1	0.3
1993	856	100.0	61.6	35.2	2.9	0.4
1991	801	100.0	63.2	33.5	3.2	0.1
1990	725	100.0	64.6	33.1	2.2	0.1
1989	843	100.0	60.3	36.9	2.5	0.4
1988	787	100.0	62.5	34.1	3.4	–
1987	987	100.0	64.9	32.8	2.2	–
1986	820	100.0	63.0	33.4	3.4	0.1
1985	864	100.0	56.5	40.0	3.4	0.1
1984	825	100.0	65.6	31.4	3.0	–
1983	961	100.0	62.4	34.3	3.2	–
1982	1051	100.0	65.3	31.9	2.7	0.2
1980	884	100.0	67.8	29.2	2.8	0.2
1978	955	100.0	65.1	32.1	2.6	0.1
1977	970	100.0	65.2	30.7	3.6	0.5
1976	973	100.0	66.8	30.8	2.4	–
1975	997	100.0	67.3	29.8	2.7	0.2
1974	1061	100.0	69.0	27.3	3.5	0.2
1973	1073	100.0	67.8	29.5	2.6	0.1

Source: General Social Surveys, National Opinion Research Center, University of Chicago; calculations by New Strategist

Table 1.49 Hours of Daily Television Viewing, 1975 to 2002

On the average day, about how many hours do you personally watch television?

(number of respondents aged 18 or older, and percent distribution by response, 1975–2002)

	number of respondents	total	none	one	two	three	four	five or more	don't know
2002	908	100.0%	3.5%	22.0%	25.7%	18.7%	11.6%	18.2%	0.3%
2000	1,832	100.0	5.8	20.7	27.8	16.9	12.7	15.8	0.2
1998	2,343	100.0	5.1	21.3	27.4	17.0	13.6	15.4	0.3
1996	1,950	100.0	4.4	19.7	28.9	17.6	13.4	15.9	0.2
1994	1,965	100.0	3.8	21.6	27.2	19.2	14.2	14.0	–
1993	1,594	100.0	3.8	20.5	28.2	19.4	12.0	16.1	–
1991	1,014	100.0	3.7	17.9	25.2	21.3	13.6	18.2	–
1990	926	100.0	3.1	21.6	28.2	18.6	12.4	16.0	0.1
1989	999	100.0	3.3	18.4	30.1	16.9	14.3	16.8	0.1
1988	981	100.0	3.3	18.8	24.8	19.2	14.2	19.7	0.2
1986	1,466	100.0	4.4	17.8	26.5	20.3	13.2	17.7	–
1985	1,524	100.0	5.1	17.7	26.0	20.4	13.7	17.1	0.1
1983	1,596	100.0	5.6	18.5	25.1	20.4	13.3	16.9	0.1
1982	1,858	100.0	4.5	20.8	25.1	19.0	13.8	16.8	–
1980	1,454	100.0	7.6	18.0	24.1	19.0	13.2	18.1	–
1978	1,529	100.0	6.0	20.7	27.3	18.8	12.7	14.5	0.1
1977	1,525	100.0	4.0	21.0	25.2	20.4	13.4	15.9	–
1975	1,483	100.0	3.8	17.3	26.6	19.6	14.6	18.0	–

Source: General Social Surveys, National Opinion Research Center, University of Chicago; calculations by New Strategist

Table 1.50 Newspaper Readership, 1972 to 2002

How often do you read the newspaper—every day, a few times a week, once a week, less than once a week, or never?

(number of respondents aged 18 or older, and percent distribution by response, 1972–2002)

	number of respondents	total	every day	few times a week	once a week	less than once a week	never
2002	908	100.0%	40.6%	24.1%	12.0%	13.3%	9.9%
2000	1,873	100.0	37.3	24.5	14.8	14.8	8.6
1998	1,870	100.0	43.0	22.5	15.7	10.8	8.0
1996	1,957	100.0	42.2	24.3	15.9	11.5	6.1
1994	1,954	100.0	49.6	23.1	13.4	10.0	3.9
1993	1,075	100.0	46.2	26.2	12.7	8.9	6.0
1991	1,022	100.0	51.4	21.5	13.6	8.5	5.0
1990	927	100.0	52.6	22.1	10.8	9.6	4.9
1989	1,005	100.0	50.0	24.7	12.9	7.6	4.9
1988	988	100.0	50.6	23.8	11.9	8.8	4.9
1987	1,814	100.0	54.4	20.5	13.0	6.5	5.6
1986	1,468	100.0	53.7	19.7	12.5	7.9	6.1
1985	1,530	100.0	52.7	21.2	12.8	7.6	5.7
1983	1,599	100.0	55.7	20.7	10.6	7.9	5.0
1982	1,856	100.0	53.7	21.9	11.9	6.8	5.8
1978	1,528	100.0	57.2	20.2	10.1	7.4	5.2
1977	1,527	100.0	62.3	16.6	9.7	6.5	4.8
1975	1,488	100.0	65.9	15.8	8.5	5.4	4.4
1972	1,611	100.0	68.6	15.0	7.9	4.3	4.2

Source: General Social Surveys, National Opinion Research Center, University of Chicago; calculations by New Strategist

Public Arena

Americans' attitudes toward the important issues of the day often run in cycles, rising and falling over time depending on current events.

With crime rates down, Americans felt less fearful about crime in their neighborhood in 2002 than in years past. In 2002, a record high 67 percent of the public said they would not be afraid to walk alone in their neighborhood at night.

Support for the death penalty is on the decline today as questions are raised about the guilt of people on death row. Thirty percent of the public opposed the death penalty for murder in 2002, a larger proportion than at any time since the mid-1970s.

Despite all the talk about guns, fewer Americans own a gun today than in the past. In 2002, only about one-third of households had a gun or revolver in their home, down from a majority or near majority in the mid-to-late 1970s.

Attitudes toward legalizing marijuana also appear to be changing, perhaps because of the publicizing of marijuana's medical benefits. In 2002, 34 percent of the public thought the use of marijuana should be made legal, up from a low of 16 percent in 1990.

Although tax rates are lower than they have been in many years, there has been little change in how Americans feel about taxes. Most believe they pay too much. In 2002, the 59 percent majority felt that the federal income tax level was too high, a figure that has been above the 50 percent mark since the GSS first asked this question in 1976.

The public's political leanings have changed only slightly over the past three decades. The percentage of Americans who say they are "moderates" stood at 38 percent in 2002—the same as in 1974. The percentage who identify themselves as liberal (from slightly to extremely) fell from 29 to 26 percent between 1974 and 2002, while the percentage identifying themselves as conservative (from slightly to extremely) rose from 28 to 34 percent.

Larger shifts have occurred in political party affiliation. In 1972, 47 percent of Americans identified themselves as Democrats and only 22 percent called themselves Republicans. By 2002, in a gradual but steady decline, a smaller 34 percent considered themselves Democrats and a larger 28 percent considered themselves Republicans. The biggest change, however, has been in the proportion of people who call themselves independents. It rose from 10 to 19 percent between 1972 and 2002.

Table 1.51 Afraid to Walk at Night in Neighborhood, 1973 to 2002

Is there any area right around here—that is, within a mile—
where you would be afraid to walk alone at night?

(number of respondents aged 18 or older, and percent distribution by response, 1973–2002)

	number of respondents	total	yes	no	don't know
2002	924	100.0%	32.0%	67.4%	0.5%
2000	1,856	100.0	39.1	59.6	1.3
1998	1,879	100.0	41.1	57.4	1.5
1996	1,923	100.0	41.8	57.2	1.0
1994	1,993	100.0	46.8	52.4	0.8
1993	1,073	100.0	43.0	56.8	0.3
1991	987	100.0	43.2	56.3	0.5
1990	914	100.0	40.9	58.0	1.1
1989	1,032	100.0	39.5	60.0	0.5
1988	975	100.0	40.1	59.0	0.9
1987	1,813	100.0	37.9	61.7	0.4
1985	1,531	100.0	40.3	58.9	0.8
1984	1,468	100.0	41.6	57.2	1.2
1982	1,857	100.0	46.4	53.4	0.2
1980	1,466	100.0	42.9	56.4	0.7
1977	1,529	100.0	44.9	54.5	0.6
1976	1,497	100.0	43.9	55.8	0.3
1974	1,480	100.0	44.8	54.7	0.5
1973	1,496	100.0	40.8	58.6	0.5

Source: General Social Surveys, National Opinion Research Center, University of Chicago; calculations by New Strategist

Table 1.52 Death Penalty for Murder, 1974 to 2002

Do you favor or oppose the death penalty
for persons convicted of murder?

(number of respondents aged 18 or older, and percent distribution by response, 1974–2002)

	number of respondents	total	favor	oppose	don't know
2002	1,365	100.0%	65.9%	30.0%	4.2%
2000	2,793	100.0	63.2	28.7	8.2
1998	2,819	100.0	67.6	24.6	7.8
1996	2,894	100.0	71.1	21.5	7.4
1994	2,979	100.0	74.4	19.5	6.2
1993	1,600	100.0	71.9	21.1	7.0
1991	1,507	100.0	71.5	22.3	6.2
1990	1,366	100.0	74.5	19.3	6.1
1989	1,532	100.0	74.0	20.5	5.5
1988	1,475	100.0	70.8	22.2	6.9
1987	1,804	100.0	69.7	24.4	5.9
1986	1,466	100.0	71.4	23.5	5.2
1985	1,526	100.0	75.6	19.5	4.9
1984	1,462	100.0	70.4	23.7	5.9
1983	1,597	100.0	73.2	22.2	4.6
1982	1,856	100.0	73.5	20.5	6.0
1980	1,461	100.0	67.2	26.7	6.1
1978	1,532	100.0	66.3	27.9	5.8
1977	1,520	100.0	67.2	26.4	6.4
1976	1,496	100.0	65.5	29.8	4.7
1975	1,483	100.0	60.1	33.2	6.7
1974	1,480	100.0	63.0	31.8	5.1

Source: General Social Surveys, National Opinion Research Center, University of Chicago; calculations by New Strategist

Table 1.53 Have Gun in Home, 1974 to 2002

Do you happen to have in your home any guns or revolvers?

(number of respondents aged 18 or older, and percent distribution by response, 1974–2002)

	number of respondents	total	yes	no	refused	don't know
2002	924	100.0%	33.5%	65.5%	1.0%	–
2000	1,858	100.0	32.5	66.3	1.2	0.1%
1998	1,876	100.0	34.9	64.8	0.3	0.1
1996	1,923	100.0	40.1	59.4	0.4	0.1
1994	1,992	100.0	40.7	58.2	1.0	0.2
1993	1,073	100.0	42.1	57.2	0.7	–
1991	986	100.0	39.9	59.1	1.0	–
1990	908	100.0	42.6	57.3	–	0.1
1989	1,030	100.0	46.1	53.9	–	–
1988	970	100.0	40.1	58.9	1.0	–
1987	1,815	100.0	45.8	53.7	0.5	–
1985	1,530	100.0	44.3	55.0	0.7	–
1984	1,467	100.0	45.1	54.2	0.6	0.1
1982	1,854	100.0	45.8	52.8	1.2	0.2
1980	1,458	100.0	47.7	52.1	0.1	0.1
1977	1,523	100.0	50.6	49.1	0.1	0.1
1976	1,493	100.0	46.7	52.2	1.1	–
1974	1,480	100.0	46.2	53.0	0.7	0.1

Source: General Social Surveys, National Opinion Research Center, University of Chicago; calculations by New Strategist

Table 1.54 Should Marijuana Be Legal, 1973 to 2002

Do you think the use of marijuana should be made legal or not?

(number of respondents aged 18 or older, and percent distribution by response, 1973–2002)

	number of respondents	total	favor	oppose	don't know
2002	912	100.0%	33.6%	59.8%	6.7%
2000	1,891	100.0	31.6	62.6	5.9
1998	1,905	100.0	27.6	66.3	6.1
1996	1,923	100.0	25.6	69.3	5.1
1994	2,000	100.0	22.9	72.5	4.7
1993	1,056	100.0	22.2	72.9	4.9
1991	1,012	100.0	18.0	78.1	4.0
1990	894	100.0	16.3	80.6	3.0
1989	1,029	100.0	16.4	80.6	3.0
1988	993	100.0	17.2	79.0	3.8
1987	1,817	100.0	16.6	80.5	2.9
1986	1,463	100.0	18.0	80.2	1.8
1984	1,465	100.0	22.7	73.3	4.0
1983	1,598	100.0	20.3	76.5	3.3
1980	1,465	100.0	24.8	72.1	3.1
1978	1,509	100.0	29.6	67.4	3.0
1976	1,497	100.0	27.8	68.9	3.3
1975	1,486	100.0	20.3	74.9	4.8
1973	1,501	100.0	18.3	79.7	2.0

Source: General Social Surveys, National Opinion Research Center, University of Chicago; calculations by New Strategist

Table 1.55 Divorce Laws, 1974 to 2002

Should divorce in this country be easier or more difficult to obtain than it is now?

(number of respondents aged 18 or older, and percent distribution by response, 1974–2002)

	number of respondents	total	easier	more difficult	stay same	don't know
2002	904	100.0%	26.3%	49.4%	21.7%	2.5%
2000	1,869	100.0	23.6	48.8	21.9	5.6
1998	1,868	100.0	22.9	51.8	18.8	6.5
1996	1,954	100.0	27.0	49.1	18.3	5.6
1994	1,968	100.0	26.0	46.5	21.7	5.7
1993	1,077	100.0	26.0	47.4	19.6	7.0
1991	1,021	100.0	27.8	48.3	19.4	4.5
1990	927	100.0	22.9	49.2	22.8	5.2
1989	1,005	100.0	25.0	50.9	17.9	6.2
1988	982	100.0	24.5	48.1	22.0	5.4
1986	1,468	100.0	26.6	51.6	17.6	4.1
1985	1,529	100.0	23.2	53.2	19.4	4.2
1983	1,597	100.0	23.7	52.3	19.4	4.6
1982	1,858	100.0	22.3	51.0	20.9	5.8
1978	1,509	100.0	26.8	41.7	27.3	4.2
1977	1,525	100.0	29.3	48.3	17.6	4.9
1976	1,496	100.0	27.3	49.7	17.6	5.3
1975	1,489	100.0	28.5	46.5	20.2	4.8
1974	1,481	100.0	31.9	42.1	20.8	5.2

Source: General Social Surveys, National Opinion Research Center, University of Chicago; calculations by New Strategist

Table 1.56 U.S. in World War, 1976 to 2002

Do you expect the United States to fight in another world war within the next ten years?

(number of respondents aged 18 or older, and percent distribution by response, 1976–2002)

	number of respondents	total	yes	no	don't know
2002	908	100.0%	63.3%	29.6%	7.0%
2000	1,869	100.0	35.7	58.1	6.2
1998	1,737	100.0	46.9	48.1	5.0
1996	1,929	100.0	39.2	56.2	4.6
1994	1,919	100.0	42.8	52.5	4.7
1993	1,079	100.0	46.8	49.7	3.5
1991	1,024	100.0	45.4	49.3	5.3
1990	927	100.0	27.5	68.5	4.0
1989	1,003	100.0	31.4	63.5	5.1
1988	987	100.0	39.9	56.2	3.9
1986	1,443	100.0	45.9	50.8	3.3
1985	778	100.0	42.9	51.0	6.0
1976	718	100.0	43.6	50.1	6.3

Source: General Social Surveys, National Opinion Research Center, University of Chicago; calculations by New Strategist

Table 1.57 Federal Income Tax Level, 1976 to 2002

Do you consider the amount of federal income tax which you have to pay as too high, about right, or too low?

(number of respondents aged 18 or older, and percent distribution by response, 1976–2002)

	number of respondents	total	too high	about right	too low	pays no tax	don't know
2002	924	100.0%	59.1%	37.3%	1.0%	–	2.6%
2000	1,845	100.0	63.8	31.2	0.9	–	4.0
1998	1,867	100.0	63.0	31.2	0.9	–	4.9
1996	1,915	100.0	64.9	30.8	0.8	–	3.6
1994	1,974	100.0	62.8	33.3	0.8	–	3.0
1993	1,060	100.0	54.9	41.1	1.2	–	2.7
1991	978	100.0	55.3	38.9	1.1	–	4.7
1990	902	100.0	58.9	36.7	0.7	–	3.8
1989	1,029	100.0	56.0	37.1	1.1	2.3%	3.5
1988	975	100.0	54.7	39.0	1.0	1.9	3.4
1987	1,804	100.0	58.9	34.9	0.7	2.0	3.5
1985	1,531	100.0	60.4	32.2	0.5	3.9	3.1
1984	1,459	100.0	62.9	32.6	0.5	2.0	2.1
1982	1,848	100.0	68.8	25.8	0.4	1.3	3.7
1980	1,449	100.0	68.2	27.0	0.3	–	4.6
1977	1,523	100.0	65.3	27.8	0.7	2.2	4.0
1976	1,491	100.0	58.4	32.7	0.6	5.0	3.3

Source: General Social Surveys, National Opinion Research Center, University of Chicago; calculations by New Strategist

Table 1.58 Political Leanings, 1974 to 2002

We hear a lot of talk these days about liberals and convervatives. On a seven-point scale from extremely liberal—point 1—to extremely conservative—point 7—where would you place yourself?

(number of respondents aged 18 or older, and percent distribution by response, 1974–2002)

	number of respondents	total	extremely liberal	liberal	slightly liberal	moderate	slightly conservative	conservative	extremely conservative	don't know
2002	1,367	100.0%	3.4%	10.5%	11.6%	38.2%	15.3%	15.4%	3.0%	2.6%
2000	2,793	100.0	3.4	10.5	11.6	38.2	15.3	15.4	3.0	2.6
1998	2,824	100.0	3.8	11.0	10.2	37.7	14.0	14.7	3.2	5.3
1996	2,898	100.0	2.3	12.6	12.4	34.9	15.3	14.7	3.0	4.7
1994	2,980	100.0	2.0	10.5	11.5	36.1	15.6	15.8	3.2	5.3
1993	1,597	100.0	2.4	11.0	12.7	35.2	15.8	16.0	3.5	3.4
1991	1,513	100.0	1.9	11.3	12.7	36.0	16.5	15.9	2.6	3.1
1990	1,368	100.0	2.4	10.2	14.1	38.6	14.4	14.0	2.6	3.6
1989	1,530	100.0	2.6	10.3	13.1	34.8	17.5	14.0	3.7	3.9
1988	1,472	100.0	2.6	11.6	12.5	37.0	16.1	12.7	1.8	5.8
1987	1,785	100.0	2.3	12.0	12.8	34.9	16.7	15.3	2.2	3.8
1986	1,468	100.0	2.2	12.0	12.8	37.4	16.2	12.6	2.4	4.5
1985	1,525	100.0	1.7	9.0	12.0	39.4	16.5	14.2	2.6	4.6
1984	1,462	100.0	2.3	10.7	11.2	37.1	17.8	14.0	2.8	4.1
1983	801	100.0	2.0	9.1	12.1	38.9	18.9	12.7	2.8	3.6
1982	1,846	100.0	2.0	8.4	12.2	39.8	17.7	13.5	2.5	3.9
1980	1,451	100.0	2.1	9.3	14.0	39.2	13.7	13.7	3.7	4.5
1978	1,505	100.0	2.5	8.3	14.3	40.1	17.8	12.4	3.0	1.5
1977	1,524	100.0	1.5	9.4	16.0	36.5	17.5	12.5	2.0	4.7
1976	1,494	100.0	2.4	11.1	14.0	37.0	16.5	11.7	2.6	4.7
1975	1,478	100.0	2.1	12.5	12.4	37.4	14.8	12.7	1.8	6.2
1974	1,480	100.0	3.1	12.1	13.3	37.8	15.7	10.1	2.4	5.5

Source: General Social Surveys, National Opinion Research Center, University of Chicago; calculations by New Strategist

Table 1.59 Political Party Affiliation, 1972 to 2002

Generally speaking, do you usually think of yourself as a Republican, Democrat, Independent, or what?

(number of respondents aged 18 or older, and percent distribution by response, 1972–2002)

	number of respondents	total	strong Democrat	not strong Democrat	independent, near Democrat	independent	independent, near Republican	not strong Republican	strong Republican	other
2002	2,729	100.0%	15.0%	18.9%	9.8%	19.3%	7.3%	16.5%	11.5%	1.8%
2000	2,805	100.0	14.8	18.1	11.6	20.2	9.3	14.2	10.2	1.7
1998	2,823	100.0	13.1	21.1	12.4	16.9	8.6	17.1	8.5	2.2
1996	2,898	100.0	13.8	19.9	12.3	15.8	8.9	17.3	10.6	1.5
1994	2,943	100.0	14.4	21.9	11.6	12.5	9.6	17.6	10.9	1.5
1993	1,597	100.0	14.2	20.1	11.9	12.8	9.9	18.7	11.3	1.1
1991	1,511	100.0	14.8	21.1	8.7	12.4	11.2	18.9	12.0	0.9
1990	1,368	100.0	12.4	23.0	9.7	11.3	10.5	20.5	11.7	0.9
1989	1,532	100.0	15.3	21.9	8.7	12.5	7.8	21.5	11.4	0.8
1988	1,481	100.0	15.9	21.1	12.2	12.6	9.5	18.6	9.9	0.3
1987	1,809	100.0	23.3	21.8	11.7	11.0	8.2	14.7	8.5	0.8
1986	1,467	100.0	16.7	22.9	10.8	12.7	10.2	16.4	9.6	0.6
1985	1,529	100.0	16.0	23.0	10.4	9.5	10.3	17.4	12.4	1.1
1984	1,465	100.0	18.1	19.1	14.3	11.1	10.6	16.7	8.5	1.5
1983	1,593	100.0	15.4	24.0	13.7	12.1	8.9	16.1	9.1	0.8
1982	1,851	100.0	20.6	26.1	13.1	12.2	8.2	11.6	7.4	0.7
1980	1,465	100.0	12.8	25.5	13.2	16.8	8.4	14.9	7.8	0.6
1978	1,527	100.0	14.1	25.5	13.0	14.5	8.8	16.1	7.3	0.7
1977	1,518	100.0	18.1	26.4	13.2	11.5	8.6	14.9	7.0	0.3
1976	1,495	100.0	15.1	27.0	13.8	16.1	7.0	14.3	6.4	0.3
1975	1,485	100.0	16.9	23.5	14.2	14.2	8.2	15.9	6.3	0.8
1974	1,471	100.0	16.7	25.4	14.1	9.8	7.2	14.7	7.5	4.0
1973	1,493	100.0	15.5	25.7	12.9	9.6	9.4	14.6	8.2	4.2
1972	1,607	100.0	20.3	27.1	10.0	9.9	6.2	14.4	7.8	4.3

Source: General Social Surveys, National Opinion Research Center, University of Chicago; calculations by New Strategist

Race Relations

Americans' attitudes toward race relations have changed dramatically over the past three decades as integration has become the rule, mixed-race marriages have become more common, and the black middle class has grown.

The percentage of the public agreeing with the notion that "blacks shouldn't push themselves where they're not wanted" has fallen from the 71 percent majority in 1972 to a 33 percent minority in 2002. Fewer than 10 percent of Americans still favor laws against interracial marriage, down from 38 percent who felt that way in 1972.

These changing attitudes stem in part from greater mixing of the races. The percentage of the public living in neighborhoods that include blacks rose from 29 to 69 percent between 1972 and 2002.

Americans are at a loss to explain why blacks have lower incomes than whites. Fewer people are willing to point the blame at any single cause. Only one-third of the public say discrimination is the main cause, down from 39 percent who felt that way in 1977. The share of those pointing the finger at a lack of education fell from 49 to 43 percent during those years. The percentage of Americans who blame a lack of will fell from 62 to 48 percent between 1977 and 2002, and the percentage of those who think it is less inborn ability to learn dropped from 25 to just 12 percent.

Americans' mixed feelings about the condition of blacks and what to do about it are especially revealed when they are asked whether government has an obligation to help blacks improve their living standards. The percentage of the public that feels both ways about the issue—that government should and should not help blacks—rose from 21 to 31 percent between 1975 and 2002. About half the public thinks blacks should receive no special treatment from the government.

Table 1.60 Should Government Aid Blacks, 1975 to 2002

Some people think that (Negroes/Blacks/African-Americans) have been discriminated against for so long that the government has a special obligation to help improve their living standards. Others believe that the government should not be giving special treatment to (Negroes/Blacks/African-Americans). Where would you place yourself on this scale?

(number of respondents aged 18 or older, and percent distribution by response, 1975–2002)

	number of respondents	total	1 government should help	2	3 agree with both	4	5 no special treatment	don't know
2002	910	100.0%	8.4%	7.9%	31.0%	19.5%	31.1%	2.2%
2000	1,881	100.0	9.4	9.2	31.8	19.2	26.2	4.3
1998	1,904	100.0	6.5	10.2	31.0	21.0	27.6	3.7
1996	1,915	100.0	8.1	8.5	28.8	23.1	28.1	3.3
1994	2,000	100.0	8.2	7.3	29.2	23.3	29.1	3.0
1993	1,050	100.0	7.1	10.0	31.7	20.7	27.6	2.9
1991	1,013	100.0	10.3	11.2	30.7	18.7	26.1	3.2
1990	1,369	100.0	10.2	10.1	33.0	16.1	27.3	3.4
1989	1,033	100.0	8.7	9.4	26.9	18.4	33.1	3.5
1988	993	100.0	7.5	10.0	28.7	17.3	33.5	3.0
1987	1,812	100.0	9.9	10.2	28.8	17.7	30.8	2.6
1986	1,466	100.0	8.2	9.5	28.6	17.7	33.2	2.7
1984	1,450	100.0	9.4	9.4	30.3	17.1	30.3	3.5
1983	1,592	100.0	7.5	9.5	25.5	20.2	33.1	4.1
1975	1,488	100.0	16.1	8.5	20.9	12.0	39.8	2.7

Source: General Social Surveys, National Opinion Research Center, University of Chicago; calculations by New Strategist

Table 1.61 Blacks Shouldn't Push, 1972 to 2002

(Negroes / Blacks / African-Americans) shouldn't push themselves where they're not wanted.

(number of respondents aged 18 or older, and percent distribution by response, 1972–2002)

	number of respondents	total	agree strongly	agree slightly	disagree slightly	disagree strongly	don't know
2002	920	100.0%	13.7%	19.3%	24.5%	34.5%	8.0%
2000	1,737	100.0	15.5	23.2	21.8	33.5	6.0
1998	1,876	100.0	13.6	25.4	22.7	32.5	5.8
1996	1,916	100.0	16.0	22.8	24.2	33.2	3.8
1994	1,509	100.0	14.2	26.8	24.9	30.4	3.6
1985	746	100.0	25.9	32.3	22.4	17.2	2.3
1984	1,464	100.0	25.5	30.1	21.2	21.0	2.3
1982	1,855	100.0	26.8	29.3	21.6	19.7	2.6
1980	1,464	100.0	33.6	30.8	19.1	14.0	2.5
1977	1,349	100.0	43.3	28.2	17.3	9.2	2.0
1976	1,363	100.0	41.9	27.7	16.4	12.0	1.9
1975	1,321	100.0	45.2	27.6	14.6	10.2	2.4
1973	1,313	100.0	43.8	29.2	14.8	11.2	1.1
1972	1,346	100.0	41.7	29.1	12.6	10.0	6.5

Source: General Social Surveys, National Opinion Research Center, University of Chicago; calculations by New Strategist

Table 1.62 Laws against Racial Intermarriage, 1972 to 2002

Do you think there should be laws against marriages between (Negroes / Blacks / African-Americans) and whites?

(number of respondents aged 18 or older, and percent distribution by response, 1972–2002)

	number of respondents	total	yes	no	don't know
2002	923	100.0%	9.5%	89.7%	0.8%
2000	1,744	100.0	9.9	87.4	2.7
1998	1,879	100.0	10.9	86.5	2.7
1996	1,922	100.0	10.9	87.0	2.1
1994	1,992	100.0	13.5	84.2	2.3
1993	1,072	100.0	16.6	80.1	3.3
1991	986	100.0	17.0	79.7	3.2
1990	916	100.0	18.7	78.5	2.8
1989	1,031	100.0	20.8	76.6	2.6
1988	974	100.0	21.9	75.2	3.0
1987	1,813	100.0	23.4	73.9	2.6
1985	1,524	100.0	25.4	72.1	2.5
1984	1,420	100.0	24.4	73.0	2.6
1982	1,856	100.0	29.3	67.8	2.9
1980	1,466	100.0	29.1	68.2	2.7
1977	1,348	100.0	27.8	70.6	1.6
1976	1,363	100.0	31.8	65.8	2.4
1975	1,321	100.0	37.8	60.0	2.2
1974	1,309	100.0	33.8	64.0	2.2
1973	1,309	100.0	37.3	61.2	1.5
1972	1,352	100.0	38.0	58.8	3.2

Source: General Social Surveys, National Opinion Research Center, University of Chicago; calculations by New Strategist

Table 1.63 Blacks Living in the Neighborhood, 1972 to 2002

Are there any (Negroes / Blacks / African-Americans) living in this neighborhood now?

(number of respondents aged 18 or older, and percent distribution by response, 1972–2002)

	number of respondents	total	yes	no	don't know
2002	1,347	100.0%	69.3%	27.1%	3.6%
2000	2,772	100.0	64.6	30.0	5.4
1998	2,777	100.0	63.0	31.9	5.1
1996	2,878	100.0	61.5	33.0	5.5
1994	2,977	100.0	61.1	34.1	4.8
1993	1,596	100.0	59.8	35.2	4.9
1991	1,502	100.0	52.5	43.1	4.4
1990	1,368	100.0	54.3	40.2	5.5
1989	1,527	100.0	51.5	43.6	4.9
1988	1,476	100.0	53.5	41.9	4.5
1987	1,814	100.0	47.8	48.7	3.5
1986	1,468	100.0	47.8	49.5	2.7
1985	1,527	100.0	48.1	47.5	4.4
1984	1,465	100.0	50.9	45.1	4.0
1983	1,596	100.0	47.1	49.9	3.1
1982	1,856	100.0	46.7	49.5	3.8
1980	1,466	100.0	46.0	50.3	3.7
1978	1,530	100.0	48.7	47.8	3.5
1977	1,350	100.0	39.4	57.6	3.0
1976	1,367	100.0	42.4	53.9	3.7
1975	1,326	100.0	32.9	62.9	4.2
1974	1,310	100.0	42.3	54.3	3.4
1973	1,320	100.0	39.7	56.4	3.9
1972	1,351	100.0	28.6	67.2	4.2

Source: General Social Surveys, National Opinion Research Center, University of Chicago; calculations by New Strategist

Table 1.64 Affirmative Action, 1994 to 2002

Some people say that because of past discrimination, blacks should be given preference in hiring and promotion. Others say that such preferences in hiring and promotion of blacks is wrong because it discriminates against whites. What about your opinion—are you for or against preferential hiring and promotion of blacks?

(number of respondents aged 18 or older, and percent distribution by response, 1994–2002)

	number of respondents	total	strongly favor	not strongly favor	not strongly oppose	strongly oppose	don't know
2002	905	100.0%	9.3%	6.4%	27.5%	54.4%	2.4%
2000	1,863	100.0	10.8	7.0	25.8	50.1	6.4
1998	1,853	100.0	7.7	6.3	22.9	55.3	7.8
1996	1,938	100.0	9.4	6.6	25.0	52.9	6.0
1994	1,457	100.0	9.3	6.9	24.3	54.2	5.4

Source: General Social Surveys, National Opinion Research Center, University of Chicago; calculations by New Strategist

Table 1.65 Blacks Should Work Way Up, 1994 to 2002

Do you agree strongly, agree somewhat, neither agree nor disagree, disagree somewhat, or disagree strongly with the following statement: Irish, Italians, Jewish and many other minorities overcame prejudice and worked their way up. Blacks should do the same without special favors.

(number of respondents aged 18 or older, and percent distribution by response, 1994–2002)

	number of respondents	total	agree strongly	agree somewhat	neither agree nor disagree	disagree somewhat	disagree strongly	don't know
2002	904	100.0%	46.7%	26.3%	12.7%	7.6%	5.5%	1.1%
2000	1,864	100.0	42.8	28.1	10.9	9.0	7.0	2.1
1998	1,864	100.0	42.1	28.9	12.1	8.5	6.1	2.3
1996	1,954	100.0	43.7	28.1	11.4	9.5	5.6	1.7
1994	1,465	100.0	43.7	28.7	10.0	9.7	5.9	2.0

Source: General Social Surveys, National Opinion Research Center, University of Chicago; calculations by New Strategist

Table 1.66 Conditions for Blacks, 1994 to 2002

In the past few years, do you think conditions for black people have improved, gotten worse, or stayed about the same?

(number of respondents aged 18 or older, and percent distribution by response, 1994–2002)

	number of respondents	total	improved	gotten worse	stayed about the same	don't know
2002	908	100.0%	65.2%	3.7%	28.9%	2.2%
2000	1,873	100.0	62.4	5.7	28.8	3.2
1998	1,865	100.0	62.6	5.0	27.7	4.7
1996	1,955	100.0	57.7	9.4	29.5	3.4
1994	1,462	100.0	53.1	12.1	32.4	2.4

Source: General Social Surveys, National Opinion Research Center, University of Chicago; calculations by New Strategist

Table 1.67 Differences between Blacks and Whites Due to Discrimination, 1977 to 2002

On the average (Negroes / Blacks / African-Americans) have worse jobs, income, and housing than white people. Do you think the differences are mainly due to discrimination?

(number of respondents aged 18 or older, and percent distribution by response, 1977–2002)

	number of respondents	total	yes	no	don't know
2002	907	100.0%	33.5%	63.4%	3.1%
2000	1,868	100.0	36.7	56.9	6.5
1998	1,864	100.0	35.1	58.5	6.4
1996	1,946	100.0	37.8	57.3	4.9
1994	1,968	100.0	40.7	54.2	5.1
1993	1,077	100.0	41.2	53.9	4.9
1991	1,020	100.0	39.9	55.7	4.4
1990	1,365	100.0	39.1	55.5	5.4
1989	999	100.0	39.8	54.6	5.6
1988	981	100.0	42.4	52.9	4.7
1986	1,464	100.0	43.6	53.6	2.9
1985	1,530	100.0	43.1	52.5	4.3
1977	1,347	100.0	39.2	56.3	4.5

Source: General Social Surveys, National Opinion Research Center, University of Chicago; calculations by New Strategist

Table 1.68 Differences between Blacks and Whites Due to Less Inborn Ability, 1977 to 2002

On the average (Negroes/Blacks/African-Americans) have worse jobs, income, and housing than white people. Do you think the differences are because most (Negroes/Blacks/African-Americans) have less in-born ability to learn?

(number of respondents aged 18 or older, and percent distribution by response, 1977–2002)

	number of respondents	total	yes	no	don't know
2002	908	100.0%	11.7%	86.0%	2.3%
2000	1,868	100.0	12.2	84.2	3.6
1998	1,865	100.0	9.5	86.3	4.1
1996	1,955	100.0	9.9	86.8	3.3
1994	1,966	100.0	12.9	83.1	4.0
1993	1,075	100.0	12.6	84.0	3.4
1991	1,018	100.0	14.0	81.6	4.3
1990	1,364	100.0	17.6	79.3	3.2
1989	1,000	100.0	18.1	77.4	4.5
1988	981	100.0	18.3	77.6	4.1
1986	1,467	100.0	19.9	76.6	3.5
1985	1,529	100.0	20.3	75.7	4.1
1977	1,347	100.0	24.8	70.3	4.9

Source: General Social Surveys, National Opinion Research Center, University of Chicago; calculations by New Strategist

Table 1.69 Differences between Blacks and Whites Due to Lack of Education, 1977 to 2002

On the average (Negroes / Blacks / African-Americans) have worse jobs, income, and housing than white people. Do you think the differences are because most (Negroes / Blacks / African-Americans) don't have the chance for education that it takes to rise out of poverty?

(number of respondents aged 18 or older, and percent distribution by response, 1977–2002)

	number of respondents	total	yes	no	don't know
2002	907	100.0%	43.0%	54.1%	2.9%
2000	1,867	100.0	45.3	50.8	4.0
1998	1,866	100.0	42.9	52.3	4.8
1996	1,954	100.0	44.7	52.0	3.3
1994	1,965	100.0	49.3	47.1	3.6
1993	1,075	100.0	52.7	43.3	4.0
1991	1,020	100.0	51.8	45.4	2.8
1990	1,365	100.0	52.0	44.6	3.4
1989	1,001	100.0	52.0	44.2	3.8
1988	982	100.0	52.1	44.1	3.8
1986	1,465	100.0	51.8	45.9	2.3
1985	1,530	100.0	52.7	44.9	2.4
1977	1,346	100.0	48.7	47.7	3.6

Source: General Social Surveys, National Opinion Research Center, University of Chicago; calculations by New Strategist

Table 1.70 Differences between Blacks and Whites Due to Lack of Will, 1977 to 2002

On the average (Negroes/Blacks/African-Americans) have worse jobs, income, and housing than white people. Do you think the differences are due to lack of will?

(number of respondents aged 18 or older, and percent distribution by response, 1977–2002)

	number of respondents	total	yes	no	don't know
2002	905	100.0%	48.1%	47.0%	5.0%
2000	1859	100.0	45.5	47.6	7.0
1998	1862	100.0	42.4	49.1	8.4
1996	1948	100.0	47.5	46.3	6.2
1994	1961	100.0	49.2	45.0	5.9
1993	1075	100.0	49.0	44.3	6.7
1991	1020	100.0	55.1	39.1	5.8
1990	1364	100.0	57.8	36.1	6.1
1989	998	100.0	56.6	37.9	5.5
1988	981	100.0	54.9	40.1	5.0
1986	1464	100.0	58.5	37.4	4.1
1985	1531	100.0	55.3	39.8	5.0
1977	1347	100.0	62.1	32.2	5.7

Source: General Social Surveys, National Opinion Research Center, University of Chicago; calculations by New Strategist

Religion

Religion is important to Americans, and the General Social Survey documents its role in daily life. One of the findings is the changing religious background of Americans as the nation becomes more diverse. Between 1973 and 2002, the proportion of Americans who say they were raised as Protestants fell from 65 to 57 percent. An even smaller 53 percent now identify themselves as Protestant. The percentage of those who claim no religious preference grew from 5 to 14 percent between 1972 and 2002, while the proportion of Americans identifying with a religion other than Protestant, Catholic, or Jewish (such as Islam) rose from 2 to 7 percent.

Attendance at religious services has fallen slightly over the past three decades. In 2002, one in four said they attend church at least once a week, down from 28 to 30 percent in the mid 1970s. Nineteen percent of adults in 2002 said they never go to church, up from 12 to 14 percent in the mid-1970s.

Although church attendance has declined somewhat, the 57 percent majority of Americans pray at least once a day. This proportion has not changed much since the question was first asked in 1983.

The 53 percent majority of the public believes the Bible is inspired by God, but is not the literal word of God. This proportion has climbed slightly since the early 1980s.

Although the United States Supreme Court ruled that no state or local government may require the reading of the Lord's Prayer or Bible verses in public schools, most Americans disagree with this decision. The proportion who disagreed stood at 57 percent in 2002, while a smaller 38 percent agreed with the ruling.

Table 1.71 Relgion in Which Raised, 1973 to 2002

In what religion were you raised?

(number of respondents aged 18 or older, and percent distribution by response, 1973–2002)

	number of respondents	total	Protestant	Catholic	Jewish	none	other	don't know
2002	2,750	100.0%	56.5%	29.9%	2.0%	7.1%	4.3%	0.2%
2000	2,803	100.0	57.4	30.1	2.3	6.8	3.3	–
1998	2,805	100.0	58.4	30.6	1.9	6.2	2.9	0.1
1996	2,899	100.0	59.8	28.9	2.3	5.8	3.1	–
1994	2,985	100.0	61.8	29.5	1.8	4.3	2.5	0.0
1993	1,596	100.0	65.1	26.4	2.2	4.4	1.8	–
1991	1,514	100.0	63.8	28.7	2.2	3.8	1.5	–
1990	1,364	100.0	64.3	26.5	2.0	5.3	2.0	–
1989	1,533	100.0	63.0	29.0	1.8	4.0	2.2	–
1988	1,481	100.0	64.3	28.0	2.1	3.6	2.1	–
1987	1,792	100.0	67.6	26.6	1.5	3.0	1.3	–
1986	1,468	100.0	64.9	28.0	2.2	3.1	1.8	–
1985	1,529	100.0	64.0	29.0	2.1	4.1	0.8	–
1984	1,452	100.0	65.8	27.5	2.1	3.0	1.7	–
1983	1,590	100.0	62.6	30.3	3.1	3.3	0.7	–
1982	1,851	100.0	65.6	27.1	2.9	3.1	1.4	–
1980	1,466	100.0	67.1	26.5	2.2	3.1	1.2	–
1978	1,525	100.0	66.7	27.4	2.0	3.1	0.7	–
1977	1,524	100.0	68.4	25.6	2.4	2.6	1.0	0.1
1976	1,497	100.0	64.9	28.6	2.2	3.1	1.2	–
1975	1,490	100.0	69.3	25.4	1.7	3.0	0.7	–
1974	1,482	100.0	66.4	27.1	3.3	2.6	0.5	–
1973	1,500	100.0	65.4	27.9	2.9	2.4	1.4	–

Source: General Social Surveys, National Opinion Research Center, University of Chicago; calculations by New Strategist

Table 1.72 Religious Preference, 1972 to 2002

What is your religious preference? Is it Protestant, Catholic, Jewish, some other religion, or no religion?

(number of respondents aged 18 or older, and percent distribution by response, 1972–2002)

	number of respondents	total	Protestant	Catholic	Jewish	none	other	don't know
2002	2,750	100.0%	53.1%	24.5%	1.7%	13.8%	6.8%	0.1%
2000	2,814	100.0	54.1	24.1	2.2	14.1	5.4	0.0
1998	2,802	100.0	54.4	25.2	1.8	14.1	4.4	0.2
1996	2,900	100.0	57.4	23.6	2.3	11.7	4.9	0.0
1994	2,981	100.0	59.5	25.5	2.0	9.2	3.9	–
1993	1,598	100.0	64.1	22.0	2.1	9.1	2.6	0.1
1991	1,515	100.0	63.8	25.5	2.1	6.7	1.9	–
1990	1,368	100.0	63.0	23.9	2.0	8.0	3.1	0.1
1989	1,533	100.0	63.3	25.2	1.5	7.8	2.2	–
1988	1,480	100.0	61.2	25.9	2.0	8.0	2.8	–
1987	1,811	100.0	65.2	24.2	1.4	7.2	2.1	–
1986	1,467	100.0	62.8	25.8	2.6	6.7	2.1	–
1985	1,529	100.0	62.5	26.7	2.1	7.1	1.6	–
1984	1,461	100.0	63.8	25.7	1.8	7.3	1.4	–
1983	1,595	100.0	60.8	27.5	2.7	7.3	1.6	–
1982	1,849	100.0	64.5	24.4	2.5	7.4	1.2	–
1980	1,465	100.0	63.9	24.7	2.2	7.2	2.0	–
1978	1,528	100.0	64.1	25.1	1.9	7.8	1.1	–
1977	1,523	100.0	65.9	24.5	2.3	6.1	1.2	–
1976	1,497	100.0	63.5	26.1	1.8	7.6	1.0	–
1975	1,488	100.0	65.5	24.4	1.5	7.6	0.9	–
1974	1,483	100.0	64.3	25.4	3.0	6.8	0.5	–
1973	1,500	100.0	62.7	25.9	2.8	6.4	2.3	–
1972	1,608	100.0	64.1	25.7	3.4	5.2	1.7	–

Source: General Social Surveys, National Opinion Research Center, University of Chicago; calculations by New Strategist

Table 1.73 Attendance at Religious Services, 1972 to 2002

How often do you attend religious services?

(number of respondents aged 18 or older, and percent distribution by response, 1972–2002)

	number of respondents	total	once a week or more	one to three times a month	several times a year	once a year	less than once a year	never	don't know
2002	2,765	100.0%	24.2%	22.6%	12.9%	13.9%	7.0%	18.6%	0.8%
2000	2,817	100.0	24.2	19.5	13.1	11.9	7.8	20.7	2.8
1998	2,832	100.0	25.0	22.5	10.8	10.5	10.4	19.3	1.6
1996	2,904	100.0	23.9	21.4	14.3	13.8	8.7	15.1	2.8
1994	2,992	100.0	26.6	21.4	12.8	13.9	7.6	16.1	1.7
1993	1,606	100.0	28.4	21.7	11.0	12.0	8.5	16.1	2.4
1991	1,517	100.0	28.7	23.0	11.8	13.3	9.0	12.5	1.6
1990	1,372	100.0	29.1	22.0	12.8	11.9	8.3	13.1	2.8
1989	1,537	100.0	29.5	21.3	12.3	12.9	7.2	16.4	0.3
1988	1,481	100.0	26.1	24.8	13.1	11.3	7.3	17.2	0.2
1987	1,819	100.0	28.4	23.1	15.3	13.9	6.7	11.9	0.7
1986	1,470	100.0	31.7	22.5	11.9	12.4	7.1	14.0	0.3
1985	1,534	100.0	32.7	18.5	12.1	15.0	7.0	14.5	0.3
1984	1,473	100.0	32.7	20.6	14.0	11.7	7.3	12.9	0.9
1983	1,599	100.0	31.4	21.6	11.6	13.1	8.1	13.9	0.3
1982	1,858	100.0	28.4	20.3	13.9	15.3	7.2	14.1	0.8
1980	1,468	100.0	29.0	20.9	15.2	15.7	7.4	11.4	0.5
1978	1,532	100.0	27.5	23.2	11.4	13.2	8.7	15.6	0.3
1977	1,530	100.0	29.5	22.1	12.4	13.3	8.3	13.9	0.6
1976	1,499	100.0	28.8	19.7	15.5	13.5	9.1	12.9	0.5
1975	1,490	100.0	29.3	22.4	14.0	12.3	7.2	14.5	0.2
1974	1,484	100.0	30.3	22.4	12.7	15.2	6.9	12.2	0.2
1973	1,504	100.0	27.9	22.2	15.0	12.9	7.8	13.6	0.6
1972	1,613	100.0	34.8	21.6	14.0	11.0	8.5	9.3	0.8

Source: General Social Surveys, National Opinion Research Center, University of Chicago; calculations by New Strategist

Table 1.74 How Often Do You Pray, 1983 to 2002

About how often do you pray?

(number of respondents aged 18 or older, and percent distribution by response, 1983–2002)

	number of respondents	total	several times a day	once a day	several times a week	once a week	less than once a week	never	don't know
2002	1,362	100.0%	25.6%	31.1%	11.3%	8.6%	22.2%	0.5%	0.7%
2000	1,386	100.0	27.1	29.0	14.1	6.5	22.3	0.9	0.1
1998	1,431	100.0	24.8	29.8	14.1	7.5	21.9	1.7	0.2
1996	985	100.0	26.0	31.7	13.6	8.0	18.1	2.5	0.1
1994	1,956	100.0	23.2	32.7	11.6	8.5	22.5	1.3	0.2
1993	1,056	100.0	26.6	29.5	13.5	7.7	21.2	1.5	–
1990	903	100.0	23.3	28.9	13.7	8.5	25.4	–	0.2
1989	994	100.0	23.1	29.6	15.1	6.6	24.9	0.6	–
1988	1,473	100.0	23.5	30.5	15.5	7.7	22.1	0.3	0.3
1987	1,786	100.0	25.3	31.7	13.5	8.7	20.2	0.6	–
1985	1,510	100.0	27.2	31.0	12.6	7.4	20.6	1.3	–
1984	1,449	100.0	28.2	29.1	13.9	7.2	20.2	1.4	0.1
1983	1,579	100.0	24.5	30.0	12.9	7.7	20.6	3.9	0.4

Source: General Social Surveys, National Opinion Research Center, University of Chicago; calculations by New Strategist

Table 1.75 Feelings about the Bible, 1984 to 2002

Which of these statements comes closest to describing your feelings about the Bible?

a) The Bible is the actual word of God and is to be taken literally, word for word;

b) The Bible is the inspired word of God but not everything in it should be taken literally, word for word;

c) The Bible is an ancient book of fables, legends, history, and moral precepts recorded by men.

(number of respondents aged 18 or older, and percent distribution by response, 1984–2002)

	number of respondents	total	word of God	inspired word	book of fables	other	don't know
2002	1,369	100.0%	28.5%	53.1%	14.0%	2.6%	1.8%
2000	2,322	100.0	33.7	46.7	15.5	1.0	3.1
1998	2,355	100.0	30.7	49.4	16.3	1.1	2.5
1996	1,948	100.0	30.4	49.8	17.1	0.6	2.1
1994	1,962	100.0	31.4	51.1	14.9	0.9	1.7
1993	1,074	100.0	33.1	48.8	15.2	0.8	2.0
1991	1,020	100.0	34.8	47.8	14.8	0.8	1.8
1990	920	100.0	32.5	49.5	15.2	0.8	2.1
1989	997	100.0	31.3	49.5	16.0	0.4	2.7
1988	1,478	100.0	34.2	47.1	16.2	0.7	1.9
1987	1,183	100.0	36.7	46.1	15.4	0.6	1.3
1985	746	100.0	36.5	48.9	12.6	0.3	1.7
1984	976	100.0	37.6	46.6	13.7	0.7	1.3

Source: General Social Surveys, National Opinion Research Center, University of Chicago; calculations by New Strategist

Table 1.76 Prayer in the Public Schools, 1974 to 2002

The United States Supreme Court has ruled that no state or local government may require the reading of the Lord's Prayer or Bible verses in public schools. Do you approve or disapprove of the court's ruling?

(number of respondents aged 18 or older, and percent distribution by response, 1984–2002)

	number of respondents	total	approve	disapprove	don't know
2002	908	100.0%	37.6%	57.0%	5.4%
2000	1,869	100.0	36.8	58.2	5.0
1998	1,867	100.0	42.5	52.9	4.6
1996	1,958	100.0	39.8	56.1	4.0
1994	1,972	100.0	37.4	58.3	4.3
1993	1,077	100.0	39.3	56.7	4.0
1991	1,021	100.0	38.4	58.2	3.4
1990	926	100.0	39.6	55.8	4.5
1989	1,005	100.0	40.9	55.9	3.2
1988	986	100.0	37.3	58.9	3.8
1986	723	100.0	37.3	61.1	1.5
1985	1,530	100.0	43.1	53.9	3.1
1983	1,595	100.0	39.6	56.7	3.8
1982	1,856	100.0	37.4	59.6	2.9
1977	1,527	100.0	33.5	64.2	2.3
1975	1,487	100.0	35.4	61.7	2.9
1974	750	100.0	30.8	66.1	3.1

Source: General Social Surveys, National Opinion Research Center, University of Chicago; calculations by New Strategist

Table 1.77 Allowing Someone Who Is against Religion to Speak, 1972 to 2002

There are always some people whose ideas are considered bad or dangerous by other people. For instance, somebody who is against all churches and religion: If such a person wanted to make a speech in your (city/town/community) against churches and religion, should he be allowed to speak, or not?

(number of respondents aged 18 or older, and percent distribution by response, 1972–2002)

	number of respondents	total	allowed	not allowed	don't know
2002	924	100.0%	76.8%	22.3%	0.9%
2000	1,856	100.0	74.4	24.2	1.3
1998	1,879	100.0	74.1	24.3	1.5
1996	1,919	100.0	73.4	25.2	1.4
1994	1,992	100.0	72.8	26.1	1.1
1993	1,073	100.0	71.2	27.0	1.8
1991	990	100.0	72.0	26.9	1.1
1990	914	100.0	72.5	25.8	1.6
1989	1,031	100.0	71.8	27.2	1.1
1988	976	100.0	69.8	28.7	1.5
1987	1,814	100.0	69.2	30.3	0.5
1985	1,532	100.0	64.7	33.9	1.4
1984	1,469	100.0	68.2	31.2	0.5
1982	1,859	100.0	63.5	34.9	1.7
1980	1,468	100.0	66.1	33.0	0.8
1977	1,527	100.0	62.3	37.1	0.6
1976	1,499	100.0	64.0	35.0	1.1
1974	1,482	100.0	61.7	36.9	1.3
1973	1,503	100.0	65.3	34.0	0.7
1972	1,613	100.0	65.0	32.7	2.3

Source: General Social Surveys, National Opinion Research Cetner, University of Chicago; calculations by New Strategist

Table 1.78 Allowing Anti-Religious Book in Local Library, 1972 to 2002

There are always some people whose ideas are considered bad or dangerous by other people. For instance, somebody who is against all churches and religion: If some people in your community suggested that a book he wrote against churches and religion should be taken out of your public library, would you favor removing this book, or not?

(number of respondents aged 18 or older, and percent distribution by response, 1972–2002)

	number of respondents	total	remove	not remove	don't know
2002	921	100.0%	24.5%	73.0%	2.5%
2000	1,855	100.0	28.4	68.0	3.6
1998	1,877	100.0	27.3	69.0	3.7
1996	1,916	100.0	28.5	68.2	3.3
1994	1,991	100.0	28.0	69.5	2.5
1993	1,069	100.0	28.7	67.4	3.8
1991	990	100.0	28.2	69.3	2.5
1990	912	100.0	29.8	66.8	3.4
1989	1,031	100.0	29.6	67.2	3.2
1988	972	100.0	34.0	64.0	2.1
1987	1,808	100.0	31.7	66.2	2.0
1985	1,532	100.0	36.9	60.5	2.5
1984	1,470	100.0	33.8	63.7	2.4
1982	1,860	100.0	36.9	60.2	3.0
1980	1,468	100.0	35.5	61.9	2.6
1977	1,525	100.0	39.6	58.6	1.8
1976	1,497	100.0	38.0	59.6	2.4
1974	1,482	100.0	37.7	59.9	2.5
1973	1,501	100.0	37.0	61.0	2.0
1972	1,607	100.0	35.9	60.7	3.4

Source: General Social Surveys, National Opinion Research Cetner, University of Chicago; calculations by New Strategist

Table 1.79 Allowing Someone Who Is against Religion to Teach College, 1972 to 2002

There are always some people whose ideas are considered bad or dangerous by other people. For instance, somebody who is against all churches and religion: Should such a person be allowed to teach in a college or university, or not?

(number of respondents aged 18 or older, and percent distribution by response, 1972–2002)

	number of respondents	total	allowed	not allowed	don't know
2002	923	100.0%	60.2%	37.9%	1.8%
2000	1,854	100.0	56.1	39.1	4.7
1998	1,875	100.0	57.0	37.7	5.3
1996	1,920	100.0	55.2	40.1	4.7
1994	1,989	100.0	52.0	43.8	4.2
1993	1,069	100.0	52.0	44.0	4.0
1991	990	100.0	52.0	44.4	3.5
1990	914	100.0	50.3	44.1	5.6
1989	1,032	100.0	51.1	44.4	4.6
1988	975	100.0	45.3	51.5	3.2
1987	1,811	100.0	46.9	49.9	3.3
1985	1,529	100.0	45.5	51.7	2.9
1984	1,469	100.0	45.8	50.9	3.3
1982	1,857	100.0	44.7	51.6	3.7
1980	1,464	100.0	45.4	51.5	3.1
1977	1,527	100.0	38.8	59.3	2.0
1976	1,499	100.0	41.3	56.5	2.2
1974	1,482	100.0	41.8	54.7	3.6
1973	1,499	100.0	40.7	56.2	3.1
1972	1,610	100.0	40.0	55.5	4.5

Source: General Social Surveys, National Opinion Research Center, University of Chicago; calculations by New Strategist

Sexual Attitudes and Behavior

Attitudes toward sexual behavior have, by and large, become more liberal over the past few decades—in part because open-minded younger generations are replacing more conservative older people. Most Americans support sex education in public schools, with the figure growing from 79 to 87 percent between 1974 and 2002. The proportion who say premarital sex is "not wrong at all" has climbed from 26 percent in 1972 to 44 percent in 2002. But the great majority of people still believe extramarital sex is "always wrong."

Attitudes toward homosexuality have changed markedly over the past thirty years. In 1973, 70 percent of Americans believed that sex between adults of the same gender was "always wrong." By 2002, however, only 53 percent felt that way. The proportion who say it is "not wrong at all" rose from 11 to 32 percent during those years. Most Americans would also allow a homosexual to speak publicly, to have a book in the local library, and to teach at a college or university.

Americans' own sexual behavior is fairly conservative. Just 15 percent of adults have had more than one sex partner in the past year. Sixty-one percent have had only one sex partner in the past year, while another 23 percent have had no sex partners. Among those who have had a sex partner in the past year, 87 percent say their partner was their spouse. A similar percentage say the last time they had sex it was with someone with whom they have an ongoing relationship. A substantial 19 percent of ever-married adults say they have had sex with someone outside of marriage, however.

Table 1.80 Sex Education in Public Schools, 1974 to 2002

Would you be for or against sex education in the public schools?

(number of respondents aged 18 or older, and percent distribution by response, 1974–2002)

	number of respondents	total	favor	oppose	depends	don't know
2002	908	100.0%	86.7%	11.3%	–	2.0%
2000	1,868	100.0	85.2	12.4	–	2.4
1998	1,863	100.0	85.1	12.7	–	2.3
1996	1,954	100.0	85.3	12.3	–	2.4
1994	1,965	100.0	85.0	12.1	–	2.9
1993	1,077	100.0	82.6	14.8	–	2.6
1991	1,022	100.0	85.1	11.8	–	3.0
1990	924	100.0	87.6	9.8	–	2.6
1989	1,003	100.0	84.4	12.2	–	3.4
1988	984	100.0	84.7	12.6	–	2.7
1986	1,468	100.0	81.7	15.5	–	2.8
1985	1,526	100.0	82.0	15.5	–	2.5
1983	1,595	100.0	83.6	13.6	–	2.8
1982	1,856	100.0	81.6	15.2	–	3.2
1977	1,524	100.0	77.0	20.9	–	2.1
1975	1,488	100.0	76.3	20.0	–	3.7
1974	1,481	100.0	78.9	17.1	0.6%	3.4

Source: General Social Surveys, National Opinion Research Cetner, University of Chicago; calculations by New Strategist

Table 1.81 Premarital Sex, 1972 to 2002

There's been a lot of discussion about the way morals and attitudes about sex are changing in this country. If a man and woman have sex relations before marriage, do you think it is always wrong, almost always wrong, wrong only sometimes, or not wrong at all?

(number of respondents aged 18 or older, and percent distribution by response, 1972–2002)

	number of respondents	total	always wrong	almost always wrong	sometimes wrong	not wrong at all	don't know
2002	903	100.0%	26.8%	8.1%	19.5%	43.6%	2.0%
2000	1,867	100.0	26.9	8.4	20.6	40.1	4.0
1998	1,869	100.0	25.5	8.9	20.2	41.9	3.5
1996	1,954	100.0	23.1	9.4	22.0	42.6	3.0
1994	1,967	100.0	25.2	9.8	19.8	42.2	3.1
1993	1,077	100.0	26.3	9.8	20.2	41.1	2.5
1991	1,021	100.0	26.8	9.6	18.2	42.6	2.7
1990	925	100.0	24.8	11.1	22.2	38.5	3.5
1989	1,002	100.0	27.1	8.4	22.1	39.3	3.1
1988	982	100.0	25.6	10.4	21.8	39.5	2.7
1986	1,464	100.0	27.0	8.7	22.4	39.2	2.7
1985	1,530	100.0	27.6	8.0	19.2	42.0	3.1
1983	1,592	100.0	26.8	9.7	23.7	37.8	1.9
1982	1,851	100.0	28.0	9.0	20.4	39.5	3.1
1978	1,528	100.0	28.6	11.5	19.9	37.8	2.2
1977	1,520	100.0	30.2	9.3	22.4	35.6	2.6
1975	1,485	100.0	29.7	11.9	23.0	31.5	3.9
1974	1,477	100.0	32.0	12.3	22.8	29.7	3.2
1972	1,602	100.0	35.1	11.4	23.3	26.2	4.1

Source: General Social Surveys, National Opinion Research Center, University of Chicago; calculations by New Strategist

Table 1.82 Extramarital Sex, 1973 to 2002

What is your opinion about a married person having sexual relations with someone other than the marriage partner—is it always wrong, almost always wrong, wrong only sometimes, or not wrong at all?

(number of respondents aged 18 or older, and percent distribution by response, 1973–2002)

	number of respondents	total	always wrong	almost always wrong	sometimes wrong	not wrong at all	don't know
2002	924	100.0%	78.5%	13.4%	4.2%	2.1%	1.8%
2000	1,855	100.0	78.1	10.7	7.0	2.5	1.7
1998	1,877	100.0	78.1	12.3	5.7	2.3	1.5
1996	1,919	100.0	76.7	14.9	5.1	1.8	1.6
1994	1,993	100.0	77.6	12.4	6.5	2.3	1.2
1993	1,070	100.0	76.2	14.2	5.6	2.4	1.6
1991	987	100.0	74.8	13.4	6.4	3.1	2.3
1990	914	100.0	77.6	12.6	6.9	1.4	1.5
1989	1,031	100.0	77.3	12.7	7.2	1.6	1.2
1988	975	100.0	78.4	12.8	5.5	2.1	1.2
1987	1,810	100.0	73.1	15.2	8.3	2.3	1.0
1985	1,530	100.0	74.0	13.5	8.5	2.8	1.2
1984	1,465	100.0	69.8	18.0	8.8	2.3	1.1
1982	1,850	100.0	72.4	13.4	10.1	2.7	1.5
1980	1,467	100.0	69.4	15.7	9.7	3.6	1.6
1977	1,523	100.0	72.4	13.5	10.0	3.2	0.9
1976	1,494	100.0	67.8	15.4	11.3	4.2	1.3
1974	1,482	100.0	73.0	11.7	11.4	2.4	1.5
1973	1,500	100.0	69.1	14.7	11.5	4.1	0.6

Source: General Social Surveys, National Opinion Research Center, University of Chicago; calculations by New Strategist

Table 1.83 Homosexual Relations, 1973 to 2002

What about sexual relations between two adults of the same sex—
do you think it is always wrong, almost always wrong,
wrong only sometimes, or not wrong at all?

(number of respondents aged 18 or older, and percent distribution by response, 1973–2002)

	number of respondents	total	always wrong	almost always wrong	sometimes wrong	not wrong at all	other	don't know
2002	919	100.0%	52.9%	4.7%	6.9%	31.8%	–	3.8%
2000	1,850	100.0	53.9	4.1	7.3	26.4	–	8.3
1998	1,874	100.0	54.3	5.3	6.5	27.5	–	6.5
1996	1,908	100.0	56.5	4.9	5.8	26.4	–	6.5
1994	1,991	100.0	62.9	3.8	5.8	22.0	–	5.4
1993	1,068	100.0	62.8	4.1	6.9	20.9	–	5.2
1991	986	100.0	70.9	3.9	4.2	15.0	–	6.1
1990	916	100.0	72.6	4.6	5.8	12.2	–	4.8
1989	1,029	100.0	70.7	3.9	5.7	15.0	–	4.8
1988	973	100.0	74.0	4.5	5.4	12.3	–	3.7
1987	1,801	100.0	74.4	4.2	6.7	12.0	–	2.7
1985	1,531	100.0	73.0	3.9	6.8	13.3	–	3.1
1984	1,466	100.0	70.6	4.8	7.2	13.8	–	3.7
1982	1,847	100.0	70.0	5.2	6.7	14.0	–	4.2
1980	1,465	100.0	69.9	5.7	5.8	13.9	–	4.6
1977	1,522	100.0	68.6	5.5	7.2	14.2	–	4.5
1976	1,488	100.0	67.1	5.9	7.5	15.3	–	4.2
1974	1,484	100.0	67.0	4.8	7.5	12.3	3.4%	4.9
1973	1,497	100.0	70.3	6.3	7.3	10.6	2.1	3.3

Source: General Social Surveys, National Opinion Research Center, University of Chicago; calculations by New Strategist

Table 1.84 Allowing Homosexuals to Speak, 1973 to 2002

There are always some people whose ideas are considered bad or dangerous by other people. And what about a man who admits that he is a homosexual? Suppose this admitted homosexual wanted to make a speech in your community. Should he be allowed to speak, or not?

(number of respondents aged 18 or older, and percent distribution by response, 1973–2002)

	number of respondents	total	allowed	not allowed	don't know
2002	921	100.0%	83.8%	15.0%	1.2%
2000	1,855	100.0	80.5	16.4	3.0
1998	1,879	100.0	80.8	16.3	2.9
1996	1,922	100.0	80.8	16.9	2.3
1994	1,988	100.0	79.4	18.3	2.4
1993	1,073	100.0	78.2	18.5	3.3
1991	990	100.0	76.0	21.6	2.4
1990	914	100.0	73.7	22.5	3.7
1989	1,030	100.0	76.3	21.1	2.6
1988	975	100.0	69.8	26.4	3.8
1987	1,813	100.0	68.2	29.2	2.5
1985	1,530	100.0	66.8	29.8	3.4
1984	1,468	100.0	68.1	28.3	3.5
1982	1,851	100.0	64.4	31.2	4.4
1980	1,468	100.0	65.9	31.0	3.1
1977	1,528	100.0	61.8	34.6	3.7
1976	1,496	100.0	62.0	34.9	3.1
1974	1,483	100.0	62.4	33.1	4.5
1973	1,501	100.0	60.8	35.4	3.7

Source: General Social Surveys, National Opinion Research Center, University of Chicago; calculations by New Strategist

Table 1.85 Allowing Homosexual Book in Local Library, 1973 to 2002

There are always some people whose ideas are considered bad or dangerous by other people. And what about a man who admits that he is a homosexual? If some people in your community suggested that a book he wrote in favor of homosexuality should be taken out of your public library, would you favor removing this book, or not?

(number of respondents aged 18 or older, and percent distribution by response, 1973–2002)

	number of respondents	total	remove	not remove	don't know
2002	921	100.0%	22.4%	75.4%	2.3%
2000	1,856	100.0	25.6	71.1	3.3
1998	1,878	100.0	25.5	70.1	4.4
1996	1,918	100.0	27.9	69.1	3.0
1994	1,989	100.0	28.3	68.7	3.1
1993	1,071	100.0	29.2	66.6	4.2
1991	989	100.0	28.5	68.6	2.9
1990	914	100.0	33.2	64.1	2.7
1989	1,028	100.0	32.8	64.1	3.1
1988	974	100.0	35.9	60.5	3.6
1987	1,811	100.0	40.2	57.4	2.4
1985	1,529	100.0	41.6	55.5	2.9
1984	1,468	100.0	37.6	59.5	2.9
1982	1,852	100.0	40.7	55.9	3.4
1980	1,466	100.0	39.6	58.2	2.2
1977	1,526	100.0	41.3	55.3	3.3
1976	1,497	100.0	41.0	55.4	3.5
1974	1,479	100.0	41.1	55.0	3.9
1973	1,502	100.0	43.9	53.5	2.6

Source: General Social Surveys, National Opinion Research Center, University of Chicago; calculations by New Strategist

Table 1.86 Allowing Homosexual to Teach College, 1973 to 2002

There are always some people whose ideas are considered bad or dangerous by other people. And what about a man who admits that he is a homosexual? Should such a person be allowed to teach in a college or university, or not?

(number of respondents aged 18 or older, and percent distribution by response, 1973–2002)

	number of respondents	total	allowed	not allowed	don't know
2002	921	100.0%	78.4%	19.3%	2.3%
2000	1,855	100.0	76.1	19.8	4.1
1998	1,879	100.0	73.8	22.1	4.1
1996	1,921	100.0	75.0	22.1	3.0
1994	1,989	100.0	70.8	26.2	2.9
1993	1,070	100.0	68.5	27.1	4.4
1991	990	100.0	63.4	32.9	3.6
1990	914	100.0	62.8	32.5	4.7
1989	1,030	100.0	63.5	31.8	4.7
1988	972	100.0	56.8	38.6	4.6
1987	1,814	100.0	56.7	39.5	3.8
1985	1,529	100.0	57.9	39.0	3.0
1984	1,468	100.0	58.9	37.1	4.0
1982	1,851	100.0	54.5	40.8	4.7
1980	1,466	100.0	54.6	41.5	3.8
1977	1,526	100.0	49.3	46.5	4.2
1976	1,496	100.0	52.1	44.7	3.2
1974	1,481	100.0	50.2	44.6	5.2
1973	1,502	100.0	47.3	48.4	4.3

Source: General Social Surveys, National Opinion Research Center, University of Chicago; calculations by New Strategist

Table 1.87 Number of Sex Partners in Past Year, 1993 to 2002

How many sex partners have you had in the last 12 months?

(number of respondents aged 18 or older, and percent distribution by response, 1993–2002)

	number of respondents	total	no partners	one partner	two partners	three partners	four partners	five or more partners	more than one	don't know	no answer
2002	2,276	100.0%	22.5%	61.4%	7.0%	3.6%	1.7%	2.1%	0.2%	0.2%	1.3%
2000	2,400	100.0	21.7	62.6	6.3	3.3	1.8	1.9	0.1	–	2.4
1998	2,451	100.0	20.9	64.7	6.7	2.3	1.6	1.9	0.5	0.0	1.4
1996	2,657	100.0	18.7	64.9	7.2	3.4	1.7	1.7	0.9	0.1	1.4
1994	2,791	100.0	21.8	63.9	6.8	2.6	1.3	1.5	0.1	–	2.0
1993	1,492	100.0	21.0	65.9	5.8	2.2	1.7	1.7	–	–	1.7

Source: General Social Surveys, National Opinion Research Center, University of Chicago

Table 1.88 How Often Do You Have Sex, 1993 to 2002

About how often did you have sex during the last 12 months?

(number of respondents aged 18 or older, and percent distribution by response, 1993–2002)

	number of respondents	total	not at all	once or twice	about once a month	two or three times/month	about once a week	two or three times/week	four or more times/week	don't know	no answer
2002	2,276	100.0%	21.3%	8.2%	9.3%	15.4%	15.0%	18.2%	7.2%	0.8%	4.7%
2000	2,400	100.0	21.2	8.4	8.5	15.0	16.3	18.6	6.3	0.0	5.6
1998	2,451	100.0	21.1	7.1	10.7	14.6	17.3	18.7	5.1	0.1	5.3
1996	2,657	100.0	17.9	7.2	9.3	15.5	17.7	21.3	6.2	0.1	4.8
1994	2,791	100.0	20.2	6.7	10.4	14.9	17.3	19.3	5.6	0.1	5.6
1993	1,492	100.0	20.7	6.2	11.0	14.8	18.2	18.3	6.5	–	4.3

Source: General Social Surveys, National Opinion Research Center, University of Chicago

Table 1.89 Was Sex Partner Husband/Wife, 1993 to 2002

Was one of the partners your husband or wife or regular sexual partner?

(number of respondents aged 18 or older with a sex partner in past 12 months, and percent distribution by response, 1993–2002)

	number of respondents	total	yes	no	don't know	no answer
2002	1,765	100.0%	87.3%	10.3%	0.1%	2.4%
2000	1,879	100.0	85.9	9.3	–	4.8
1998	1,939	100.0	87.6	9.6	–	2.8
1996	2,159	100.0	88.1	8.4	–	3.5
1994	2,183	100.0	87.9	8.5	–	3.7
1993	1,179	100.0	89.5	6.8	–	3.7

Source: General Social Surveys, National Opinion Research Center, University of Chicago

Table 1.90 Sex in an Ongoing Relationship, 1996 to 2002

The last time you had sex, was it with someone you were in an ongoing relationship with, or was it with someone else? Remember that by sex we mean only vaginal, oral, or anal sex.

(number of respondents aged 18 or older, and percent distribution by response, 1996–2002)

	number of respondents	total	yes	no	don't know	no answer
2002	2,289	100.0%	86.5%	6.9%	0.5%	6.1%
2000	2,400	100.0	81.6	9.8	0.0	8.5
1998	2,451	100.0	83.6	9.6	0.1	6.7
1996	2,657	100.0	85.1	7.4	–	7.6

Source: General Social Surveys, National Opinion Research Center, University of Chicago

Table 1.91 Extramarital Sex, 1993 to 2002

Have you ever had sex with someone other than your husband or wife while you were married?

(number of respondents aged 18 or older who have ever been married, and percent distribution by response, 1993–2002)

	number of respondents	total	yes	no	don't know	no answer
2002	1,669	100.0%	18.6%	78.3%	0.1%	2.9%
2000	1,798	100.0	17.1	78.9	0.1	3.9
1998	1,864	100.0	17.4	79.5	–	3.2
1996	2,042	100.0	18.1	79.2	0.0	2.6
1994	2,205	100.0	16.1	80.8	–	3.2
1993	1,234	100.0	15.8	79.6	–	4.6

Source: General Social Surveys, National Opinion Research Center, University of Chicago

Social Relations

Although it is popularly thought that American families are scattered far and wide, most Americans live close enough to relatives to socialize with them frequently. Americans are more likely to socialize with relatives than with friends or neighbors, according to the General Social Survey.

Thirty-six percent of adults say they spend a social evening with relatives at least several times a week, a figure that has not changed much over the past three decades. The 55 percent majority socializes with relatives at least several times a month. A smaller 25 percent of adults spend a social evening with friends at least several times a week, and about half do so at least several times a month.

Socializing with neighbors is less common. Only 36 percent of adults socialize with neighbors at least several times a month. A much smaller 18 percent spend an evening at a bar at least several times a month.

Only 5 to 7 percent of adults say they "never" spend a social evening with relatives or friends, but a much larger 30 percent never socialize with neighbors. An even larger 44 percent of the public never spend an evening at a bar.

Table 1.92 Spending an Evening with Relatives, 1974 to 2002

How often do you spend a social evening with relatives?

(number of respondents aged 18 or older, and percent distribution by response, 1974–2002)

	number of respondents	total	almost daily	several times a week	several times a month	once a month	severak times a year	once a year	never	don't know
2002	907	100.0%	11.4%	24.6%	19.3%	16.5%	16.9%	6.2%	5.0%	0.2%
2000	1,867	100.0	9.6	26.4	19.8	15.6	17.9	5.7	4.9	0.2
1998	1,867	100.0	8.0	27.0	16.9	17.5	18.9	7.4	4.1	0.2
1996	1,959	100.0	9.1	26.9	16.5	17.3	18.7	6.7	4.7	0.1
1994	1,971	100.0	7.9	25.7	18.4	17.8	18.9	7.1	4.1	0.2
1993	1,077	100.0	7.8	24.4	19.4	19.6	17.2	7.7	3.7	0.2
1991	1,021	100.0	9.8	25.3	19.8	15.1	19.1	6.5	4.4	0.1
1990	926	100.0	7.9	27.0	19.3	15.4	19.8	7.0	3.5	0.1
1989	1,003	100.0	7.4	26.4	16.4	16.2	20.5	7.2	5.8	0.2
1988	985	100.0	9.5	26.7	18.5	14.6	18.5	7.5	4.6	0.1
1986	1,465	100.0	9.8	26.8	15.3	16.7	18.5	7.8	5.2	0.1
1985	1,530	100.0	7.0	27.8	19.3	16.4	18.4	6.8	4.0	0.3
1983	1,596	100.0	6.3	26.4	20.1	15.9	18.8	7.3	5.2	0.1
1982	1,851	100.0	7.9	27.2	17.3	16.4	18.6	8.2	4.3	0.2
1978	1,528	100.0	7.0	28.7	18.9	14.4	18.9	8.2	3.7	0.1
1977	1,527	100.0	8.4	28.9	17.7	17.4	16.4	6.1	4.9	0.1
1975	1,488	100.0	7.2	31.9	16.7	16.5	16.3	6.9	4.5	–
1974	1,482	100.0	9.1	28.6	19.3	16.0	15.8	7.8	3.4	–

Source: General Social Surveys, National Opinion Research Center, University of Chicago; calculations by New Strategist

Table 1.93 Spending an Evening with Friends, 1974 to 2002

How often do you spend a social evening with friends?

(number of respondents aged 18 or older, and percent distribution by response, 1974–2002)

	number of respondents	total	almost daily	several times a week	several times a month	once a month	severak times a year	once a year	never	don't know
2002	908	100.0%	5.0%	19.6%	24.3%	21.6%	15.3%	6.6%	7.4%	0.2%
2000	1,869	100.0	3.7	19.1	20.3	21.5	18.1	7.3	9.7	0.4
1998	1,866	100.0	3.4	18.6	21.4	20.5	20.3	6.8	8.5	0.5
1996	1,959	100.0	3.6	20.9	20.4	21.8	16.7	7.2	9.0	0.2
1994	1,967	100.0	2.4	19.9	20.7	22.6	18.0	7.1	9.2	0.1
1993	1,077	100.0	3.2	21.1	20.4	19.9	20.2	6.0	9.0	0.1
1991	1,020	100.0	3.7	21.0	18.3	23.7	15.1	7.3	10.8	0.1
1990	926	100.0	2.5	17.3	20.8	23.7	18.9	6.3	10.5	0.1
1989	1,004	100.0	4.0	18.3	17.9	22.8	18.0	7.3	11.5	0.2
1988	986	100.0	2.9	17.6	20.8	23.5	18.7	6.3	10.1	–
1986	1,466	100.0	1.6	20.4	18.3	22.6	19.9	5.4	11.7	0.1
1985	1,530	100.0	2.9	19.0	19.9	20.9	18.4	9.1	9.8	0.1
1983	1,596	100.0	2.6	18.9	21.2	22.2	18.3	6.1	10.6	0.1
1982	1,852	100.0	3.3	18.2	21.0	21.7	19.2	7.3	9.2	0.2
1978	1,529	100.0	2.2	18.9	20.9	16.5	21.2	8.5	11.7	0.2
1977	1,526	100.0	2.8	18.8	19.7	22.1	19.1	7.2	10.0	0.2
1975	1,488	100.0	3.4	17.9	17.4	22.6	18.3	7.7	12.5	0.2
1974	1,483	100.0	2.4	19.6	18.3	22.0	18.2	8.2	11.1	0.3

Source: General Social Surveys, National Opinion Research Center, University of Chicago; calculations by New Strategist

Table 1.94 Spending an Evening with Neighbors, 1974 to 2002

How often do you spend a social evening with neighbors?

(number of respondents aged 18 or older, and percent distribution by response, 1974–2002)

	number of respondents	total	almost daily	several times a week	several times a month	once a month	severak times a year	once a year	never	don't know
2002	908	100.0%	9.0%	14.6%	12.4%	11.9%	11.3%	10.4%	30.0%	0.3%
2000	1,870	100.0	5.2	16.7	11.0	13.6	11.8	10.5	30.6	0.5
1998	1,868	100.0	5.2	16.0	10.5	15.6	14.0	10.3	28.0	0.3
1996	1,958	100.0	5.2	16.9	11.4	15.7	12.7	9.3	28.7	0.3
1994	1,968	100.0	5.2	16.0	11.5	14.1	12.6	9.6	30.8	0.2
1993	1,078	100.0	4.5	16.8	12.1	14.5	12.8	9.5	29.7	0.2
1991	1,021	100.0	5.4	18.7	11.7	13.7	12.2	7.6	30.5	0.2
1990	926	100.0	5.6	17.8	11.3	14.5	11.1	9.5	29.6	0.5
1989	1,004	100.0	5.1	16.9	9.6	14.8	12.2	10.6	30.4	0.5
1988	986	100.0	4.7	20.6	11.2	15.1	13.0	7.0	28.3	0.2
1986	1,467	100.0	7.1	21.0	11.2	14.7	11.0	9.3	25.8	–
1985	1,530	100.0	5.6	18.0	13.1	13.8	13.0	10.5	25.8	0.2
1983	1,595	100.0	5.7	19.8	12.2	14.4	12.4	9.3	26.0	0.2
1982	1,850	100.0	5.6	19.1	12.3	17.2	13.8	10.2	21.8	–
1978	1,528	100.0	6.0	23.5	10.9	12.4	13.5	8.5	24.8	0.4
1977	1,526	100.0	5.6	21.7	12.1	15.7	12.5	8.1	24.2	0.1
1975	1,488	100.0	6.0	22.4	13.2	14.7	12.2	7.9	23.5	0.2
1974	1,482	100.0	7.4	23.4	12.8	16.8	11.3	6.1	21.7	0.4

Source: General Social Surveys, National Opinion Research Center, University of Chicago; calculations by New Strategist

Table 1.95 Spending an Evening at a Bar, 1974 to 2002

How often do you spend the evening at a bar?

(number of respondents aged 18 or older, and percent distribution by response, 1974–2002)

	number of respondents	total	almost daily	several times a week	several times a month	once a month	severak times a year	once a year	never	don't know
2002	907	100.0%	1.2%	8.6%	8.2%	12.6%	11.9%	13.1%	44.2%	0.2%
2000	1,871	100.0	1.1	7.6	7.5	9.6	11.9	12.5	49.3	0.6
1998	1,864	100.0	1.4	6.7	6.7	10.7	12.4	12.8	49.1	0.2
1996	1,959	100.0	1.3	7.4	6.9	10.1	12.8	12.8	48.4	0.4
1994	1,967	100.0	1.0	7.2	7.4	9.2	13.3	12.4	49.4	0.3
1993	1,077	100.0	0.6	7.9	7.2	10.2	11.1	11.1	51.6	0.1
1991	1,020	100.0	1.8	6.9	6.1	10.7	9.9	11.7	52.8	0.2
1990	925	100.0	0.6	8.0	6.4	10.2	11.5	11.5	51.8	0.1
1989	1,004	100.0	1.0	8.2	5.6	8.5	10.3	10.9	55.7	–
1988	984	100.0	1.0	8.3	6.6	9.9	10.7	12.5	50.9	0.1
1986	1,465	100.0	1.1	8.1	6.0	9.7	11.7	9.9	53.4	0.1
1985	1,530	100.0	1.8	7.8	8.3	11.0	11.4	10.7	48.8	0.1
1983	1,595	100.0	1.6	9.7	8.7	8.2	11.4	10.1	50.2	0.1
1982	1,853	100.0	1.6	10.0	6.9	9.2	12.1	10.8	48.9	0.4
1978	1,529	100.0	1.9	8.7	9.2	7.3	12.2	10.0	50.7	0.1
1977	1,526	100.0	2.6	9.1	8.1	10.0	10.7	9.4	50.0	0.1
1975	1,486	100.0	1.5	7.7	6.6	9.2	9.0	9.4	56.0	0.7
1974	1,480	100.0	2.2	9.4	6.2	8.9	12.0	7.6	52.5	1.2

Source: General Social Surveys, National Opinion Research Center, University of Chicago; calculations by New Strategist

Suicide

In most circumstances, the majority of the public does not believe in a right to commit suicide. If a person has dishonored his or her family, 90 percent of Americans say he or she does not have a right to commit suicide. If a person has gone bankrupt, again 90 percent oppose his or her right to commit suicide. If a person is simply tired of living and ready to die, 84 percent oppose the right to die. These figures have changed little in the twenty-five years that the General Social Survey has been exploring the issue.

If someone has an incurable disease, however, attitudes toward suicide have changed. In 2002, 58 percent supported the right of someone with an incurable disease to end his or her own life, up from 38 percent in 1977. Only 40 percent oppose suicide in the event of an incurable disease, down from 59 percent who opposed it in 1977.

Table 1.96 Suicide If Person Has Dishonored Family, 1977 to 2002

Do you think a person has the right to end his or her own life if this person has dishonored his or her family?

(number of respondents aged 18 or older, and percent distribution by response, 1977–2002)

	number of respondents	total	yes	no	don't know
2002	908	100.0%	8.7%	90.2%	1.1%
2000	1,872	100.0	8.2	89.8	2.0
1998	1,865	100.0	9.7	88.2	2.1
1996	1,956	100.0	9.9	88.3	1.7
1994	1,968	100.0	9.5	88.7	1.8
1993	1,077	100.0	7.5	90.3	2.2
1991	1,021	100.0	6.1	92.0	2.0
1990	925	100.0	8.0	89.0	3.0
1989	1,000	100.0	7.0	91.3	1.7
1988	982	100.0	6.7	91.4	1.8
1986	1,467	100.0	5.9	92.8	1.3
1985	1,530	100.0	7.9	89.7	2.4
1983	1,590	100.0	6.7	91.8	1.5
1982	1,851	100.0	8.5	89.7	1.8
1978	1,531	100.0	6.3	93.3	0.5
1977	1,523	100.0	7.5	91.3	1.2

Source: General Social Surveys, National Opinion Research Center, University of Chicago; calculations by New Strategist

Table 1.97 Suicide If Bankrupt, 1977 to 2002

Do you think a person has the right to end his or her own life if this person has gone bankrupt?

(number of respondents aged 18 or older, and percent distribution by response, 1977–2002)

	number of respondents	total	yes	no	don't know
2002	907	100.0%	8.4%	90.4%	1.2%
2000	1,873	100.0	8.7	89.6	1.7
1998	1,867	100.0	9.6	88.5	1.8
1996	1,955	100.0	9.5	88.8	1.7
1994	1,969	100.0	9.2	89.3	1.5
1993	1,077	100.0	8.4	90.1	1.6
1991	1,021	100.0	6.8	91.4	1.9
1990	925	100.0	7.5	89.4	3.1
1989	1,002	100.0	7.0	91.5	1.5
1988	982	100.0	5.6	92.8	1.6
1986	1,467	100.0	6.7	92.7	0.6
1985	1,530	100.0	7.8	90.5	1.7
1983	1,589	100.0	6.5	92.2	1.3
1982	1,852	100.0	8.2	90.2	1.6
1978	1,531	100.0	5.5	93.9	0.7
1977	1,523	100.0	6.8	92.1	1.1

Source: General Social Surveys, National Opinion Research Center, University of Chicago; calculations by New Strategist

Table 1.98 Suicide If Ready to Die, 1977 to 2002

Do you think a person has the right to end his or her own life if this person is tired of living and ready to die?

(number of respondents aged 18 or older, and percent distribution by response, 1977–2002)

	number of respondents	total	yes	no	don't know
2002	908	100.0%	15.0%	83.6%	1.4%
2000	1,870	100.0	16.4	79.9	3.7
1998	1,866	100.0	16.1	80.0	3.9
1996	1,954	100.0	17.5	79.6	2.9
1994	1,966	100.0	17.8	79.2	3.0
1993	1,076	100.0	15.5	80.9	3.5
1991	1,021	100.0	12.6	84.7	2.6
1990	925	100.0	14.4	81.5	4.1
1989	1,001	100.0	13.4	84.5	2.1
1988	980	100.0	12.2	85.1	2.7
1986	1,466	100.0	15.0	83.6	1.4
1985	1,530	100.0	12.5	85.2	2.3
1983	1,590	100.0	14.6	82.8	2.6
1982	1,852	100.0	13.8	83.0	3.2
1978	1,531	100.0	11.8	86.9	1.3
1977	1,523	100.0	13.3	85.0	1.8

Source: General Social Surveys, National Opinion Research Center, University of Chicago; calculations by New Strategist

Table 1.99 Suicide If Person Has an Incurable Disease, 1977 to 2002

Do you think a person has the right to end his or her own life if this person has an incurable disease?

(number of respondents aged 18 or older, and percent distribution by response, 1977–2002)

	number of respondents	total	yes	no	don't know
2002	907	100.0%	57.8%	40.1%	2.1%
2000	1,871	100.0	54.8	39.8	5.4
1998	1,867	100.0	60.6	34.5	4.9
1996	1,956	100.0	61.2	33.8	5.0
1994	1,969	100.0	61.5	33.7	4.8
1993	1,077	100.0	56.7	38.6	4.6
1991	1,022	100.0	56.7	39.9	3.4
1990	927	100.0	56.0	38.2	5.8
1989	1,004	100.0	46.7	48.6	4.7
1988	983	100.0	50.1	46.2	3.8
1986	1,467	100.0	51.7	45.1	3.2
1985	1,532	100.0	44.1	52.5	3.4
1983	1,591	100.0	47.8	48.4	3.8
1982	1,853	100.0	44.5	50.8	4.7
1978	1,532	100.0	38.4	58.4	3.2
1977	1,524	100.0	37.9	58.9	3.2

Source: General Social Surveys, National Opinion Research Center, University of Chicago; calculations by New Strategist

Generation Social Survey Core Questions:

Women's Roles

Attitudes toward the roles of men and women have changed dramatically over the past twenty-five years as younger people have replaced older, more traditional generations. The General Social Survey has tracked the changes.

In 2002, only 38 percent of the public agreed that it is better for men to work and women to stay home. This share declined from the 65 percent majority who agreed with this statement in 1977. Conversely, 61 percent of the public disagreed with this idea in 2002, up from just 34 percent in 1977.

Working mothers are no longer regarded with the suspicion they once were, perhaps because most mothers now work. In 2002, the 63 percent majority of the public said that a working mother could have just as warm a relationship with her children as a mother who does not work. In 1977, a 48 percent minority of the public felt that way. In 1977, two-thirds of the public thought preschool children suffered if their mother worked. By 2002, a 45 percent minority still agreed.

Despite greater acceptance of the changing roles of women and men, 20 percent of Americans still think men are better suited for politics than women. This figure is lower than the 44 percent who felt that way in 1974, however.

Table 1.100 Better for Man to Work and Woman to Stay Home, 1977 to 2002

It is much better for everyone involved if the man is the achiever outside the home and the woman takes care of the home and family. Do you agree or disagree?

(number of respondents aged 18 or older, and percent distribution by response, 1977–2002)

	number of respondents	total	strongly agree	agree	disagree	strongly disagree	don't know
2002	907	100.0%	10.0%	28.3%	42.1%	18.5%	1.0%
2000	1,857	100.0	11.0	28.6	39.4	18.2	2.9
1998	1,861	100.0	7.0	27.4	44.9	18.4	2.3
1996	2,417	100.0	7.4	30.0	42.8	17.2	2.6
1994	1,969	100.0	6.7	27.4	45.5	17.7	2.7
1993	1,077	100.0	5.9	29.5	45.6	16.8	2.1
1991	1,020	100.0	7.5	33.7	39.7	16.8	2.4
1990	927	100.0	6.9	32.5	43.7	14.1	2.8
1989	1,003	100.0	9.5	30.4	41.2	16.4	2.6
1988	983	100.0	9.0	32.3	40.6	16.2	1.9
1986	1,468	100.0	9.0	37.9	39.2	12.2	1.6
1985	1,528	100.0	9.8	37.8	37.6	13.2	1.7
1977	1,526	100.0	18.0	46.8	27.7	6.0	1.5

Source: General Social Surveys, National Opinion Research Center, University of Chicago; calculations by New Strategist

Table 1.101 A Working Mother's Relationship with Children, 1977 to 2002

A working mother can establish just as warm and secure a relationship with her children as a mother who does not work. Do you agree or disagree?

(number of respondents aged 18 or older, and percent distribution by response, 1977–2002)

	number of respondents	total	strongly agree	agree	disagree	strongly disagree	don't know
2002	908	100.0%	24.0%	39.1%	26.9%	9.3%	0.8%
2000	1,868	100.0	20.1	40.3	28.9	9.5	1.2
1998	1,866	100.0	21.8	45.1	25.2	6.5	1.4
1996	2,422	100.0	23.9	41.8	25.8	7.3	1.2
1994	1,972	100.0	23.1	45.7	25.2	4.9	1.2
1993	1,078	100.0	20.1	46.0	26.3	6.2	1.4
1991	1,022	100.0	19.8	44.8	28.1	6.3	1.1
1990	927	100.0	21.7	41.2	28.8	7.7	0.6
1989	1,002	100.0	21.4	41.9	28.5	7.0	1.2
1988	986	100.0	23.6	38.9	27.5	9.0	0.9
1986	1,469	100.0	22.0	40.1	29.5	7.8	0.6
1985	1,529	100.0	21.1	39.2	28.6	10.3	0.7
1977	1,527	100.0	15.5	32.8	33.1	17.2	1.4

Source: General Social Surveys, National Opinion Research Center, University of Chicago; calculations by New Strategist

Table 1.102 Preschool Children Suffer When Mother Works, 1977 to 2002

A preschool child is likely to suffer if his or her mother works.
Do you agree or disagree?

(number of respondents aged 18 or older, and percent distribution by response, 1977–2002)

	number of respondents	total	strongly agree	agree	disagree	strongly disagree	don't know
2002	908	100.0%	9.7%	35.5%	43.2%	10.6%	1.1%
2000	1,862	100.0	9.4	36.6	40.9	10.1	3.0
1998	1,862	100.0	8.3	32.8	46.3	9.7	2.8
1996	2,418	100.0	8.4	36.4	41.5	10.6	3.1
1994	1,968	100.0	7.4	34.3	45.6	11.0	1.6
1993	1,076	100.0	7.0	35.0	45.8	9.6	2.6
1991	1,020	100.0	8.9	37.7	41.3	9.7	2.4
1990	926	100.0	7.9	40.2	40.7	8.4	2.8
1989	1,001	100.0	8.8	38.0	41.1	9.5	2.7
1988	984	100.0	10.6	36.7	40.0	10.8	1.9
1986	1,469	100.0	10.6	39.6	38.9	9.0	1.8
1985	1,527	100.0	12.8	40.2	35.6	9.6	1.8
1977	1,526	100.0	20.4	45.7	27.7	4.5	1.8

Source: General Social Surveys, National Opinion Research Center, University of Chicago; calculations by New Strategist

Table 1.103 Women Not Suited for Politics, 1974 to 2002

Most men are better suited emotionally for politics than are most women. Do you agree or disagree?

(number of respondents aged 18 or older, and percent distribution by response, 1974–2002)

	number of respondents	total	agree	disagree	not sure
2002	907	100.0%	20.4%	73.0%	6.6%
2000	1,863	100.0	21.6	71.2	7.1
1998	1,863	100.0	21.7	72.0	6.2
1996	1,955	100.0	20.9	74.6	4.6
1994	1,970	100.0	19.7	74.7	5.6
1993	1,078	100.0	20.1	74.5	5.4
1991	1,021	100.0	25.0	70.4	4.6
1990	926	100.0	25.3	68.6	6.2
1989	1,000	100.0	28.5	65.4	6.1
1988	984	100.0	32.1	64.4	3.5
1986	1,466	100.0	36.1	60.4	3.5
1985	1,524	100.0	37.1	59.1	3.8
1983	1,589	100.0	34.2	61.9	4.0
1982	917	100.0	34.9	59.3	5.8
1978	1,530	100.0	42.0	53.9	4.1
1977	1,529	100.0	46.9	48.2	4.9
1975	1,488	100.0	47.7	48.3	4.0
1974	752	100.0	43.6	49.2	7.2

Source: General Social Surveys, National Opinion Research Center, University of Chicago; calculations by New Strategist

Work and Money

Americans have always felt ambivalent about their economic status, but their economic insecurity was greater in 2002 than in years past as the recent recession and job losses took their toll.

The polarization of incomes is evident when people are asked how they stack up economically relative to others. Only 47 percent of Americans believe their family income is average compared to other families—the lowest level ever recorded by the General Social Survey. This figure has declined from a high of 58 percent who felt they were average in 1973. The percentage of those who say their family income is below average has grown from 25 to 31 percent during the past thirty years. The proportion saying their income is above average has also grown, rising from 17 to 21 percent.

On the issue of finances, 41 percent of Americans were "more or less satisfied" with their financial situation in 2002. This figure was slightly lower than the 45 percent of 1972. Nearly 29 percent of the public is dissatisfied with its financial situation, up from 23 percent in 1972.

Job satisfaction has barely budged over the past thirty years, however, with the great majority of workers claiming to be at least moderately satisfied. The 62 percent majority of working Americans in 2002 said it was unlikely they would lose their job or be laid off in the next twelve months. If they did lose their job, however, only 27 percent said it would be "very easy" to find another job with about the same pay and fringe benefits. This figure is lower than the 37 percent who said it would be very easy in 2000.

Americans still believe in the rewards of hard work. Sixty-three percent of the public said "hard work" is the way people get ahead, a proportion that has not changed significantly in thirty years. If they had enough money to live comfortably for the rest of their life, the 68 percent majority would continue to work.

Table 1.104 Opinion of Family Income, 1972 to 2002

Compared with American families in general, would you say your family income is far below average, below average, average, above average, or far above average?

(number of respondents aged 18 or older, and percent distribution by response, 1972–2002)

	number of respondents	total	far below average	below average	average	above average	far above average	don't know
2002	1,371	100.0%	6.3%	24.8%	47.1%	18.6%	2.6%	0.6%
2000	2,812	100.0	5.9	21.9	48.2	20.0	3.1	1.0
1998	2,827	100.0	5.9	22.6	46.8	21.0	2.3	1.4
1996	2,895	100.0	6.1	24.2	47.8	18.4	2.5	0.9
1994	2,978	100.0	4.6	24.0	48.2	19.9	2.3	1.0
1993	1,599	100.0	6.4	23.3	48.5	19.1	1.9	0.8
1991	1,510	100.0	5.1	22.9	50.5	18.8	1.8	0.9
1990	1,371	100.0	4.9	23.3	49.9	19.4	2.0	0.5
1989	1,536	100.0	4.2	22.9	50.2	20.4	1.6	0.7
1988	1,478	100.0	4.5	23.2	51.5	18.1	2.1	0.6
1987	1,815	100.0	4.8	24.1	48.9	20.3	1.3	0.7
1986	1,469	100.0	5.7	23.8	49.5	18.4	2.0	0.7
1985	1,531	100.0	5.8	22.9	51.1	17.6	1.9	0.6
1984	1,469	100.0	5.2	23.6	51.5	17.8	1.5	0.5
1983	1,595	100.0	6.2	23.1	48.7	18.4	2.3	1.3
1982	1,852	100.0	5.3	26.1	50.7	15.7	1.2	1.0
1980	1,465	100.0	4.8	23.3	52.1	16.8	2.3	0.8
1978	1,532	100.0	4.6	22.3	52.9	18.0	1.7	0.6
1977	1,525	100.0	5.2	23.5	51.1	17.6	1.8	0.6
1976	1,496	100.0	4.1	24.9	54.7	14.6	0.9	0.8
1975	1,487	100.0	4.4	23.5	52.3	18.0	1.3	0.6
1974	1,480	100.0	3.9	20.7	55.7	18.0	1.2	0.5
1973	1,504	100.0	3.6	18.8	58.2	17.2	1.5	0.8
1972	1,608	100.0	3.6	21.8	57.1	15.8	1.1	0.6

Source: General Social Surveys, National Opinion Research Center, University of Chicago; calculations by New Strategist

Table 1.105 Satisfaction with Financial Situation, 1972 to 2002

As far as you and your family are concerned, would you say that you are pretty well satisfied with your present financial situation, more or less satisfied, or not satisfied at all?

(number of respondents aged 18 or older, and percent distribution by response, 1972–2002)

	number of respondents	total	satisfied	more or less satisfied	not at all satisfied	don't know
2002	1,371	100.0%	29.9%	41.4%	28.5%	0.1%
2000	2,812	100.0	29.7	44.8	25.2	0.3
1998	2,829	100.0	30.0	44.4	25.5	0.2
1996	2,900	100.0	27.7	44.4	27.8	0.1
1994	2,981	100.0	27.9	45.8	26.1	0.2
1993	1,603	100.0	26.8	44.4	28.3	0.4
1991	1,511	100.0	27.6	45.5	26.6	0.3
1990	1,370	100.0	29.6	43.1	27.0	0.2
1989	1,536	100.0	30.5	44.1	25.1	0.3
1988	1,477	100.0	30.5	44.9	24.4	0.2
1987	1,814	100.0	29.7	47.9	22.3	0.1
1986	1,469	100.0	30.3	42.6	26.9	0.2
1985	1,530	100.0	29.6	43.9	26.2	0.3
1984	1,467	100.0	28.3	45.5	26.0	0.2
1983	1,597	100.0	28.6	41.1	30.0	0.3
1982	1,853	100.0	26.5	45.0	28.3	0.2
1980	1,466	100.0	28.4	44.5	26.8	0.3
1978	1,531	100.0	33.8	42.2	23.8	0.1
1977	1,524	100.0	34.1	43.6	22.1	0.2
1976	1,496	100.0	30.6	45.9	23.3	0.3
1975	1,483	100.0	30.9	42.3	26.6	0.3
1974	1,480	100.0	31.1	45.5	23.2	0.1
1973	1,502	100.0	30.7	45.5	23.8	0.1
1972	1,609	100.0	32.4	44.7	22.7	0.1

Source: General Social Surveys, National Opinion Research Center, University of Chicago; calculations by New Strategist

Table 1.106 Change in Financial Situation, 1972 to 2002

During the last few years, has your financial situation been getting better, worse, or has it stayed the same?

(number of respondents aged 18 or older, and percent distribution by response, 1972–2002)

	number of respondents	total	better	worse	stayed the same	don't know
2002	1,371	100.0%	40.7%	23.1%	36.0%	0.1%
2000	2,811	100.0	44.9	16.9	37.9	0.3
1998	2,823	100.0	44.7	15.7	39.1	0.5
1996	2,898	100.0	38.8	21.0	40.0	0.2
1994	2,980	100.0	36.1	22.6	41.0	0.3
1993	1,602	100.0	34.5	26.3	38.6	0.6
1991	1,511	100.0	35.0	22.1	42.6	0.3
1990	1,370	100.0	38.5	20.6	40.7	0.2
1989	1,532	100.0	42.7	17.8	39.4	0.1
1988	1,477	100.0	40.1	18.4	41.2	0.3
1987	1,814	100.0	40.6	18.9	40.4	0.2
1986	1,464	100.0	40.3	21.4	38.0	0.3
1985	1,531	100.0	38.5	21.7	39.5	0.3
1984	1,465	100.0	38.8	21.6	39.4	0.3
1983	1,587	100.0	34.8	26.8	37.4	0.9
1982	1,855	100.0	31.1	29.3	39.4	0.2
1980	1,464	100.0	34.3	25.3	40.2	0.1
1978	1,531	100.0	41.3	18.7	39.6	0.3
1977	1,524	100.0	38.2	21.7	39.6	0.5
1976	1,496	100.0	36.0	22.8	41.0	0.2
1975	1,485	100.0	35.0	28.1	36.4	0.4
1974	1,478	100.0	39.4	21.7	38.6	0.3
1973	1,463	100.0	42.2	16.3	41.4	0.1
1972	1,598	100.0	43.0	18.0	38.5	0.5

Source: General Social Surveys, National Opinion Research Center, University of Chicago; calculations by New Strategist

Table 1.107 Job Satisfaction, 1972 to 2002

On the whole, how satisfied are you with the work you do?
(Note: Asked only of those currently working, temporarily not at work, or keeping house.)

(number of respondents aged 18 or older, and percent distribution by response, 1972–2002)

	number of respondents	total	very satisfied	moderately satisfied	a little dissatisfied	very dissatisfied	don't know
2002	1,074	100.0%	49.7%	35.9%	9.3%	3.8%	1.2%
2000	2,170	100.0	45.2	42.3	8.6	3.5	0.4
1998	2,223	100.0	48.0	38.3	10.0	3.4	0.3
1996	2,316	100.0	44.9	39.6	10.9	4.4	0.1
1994	2,345	100.0	46.0	39.7	10.5	3.5	0.3
1993	1,229	100.0	43.3	41.1	10.8	4.7	0.1
1991	1,152	100.0	44.3	41.8	9.4	4.3	0.3
1990	1,041	100.0	46.2	39.7	10.5	3.7	–
1989	1,208	100.0	46.1	39.1	10.3	4.3	0.2
1988	1,155	100.0	46.5	39.4	10.1	3.8	0.2
1987	1,449	100.0	44.4	38.4	12.4	4.7	–
1986	1,163	100.0	49.0	39.4	8.9	2.6	0.1
1985	1,237	100.0	47.8	37.8	9.9	4.4	0.2
1984	1,208	100.0	45.9	35.0	12.1	7.0	–
1983	1,333	100.0	49.3	37.4	8.8	4.5	–
1982	1,510	100.0	46.9	37.7	9.7	5.6	0.1
1980	1,247	100.0	46.8	35.6	12.8	4.7	0.1
1978	1,281	100.0	50.8	36.1	8.4	4.5	0.1
1977	1,263	100.0	47.6	39.3	10.3	2.8	0.1
1976	1,188	100.0	51.9	34.3	9.1	4.5	0.3
1975	1,168	100.0	54.0	32.6	9.0	4.1	0.3
1974	1,228	100.0	47.7	37.3	9.9	4.6	0.4
1973	1,143	100.0	49.3	38.1	8.0	4.3	0.2
1972	947	100.0	48.4	36.6	11.2	3.5	0.3

Source: General Social Surveys, National Opinion Research Center, University of Chicago; calculations by New Strategist

Table 1.108 Likely to Lose Job, 1977 to 2002

Thinking about the next 12 months, how likely do you think it is that you will lose your job or be laid off? (Note: Asked only of those with jobs.)

(number of respondents aged 18 or older, and percent distribution by response, 1977–2002)

	number of respondents	total	very likely	fairly likely	not too likely	not likely	leaving labor force	don't know
2002	581	100.0%	6.4%	7.1%	23.9%	62.0%	–	0.7%
2000	1,246	100.0	3.5	4.3	21.7	69.0	–	1.5
1998	1,252	100.0	3.7	4.2	26.1	64.4	–	1.6
1996	1,364	100.0	4.3	6.7	27.7	59.5	–	1.8
1994	1,299	100.0	5.5	4.5	26.7	62.1	–	1.2
1993	677	100.0	4.4	8.0	26.4	59.8	–	1.3
1991	609	100.0	6.1	6.6	25.0	61.4	–	1.0
1990	601	100.0	3.2	5.5	24.1	65.7	–	1.5
1989	613	100.0	4.1	3.8	22.2	69.2	–	0.8
1988	617	100.0	4.1	4.4	24.8	65.6	–	1.1
1986	869	100.0	3.6	6.6	22.0	65.7	–	2.2
1985	942	100.0	6.7	4.5	23.1	64.6	–	1.1
1983	940	100.0	6.0	7.7	24.8	60.0	–	1.6
1982	1,080	100.0	7.2	6.2	26.1	58.8	–	1.7
1978	889	100.0	4.0	3.7	20.5	70.8	–	1.0
1977	917	100.0	4.0	5.9	23.9	63.9	0.5%	1.7

Source: General Social Surveys, National Opinion Research Center, University of Chicago; calculations by New Strategist

Table 1.109 Could Find Equally Good Job, 1977 to 2002

About how easy would it be for you to find a job with another employer with approximately the same income and fringe benefits you now have? (Note: Asked only of those with jobs.)

(number of respondents aged 18 or older, and percent distribution by response, 1972–2002)

	number of respondents	total	very easy	somewhat easy	not easy	don't know
2002	582	100.0%	26.8%	36.3%	35.4%	1.5%
2000	1,246	100.0	37.0	32.3	28.9	1.8
1998	1,249	100.0	30.1	35.0	32.7	2.2
1996	1,362	100.0	26.7	32.1	39.1	2.1
1994	1,302	100.0	20.6	32.2	44.9	2.3
1993	676	100.0	21.7	32.5	44.1	1.6
1991	608	100.0	23.4	35.2	39.6	1.8
1990	600	100.0	31.7	30.0	37.2	1.2
1989	613	100.0	33.8	27.1	37.4	1.8
1988	615	100.0	27.5	35.8	34.5	2.3
1986	870	100.0	27.4	32.3	38.5	1.8
1985	940	100.0	25.0	31.1	42.2	1.7
1983	940	100.0	18.7	28.8	50.3	2.1
1982	1,077	100.0	21.8	25.7	49.8	2.7
1978	888	100.0	27.7	31.9	38.3	2.1
1977	909	100.0	26.5	29.8	41.7	2.0

Source: General Social Surveys, National Opinion Research Center, University of Chicago; calculations by New Strategist

Table 1.110 Opinion of How People Get Ahead, 1973 to 2002

Some people say that people get ahead by their own hard work; others say that lucky breaks or help from other people are more important. Which do you think is most important?

(number of respondents aged 18 or older, and percent distribution by response, 1973–2002)

	number of respondents	total	hard work	both equally	luck or help	other	don't know
2002	923	100.0%	62.6%	26.9%	10.0%	–	0.5%
2000	1,851	100.0	64.5	24.4	10.4	–	0.7
1998	1,872	100.0	66.6	22.3	10.4	–	0.7
1996	1,915	100.0	69.6	18.0	11.4	–	1.0
1994	1,988	100.0	69.2	19.4	10.7	–	0.7
1993	1,071	100.0	65.6	21.6	12.5	–	0.3
1991	986	100.0	66.0	20.6	12.7	–	0.7
1990	915	100.0	65.4	20.8	13.3	–	0.5
1989	1,029	100.0	65.7	19.6	13.9	–	0.8
1988	976	100.0	66.7	20.9	11.9	–	0.5
1987	1,813	100.0	66.0	18.4	14.9	–	0.7
1985	1,531	100.0	65.5	18.7	14.4	–	1.4
1984	1,466	100.0	66.6	18.0	14.9	–	0.5
1982	1,857	100.0	59.9	25.5	13.1	–	1.5
1980	1,465	100.0	63.3	27.9	8.1	–	0.8
1977	1,526	100.0	60.7	28.2	10.4	–	0.7
1976	1,496	100.0	62.2	23.9	13.2	–	0.7
1974	1,480	100.0	60.9	28.6	8.6	1.3%	0.6
1973	1,502	100.0	64.8	23.6	10.0	1.1	0.5

Source: General Social Surveys, National Opinion Research Center, University of Chicago; calculations by New Strategist

Table 1.111 Continue to Work If Rich, 1973 to 2002

If you were to get enough money to live as comfortably as you would like for the rest of your life, would you continue to work or would you stop working? (Note: Asked only of those currently working or temporarily not at work.)

(number of respondents aged 18 or older, and percent distribution by response, 1973–2002)

	number of respondents	total	continue working	stop working	don't know
2002	649	100.0%	68.4%	31.0%	0.6%
2000	1,267	100.0	65.7	32.5	1.7
1998	1,303	100.0	68.6	30.0	1.4
1996	1,386	100.0	66.9	31.5	1.6
1994	1,376	100.0	65.0	33.8	1.2
1993	700	100.0	67.7	30.4	1.9
1991	624	100.0	66.0	32.7	1.3
1990	594	100.0	71.7	26.9	1.3
1989	649	100.0	71.2	27.4	1.4
1988	626	100.0	70.3	28.8	1.0
1987	1,206	100.0	74.3	25.1	0.6
1985	988	100.0	68.8	30.2	1.0
1984	955	100.0	75.5	23.9	0.6
1982	1,164	100.0	71.5	27.3	1.2
1980	886	100.0	76.1	22.9	1.0
1977	954	100.0	69.0	29.6	1.5
1976	757	100.0	68.0	30.5	1.5
1974	837	100.0	63.6	34.5	1.9
1973	831	100.0	68.1	30.4	1.4

Source: General Social Surveys, National Opinion Research Center, University of Chicago; calculations by New Strategist

CHAPTER

2

General Social Survey 2002 Topical Modules

The General Social Survey consists of three types of questions: core questions asked in most surveys; Topical Modules with questions that probe certain subjects and change from survey to survey; and the cross-national International Social Survey Program (ISSP) questions—which are also included in surveys conducted in dozens of other countries, allowing international comparisons.

The Topical Modules comprise about one-third of GSS questions in any given year. Responses to the 2002 Topical Modules are shown here, probing topics such as altruism, employee compensation, and Internet use. The ISSP questions comprise about one-sixth of GSS questions, and responses to the two ISSP modules included in the 2002 GSS are shown here. They explore social relations and working women.

Adult Transitions

What does it take for a young person to become an adult? The General Social Survey asked Americans this question and found surprising answers. A larger share of Americans considers finishing school more important to becoming an adult than financial independence.

The 72 percent majority of the public believes it to be "extremely important" for young people to have completed their schooling before they can be considered adults. Most think this should happen before age 25.

Smaller majorities say it is extremely important for young people to have full-time employment (60 percent) or be able to support a family financially (59 percent) before they can be considered adults. Most think full-time employment should happen before age 25. Being able to support a family financially is expected later in life, however, the majority saying this should normally occur at age 25 or older.

Interestingly, a smaller 46 percent of the public think it is extremely important for young people to be financially independent before they can be considered adults. Only 28 percent say it is extremely important for young people to have their own household, and just 18 percent say marriage is extremely important. The smallest share (15 percent) says having a child is extremely important to becoming an adult.

Table 2.1 Financial Independence to Become an Adult, 2002

People differ in their ideas about what it takes for a young person to become an adult these days. How important is it for them to be financially independent from their parents / guardians?

(number of respondents aged 18 or older and percent distribution by response, 2002)

	number of respondents	percent distribution
Total	**1,393**	**100.0%**
Extremely important	637	45.7
Quite important	465	33.4
Somewhat important	228	16.4
Not too important	28	2.0
Not at all important	14	1.0
Don't know	16	1.1
No answer	5	0.4

By what age should this normally occur?

	number of respondents	percent distribution
Total	**1,330**	**100.0%**
Before age 18	98	7.4
Aged 18–19	353	26.5
Aged 20–24	679	51.1
Aged 25–29	155	11.7
Aged 30 to 34	18	1.4
Aged 35 or older	3	0.2
Don't know	20	1.5
No answer	4	0.3

Source: General Social Survey, National Opinion Research Center, University of Chicago

Table 2.2 Independent Household to Become an Adult, 2002

People differ in their ideas about what it takes for a young person to become an adult these days. How important is it for them to be no longer living in their parents' household?

(number of respondents aged 18 or older and percent distribution by response, 2002)

	number of respondents	percent distribution
Total	**1,393**	**100.0%**
Extremely important	396	28.4
Quite important	387	27.8
Somewhat important	347	24.9
Not too important	180	12.9
Not at all important	55	3.9
Don't know	23	1.7
No answer	5	0.4

By what age should this normally occur?

	number of respondents	percent distribution
Total	**1,130**	**100.0%**
Before age 18	11	1.0
Aged 18–19	325	28.8
Aged 20–24	616	54.5
Aged 25–29	156	13.8
Aged 30–34	4	0.4
Aged 35 or older	1	0.1
Don't know	16	1.4
No answer	1	0.1

Source: General Social Survey, National Opinion Research Center, University of Chicago

Table 2.3 Complete Schooling to Become an Adult, 2002

People differ in their ideas about what it takes for a young person to become an adult these days. How important is it for them to have completed their formal schooling?

(number of respondents aged 18 or older and percent distribution by response, 2002)

	number of respondents	percent distribution
Total	**1,393**	**100.0%**
Extremely important	999	71.7
Quite important	246	17.7
Somewhat important	89	6.4
Not too important	30	2.2
Not at all important	13	0.9
Don't know	11	0.8
No answer	5	0.4

By what age should this normally occur?

	number of respondents	percent distribution
Total	**1,334**	**100.0%**
Before age 18	35	2.6
Aged 18–19	294	22.0
Aged 20–24	672	50.4
Aged 25–29	252	18.9
Aged 30–34	30	2.2
Aged 35 or older	10	0.7
Don't know	36	2.7
No answer	5	0.4

Source: General Social Survey, National Opinion Research Center, University of Chicago

Table 2.4 Full-Time Employment to Become an Adult, 2002

People differ in their ideas about what it takes for a young person to become an adult these days. How important is it for them to be employed full-time?

(number of respondents aged 18 or older and percent distribution by response, 2002)

	number of respondents	percent distribution
Total	**1,393**	**100.0%**
Extremely important	831	59.7
Quite important	325	23.3
Somewhat important	156	11.2
Not too important	51	3.7
Not at all important	12	0.9
Don't know	13	0.9
No answer	5	0.4

By what age should this normally occur?

	number of respondents	percent distribution
Total	**1,312**	**100.0%**
Before age 18	58	4.4
Aged 18–19	349	26.6
Aged 20–24	674	51.4
Aged 25–29	194	14.8
Aged 30–34	8	0.6
Aged 35 or older	2	0.2
Don't know	26	2.0
No answer	1	0.1

Source: General Social Survey, National Opinion Research Center, University of Chicago

Table 2.5 Support Family Financially to Become an Adult, 2002

People differ in their ideas about what it takes for a young person to become an adult these days. How important is it for them to be capable of supporting a family financially?

(number of respondents aged 18 or older and percent distribution by response, 2002)

	number of respondents	percent distribution
Total	**1,393**	**100.0%**
Extremely important	824	59.2
Quite important	306	22.0
Somewhat important	152	10.9
Not too important	57	4.1
Not at all important	27	1.9
Don't know	21	1.5
No answer	6	0.4

By what age should this normally occur?

	number of respondents	percent distribution
Total	**1,282**	**100.0%**
Before age 18	10	0.8
Aged 18–19	70	5.5
Aged 20–24	435	33.9
Aged 25–29	535	41.7
Aged 30–34	146	11.4
Aged 35 or older	18	1.4
Don't know	65	5.1
No answer	3	0.2

Source: General Social Survey, National Opinion Research Center, University of Chicago

Table 2.6 Have a Child to Become an Adult, 2002

People differ in their ideas about what it takes for a young person to become an adult these days. How important is it for them to have a child?

(number of respondents aged 18 or older and percent distribution by response, 2002)

	number of respondents	percent distribution
Total	**1,393**	**100.0%**
Extremely important	211	15.1
Quite important	168	12.1
Somewhat important	321	23.0
Not too important	344	24.7
Not at all important	302	21.7
Don't know	38	2.7
No answer	9	0.6

By what age should this normally occur?

	number of respondents	percent distribution
Total	**700**	**100.0%**
Before age 18	1	0.1
Aged 18–19	15	2.1
Aged 20–24	142	20.3
Aged 25–29	345	49.3
Aged 30–34	142	20.3
Aged 35 or older	22	3.1
Don't know	32	4.6
No answer	1	0.1

Source: General Social Survey, National Opinion Research Center, University of Chicago

Table 2.7 Get Married to Become an Adult, 2002

People differ in their ideas about what it takes for a young person to become an adult these days. How important is it for them to get married?

(number of respondents aged 18 or older and percent distribution by response, 2002)

	number of respondents	percent distribution
Total	**1,393**	**100.0%**
Extremely important	256	18.4
Quite important	191	13.7
Somewhat important	284	20.4
Not too important	330	23.7
Not at all important	290	20.8
Don't know	34	2.4
No answer	8	0.6

By what age should this normally occur?

	number of respondents	percent distribution
Total	**731**	**100.0%**
Before age 18	0	0.0
Aged 18–19	18	2.5
Aged 20–24	213	29.1
Aged 25–29	328	44.9
Aged 30–34	120	16.4
Aged 35 or older	20	2.7
Don't know	31	4.2
No answer	1	0.1

Source: General Social Survey, National Opinion Research Center, University of Chicago

Altruism

When the General Social Survey probed the public's level of altruism in 2002, it found that most people consider themselves caring and concerned about the welfare of others. Their behavior and attitudes sometimes contradict this notion, however.

When asked whether the statement, "I often have tender feelings for people less fortunate than me," applied to them, the 71 percent majority of adults placed themselves at a four or five on a scale of one to five, with five meaning "describes me very well." Conversely, when asked how well the statement, "Other people's misfortunes do not usually disturb me a great deal," describes them, the 57 percent majority placed themselves at a one or two, with one meaning "does not describe me very well."

But when the GSS probed altruistic behavior, there appeared to be less caring for others in practice than in preaching. Only 15 percent of adults said they had given blood in the past year, for example. The majority had not done volunteer work for a charity. Most had not offered their seat in a public place to a stranger who was standing. But the majority of Americans had given money to a homeless person in the past year, most had allowed a stranger ahead of them in line, and most had given money to a charity.

Still, there is ambivalence in Americans' attitude toward people who need help. The 88 percent majority agrees with the statement, "People should be willing to help others who are less fortunate." But the 53 percent majority also agree that "those in need have to learn to take care of themselves and not depend on others."

Table 2.8 Feel for People Less Fortunate, 2002

"I often have tender feelings for people less fortunate than me." How well does this statement describe you, where 1 indicates that it does not describe you very well and 5 means that it does describe you very well? Numbers 2–4 indicate that how well it describes you are in between these points.

(number of respondents aged 18 or older and percent distribution by response, 2002)

	number of respondents	percent distribution
Total	**1,372**	**100.0%**
1. Does not describe very well	64	4.7
2	68	5.0
3	253	18.4
4	341	24.9
5. Describes very well	627	45.7
Don't know	13	0.9
No answer	6	0.4

Source: General Social Survey, National Opinion Research Center, University of Chicago

Table 2.9 Feel Sorry for Those with Problems, 2002

"Sometimes I don't feel very sorry for other people when they are having problems."

How well does this statement describe you, where 1 indicates that it does not describe you very well and 5 means that it does describe you very well? Numbers 2–4 indicate that how well it describes you are in between these points.

(number of respondents aged 18 or older and percent distribution by response, 2002)

	number of respondents	percent distribution
Total	**1,372**	**100.0%**
1. Does not describe very well	493	35.9
2	291	21.2
3	324	23.6
4	142	10.3
5. Describes very well	101	7.4
Don't know	14	1.0
No answer	7	0.5

Source: General Social Survey, National Opinion Research Center, University of Chicago

Table 2.10 Feel Protective of Those Being Taken Advantage Of, 2002

"When I see someone being taken advantage of, I feel kind of protective towards them."

How well does this statement describe you, where 1 indicates that it does not describe you very well and 5 means that it does describe you very well? Numbers 2–4 indicate that how well it describes you are in between these points.

(number of respondents aged 18 or older and percent distribution by response, 2002)

	number of respondents	percent distribution
Total	**1,372**	**100.0%**
1. Does not describe very well	58	4.2
2	60	4.4
3	168	12.2
4	422	30.8
5. Describes very well	644	46.9
Don't know	14	1.0
No answer	6	0.4

Source: General Social Survey, National Opinion Research Center, University of Chicago

Table 2.11 Feeling the Misfortunes of Others, 2002

"Other people's misfortunes do not usually disturb me a great deal."
How well does this statement describe you, where 1 indicates that it does not describe you very well and 5 means that it does describe you very well? Numbers 2–4 indicate that how well it describes you are in between these points.

(number of respondents aged 18 or older and percent distribution by response, 2002)

	number of respondents	percent distribution
Total	**1,372**	**100.0%**
1. Does not describe very well	485	35.3
2	341	24.9
3	302	22.0
4	141	10.3
5. Describes very well	83	6.0
Don't know	14	1.0
No answer	6	0.4

Source: General Social Survey, National Opinion Research Center, University of Chicago

Table 2.12 Feelings When Others Are Treated Unfairly, 2002

"When I see someone being treated unfairly,
I sometimes don't feel very much pity for them."

How well does this statement describe you, where 1 indicates that it does not describe you very well and 5 means that it does describe you very well? Numbers 2–4 indicate that how well it describes you are in between these points.

(number of respondents aged 18 or older and percent distribution by response, 2002)

	number of respondents	percent distribution
Total	**1,372**	**100.0%**
1. Does not describe very well	613	44.7
2	373	27.2
3	191	13.9
4	90	6.6
5. Describes very well	76	5.5
Don't know	21	1.5
No answer	8	0.6

Source: General Social Survey, National Opinion Research Center, University of Chicago

Table 2.13 Touched by Things That Happen, 2002

"I am often quite touched by things that I see happen."
How well does this statement describe you, where 1 indicates that it does not describe you very well and 5 means that it does describe you very well? Numbers 2–4 indicate that how well it describes you are in between these points.

(number of respondents aged 18 or older and percent distribution by response, 2002)

	number of respondents	percent distribution
Total	**1,372**	**100.0%**
1. Does not describe very well	46	3.4
2	49	3.6
3	241	17.6
4	364	26.5
5. Describes very well	651	47.4
Don't know	14	1.0
No answer	7	0.5

Source: General Social Survey, National Opinion Research Center, University of Chicago

Table 2.14 Describe Self as Soft-Hearted, 2002

"I would describe myself as a pretty soft-hearted person."
How well does this statement describe you, where 1 indicates that it does not describe you very well and 5 means that it does describe you very well? Numbers 2–4 indicate that how well it describes you are in between these points.

(number of respondents aged 18 or older and percent distribution by response, 2002)

	number of respondents	percent distribution
Total	**1,372**	**100.0%**
1. Does not describe very well	50	3.6
2	69	5.0
3	234	17.1
4	337	24.6
5. Describes very well	666	48.5
Don't know	10	0.7
No answer	6	0.4

Source: General Social Survey, National Opinion Research Center, University of Chicago

Table 2.15 Blood Donation, 2002

During the past 12 months, how often have you donated blood?

(number of respondents aged 18 or older and percent distribution by response, 2002)

	number of respondents	percent distribution
Total	**1,372**	**100.0%**
More than once a week	3	0.2
Once a week	0	0.0
Once a month	5	0.4
At least 2 or 3 times in the past year	81	5.9
Once in the past year	121	8.8
Not at all in the past year	1,152	84.0
Don't know	6	0.4
No answer	4	0.3

Source: General Social Survey, National Opinion Research Center, University of Chicago

Table 2.16 Give to the Homeless, 2002

During the past 12 months, how often have you given food or money to a homeless person?

(number of respondents aged 18 or older and percent distribution by response, 2002)

	number of respondents	percent distribution
Total	**1,372**	**100.0%**
More than once a week	30	2.2
Once a week	53	3.9
Once a month	164	12.0
At least 2 or 3 times in the past year	407	29.7
Once in the past year	194	14.1
Not at all in the past year	505	36.8
Don't know	15	1.1
No answer	4	0.3

Source: General Social Survey, National Opinion Research Center, University of Chicago

Table 2.17 Returned Money to Cashier, 2002

During the past 12 months, how often have you returned money to a cashier after getting too much change?

(number of respondents aged 18 or older and percent distribution by response, 2002)

	number of respondents	percent distribution
Total	**1,372**	**100.0%**
More than once a week	8	0.6
Once a week	6	0.4
Once a month	28	2.0
At least 2 or 3 times in the past year	256	18.7
Once in the past year	330	24.1
Not at all in the past year	709	51.7
Don't know	30	2.2
No answer	5	0.4

Source: General Social Survey, National Opinion Research Center, University of Chicago

Table 2.18 Allowed a Stranger Ahead of You in Line, 2002

During the past 12 months, how often have you allowed a stranger to go ahead of you in line?

(number of respondents aged 18 or older and percent distribution by response, 2002)

	number of respondents	percent distribution
Totaxl	**1,372**	**100.0%**
More than once a week	56	4.1
Once a week	95	6.9
Once a month	273	19.9
At least 2 or 3 times in the past year	581	42.3
Once in the past year	152	11.1
Not at all in the past year	193	14.1
Don't know	17	1.2
No answer	5	0.4

Source: General Social Survey, National Opinion Research Center, University of Chicago

Table 2.19 Volunteer Work for Charity, 2002

During the past 12 months, how often have you done volunteer work for a charity?

(number of respondents aged 18 or older and percent distribution by response, 2002)

	number of respondents	percent distribution
Total	**1,372**	**100.0%**
More than once a week	60	4.4
Once a week	50	3.6
Once a month	107	7.8
At least 2 or 3 times in the past year	222	16.2
Once in the past year	167	12.2
Not at all in the past year	754	55.0
Don't know	8	0.6
No answer	4	0.3

Source: General Social Survey, National Opinion Research Center, University of Chicago

Table 2.20 Give Money to Charity, 2002

During the past 12 months, how often have you given money to a charity?

(number of respondents aged 18 or older and percent distribution by response, 2002)

	number of respondents	percent distribution
Total	**1,372**	**100.0%**
More than once a week	32	2.3
Once a week	108	7.9
Once a month	258	18.8
At least 2 or 3 times in the past year	465	33.9
Once in the past year	197	14.4
Not at all in the past year	298	21.7
Don't know	10	0.7
No answer	4	0.3

Source: General Social Survey, National Opinion Research Center, University of Chicago

Table 2.21 Give Seat to Stranger, 2002

During the past 12 months, how often have you offered your seat on a bus or in a public place to a stranger who was standing?

(number of respondents aged 18 or older and percent distribution by response, 2002)

	number of respondents	percent distribution
Total	**1,372**	**100.0%**
More than once a week	20	1.5
Once a week	26	1.9
Once a month	70	5.1
At least 2 or 3 times in the past year	259	18.9
Once in the past year	185	13.5
Not at all in the past year	788	57.4
Don't know	18	1.3
No answer	6	0.4

Source: General Social Survey, National Opinion Research Center, University of Chicago

Table 2.22 Look After a Person's Plants, Mail, or Pets, 2002

During the past 12 months, how often have you looked after a person's plants, mail, or pets while they were away?

(number of respondents aged 18 or older and percent distribution by response, 2002)

	number of respondents	percent distribution
Total	**1,372**	**100.0%**
More than once a week	31	2.3
Once a week	19	1.4
Once a month	67	4.9
At least 2 or 3 times in the past year	426	31.0
Once in the past year	213	15.5
Not at all in the past year	600	43.7
Don't know	12	0.9
No answer	4	0.3

Source: General Social Survey, National Opinion Research Center, University of Chicago

Table 2.23 Carry a Stranger's Belongings, 2002

During the past 12 months, how often have you carried a stranger's belongings, like groceries, a suitcase, or shopping bag?

(number of respondents aged 18 or older and percent distribution by response, 2002)

	number of respondents	percent distribution
Total	**1,372**	**100.0%**
More than once a week	19	1.4
Once a week	23	1.7
Once a month	61	4.4
At least 2 or 3 times in the past year	273	19.9
Once in the past year	217	15.8
Not at all in the past year	762	55.5
Don't know	13	0.9
No answer	4	0.3

Source: General Social Survey, National Opinion Research Center, University of Chicago

Table 2.24 Give Directions to a Stranger, 2002

During the past 12 months, how often have you given directions to a stranger?

(number of respondents aged 18 or older and percent distribution by response, 2002)

	number of respondents	percent distribution
Total	**1,372**	**100.0%**
More than once a week	75	5.5
Once a week	77	5.6
Once a month	238	17.3
At least 2 or 3 times in the past year	607	44.2
Once in the past year	183	13.3
Not at all in the past year	173	12.6
Don't know	15	1.1
No answer	4	0.3

Source: General Social Survey, National Opinion Research Center, University of Chicago

Table 2.25 Let Someone Borrow an Item, 2002

During the past 12 months, how often have you let someone you didn't know well borrow an item of some value like dishes or tools?

(number of respondents aged 18 or older and percent distribution by response, 2002)

	number of respondents	percent distribution
Total	**1,372**	**100.0%**
More than once a week	11	0.8
Once a week	20	1.5
Once a month	49	3.6
At least 2 or 3 times in the past year	221	16.1
Once in the past year	231	16.8
Not at all in the past year	820	59.8
Don't know	14	1.0
No answer	6	0.4

Source: General Social Survey, National Opinion Research Center, University of Chicago

Table 2.26 Feel a Selfless Caring, 2002

The following are things that you may experience in your daily life. Please tell me how often this occurs:

I feel a selfless caring.

(number of respondents aged 18 or older and percent distribution by response, 2002)

	number of respondents	percent distribution
Total	**1,372**	**100.0%**
Many times a day	128	9.3
Every day	177	12.9
Most days	266	19.4
Some days	328	23.9
Once in a while	288	21.0
Never or almost never	136	9.9
Don't know	42	3.1
No answer	7	0.5

Source: General Social Survey, National Opinion Research Center, University of Chicago

Table 2.27 Accept Others, 2002

The following are things that you may experience in your daily life. Please tell me how often this occurs:
I accept others even when they do things I think are wrong.

(number of respondents aged 18 or older and percent distribution by response, 2002)

	number of respondents	percent distribution
Total	**1,372**	**100.0%**
Many times a day	119	8.7
Every day	207	15.1
Most days	437	31.9
Some days	310	22.6
Once in a while	206	15.0
Never or almost never	66	4.8
Don't know	20	1.5
No answer	7	0.5

Source: General Social Survey, National Opinion Research Center, University of Chicago

Table 2.28 People Should Help Others, 2002

Please tell me whether you strongly agree, agree, neither agree nor disagree, disagree, or strongly disagree with the following statement: People should be willing to help others who are less fortunate.

(number of respondents aged 18 or older and percent distribution by response, 2002)

	number of respondents	percent distribution
Total	**1,372**	**100.0%**
Strongly agree	567	41.3
Agree	638	46.5
Neither agree nor disagree	123	9.0
Disagree	15	1.1
Strongly disagree	9	0.7
Don't know	12	0.9
No answer	8	0.6

Source: General Social Survey, National Opinion Research Center, University of Chicago

Table 2.29 People in Need Must Help Themselves, 2002

Please tell me whether you strongly agree, agree, neither agree nor disagree, disagree, or strongly disagree with the following statement:

Those in need have to learn to take care of themselves and not depend on others.

(number of respondents aged 18 or older and percent distribution by response, 2002)

	number of respondents	percent distribution
Total	**1,372**	**100.0%**
Strongly agree	175	12.8
Agree	552	40.2
Neither agree nor disagree	319	23.3
Disagree	254	18.5
Strongly disagree	52	3.8
Don't know	13	0.9
No answer	7	0.5

Source: General Social Survey, National Opinion Research Center, University of Chicago

Table 2.30 Important to Help People in Trouble, 2002

Please tell me whether you strongly agree, agree, neither agree nor disagree, disagree, or strongly disagree with the following statement: Personally assisting people in trouble is very important to me.

(number of respondents aged 18 or older and percent distribution by response, 2002)

	number of respondents	percent distribution
Total	**1,372**	**100.0%**
Strongly agree	328	23.9
Agree	672	49.0
Neither agree nor disagree	275	20.0
Disagree	67	4.9
Strongly disagree	12	0.9
Don't know	12	0.9
No answer	6	0.4

Source: General Social Survey, National Opinion Research Center, University of Chicago

Table 2.31 People Should Look After Themselves, 2002

Please tell me whether you strongly agree, agree, neither agree nor disagree, disagree, or strongly disagree with the following statement:

These days people need to look after themselves and not overly worry about others.

(number of respondents aged 18 or older and percent distribution by response, 2002)

	number of respondents	percent distribution
Total	**1,372**	**100.0%**
Strongly agree	86	6.3
Agree	358	26.1
Neither agree nor disagree	289	21.1
Disagree	508	37.0
Strongly disagree	114	8.3
Don't know	11	0.8
No answer	6	0.4

Source: General Social Survey, National Opinion Research Center, University of Chicago

Cultural Participation

Americans' participation in the arts is tepid at best. With television and the Internet absorbing so much of the time of so many people, there is little left for experiencing the real thing.

In 2002, only 37 percent of the public had visited an art museum or gallery in the past twelve months. Just 23 percent had gone to a live dance performance, and an even smaller 18 percent had attended a classical music concert.

Personal participation in the arts is also not the norm. In 2002, a 41 percent minority of the public had made an art or craft object in the past twelve months. About half that proportion—21 percent—had played a musical instrument, and only 10 percent had taken part in a music, dance, or theatrical performance.

Going to the movies is the only arts activity in which most Americans participate. Seventy-two percent of the public had attended a movie at least once in the past year.

The rising educational level of the population suggests that arts participation should be growing, but the numbers show little, if any, growth over a ten-year period. Perhaps the only good news in these statistics for the arts community is the stability of participation over the past decade despite the proliferation of television channels and widespread Internet use.

Table 2.32 Cultural Participation, 1993 to 2002

I'd like to ask about some leisure or recreational activities that people do during their free time. As I read each activity, can you tell me if it is something you have done in the past 12 months?

(number of respondents aged 18 or older and percent distribution by response, 1993-2002)

	number of respondents	total	yes	no	don't know	no answer
Visit an art museum or gallery:						
2002	2,765	100.0%	36.8%	62.2%	0.5%	0.4%
1998	1,445	100.0	36.5	62.8	0.1	0.7
1993	1,606	100.0	40.2	59.0	0.1	0.7
Make art or craft objects such as pottery, woodworking, quilts, or paintings:						
2002	1,372	100.0	41.3	57.7	0.6	0.4
1998	1,445	100.0	37.6	61.6	0.0	0.8
1993	1,606	100.0	40.0	59.2	0.1	0.7
Go to a live ballet or dance performance, not including school performances:						
2002	1,372	100.0	22.7	76.2	0.7	0.4
1998	1,445	100.0	19.6	79.7	0.0	0.8
1993	1,606	100.0	19.6	79.6	0.1	0.7
Go to a classical music or opera performance, not including school performances:						
2002	2,765	100.0	17.5	81.6	0.5	0.4
1998	1,445	100.0	16.8	82.5	0.0	0.7
1993	1,606	100.0	15.8	83.3	0.1	0.8
Take part in a music, dance, or theatrical performance:						
2002	1,372	100.0	10.3	88.7	0.6	0.4
1998	1,445	100.0	10.5	88.6	0.0	0.9
1993	1,606	100.0	9.6	89.4	0.1	0.9
Go out to see a movie in a theater:						
2002	1,372	100.0	72.4	26.6	0.6	0.4
1998	1,445	100.0	65.9	33.3	0.0	0.8
1993	1,606	100.0	69.4	29.9	0.1	0.7
Play a musical instrument like a piano, guitar, or violin:						
2002	1,372	100.0	20.8	78.1	0.6	0.4
1998	1,445	100.0	23.3	75.8	0.0	0.9
1993	1,606	100.0	23.2	75.8	0.1	0.9

Source: General Social Surveys, National Opinion Research Center, University of Chicago

Employee Compensation

For all the talk about 401(k)s, profit sharing, stock options, and bonuses, you would think most Americans' fortunes depend on these forms of compensation. In fact, few workers participate. Once you boil down the number to those who work for private companies that offer stock and who own stock in the company, you're left with a fraction of the American labor force.

Among all workers aged 18 or older, 76 percent work for a private company. Among those working for private companies, only 23 percent own stock in the company. Among those owning stock in their company, only 18 percent own stock worth $50,000 or more (18 percent do not know how much stock they own, and 12 percent would not answer the question). Ignoring the "don't knows" and "no answers," it appear that just 3 percent of American workers own stock worth $50,000 or more in the company for which they work.

Only 33 percent of workers aged 18 or older are eligible for bonuses or profit-sharing. Among those in companies with performance-based pay, 64 percent received bonuses in the previous year. Overall, only 22 percent of the nation's workers received bonuses in the past year. Among those receiving them, the majority got less than $3,000.

Table 2.33 Work by Type of Organization, 2002

Do you work for a private company, a nonprofit organization, or for the government or a government agency?

(number of working respondents aged 18 or older and percent distribution by response, 2002)

	number of respondents	percent distribution
Total	**1,796**	**100.0%**
Private company	1,370	76.3
Nonprofit organization	114	6.3
Government or government agency	305	17.0
Don't know	1	0.1
No answer	6	0.3

Source: General Social Survey, National Opinion Research Center, University of Chicago

Table 2.34 Own Stock in Company, 2002

Do you own any shares of stock in the company where you now work, either directly or through some type of retirement or stock plan?

(number of respondents aged 18 or older working in private companies and percent distribution by response, 2002)

	number of respondents	percent distribution
Total in private companies	**1,376**	**100.0%**
Yes	314	22.8
No, I work for a company that does not have stock	598	43.5
No, my company has stock but I do not own any of my company's stock	179	13.0
No, I do not own stock and I do not know if my company has stock	188	13.7
I do not know if I own stock in my company	74	5.4
Don't know	7	0.5
No answer	16	1.2

Source: General Social Survey, National Opinion Research Center, University of Chicago

Table 2.35 Value of Company Stock Owned, 2002

Please give a general estimate of how much cash you would get if all this stock were sold today?

(number of respondents aged 18 or older working in private companies who own company stock and percent distribution by response, 2002)

	number of respondents	percent distribution
Total who own stock in company	**330**	**100.0%**
Under $1,000	21	6.4
$1,000 to $2,999	32	9.7
$3,000 to $4,999	11	3.3
$5,000 to $9,999	29	8.8
$10,000 to $19,999	32	9.7
$20,000 to $29,999	18	5.5
$30,000 to $39,999	11	3.3
$40,000 to $49,999	5	1.5
$50,000 to $99,999	18	5.5
$100,000 to $499,999	28	8.5
$500,000 to $999,999	4	1.2
$1,000,000 or more	8	2.4
Other	14	4.2
Don't know	59	17.9
No answer	40	12.1

Source: General Social Survey, National Opinion Research Center, University of Chicago

Table 2.36 Stock Options, 2002

Do you currently hold any stock options in your company (vested or unvested)?

(number of respondents aged 18 or older working in private companies that have stock and percent distribution by response, 2002)

	number of respondents	percent distribution
Total in private companies that have stock	**778**	**100.0%**
Yes	178	22.9
No	568	73.0
Don't know	14	1.8
No answer	18	2.3

Source: General Social Survey, National Opinion Research Center, University of Chicago

Table 2.37 Performance-Based Pay, 2002

In your job are you eligible for any type of performance-based pay, such as individual or group bonuses or any type of profit-sharing?

(number of working respondents aged 18 or older and percent distribution by response, 2002)

	number of respondents	percent distribution
Total	**1,796**	**100.0%**
Yes	597	33.2
No	1,164	64.8
Don't know	19	1.1
No answer	16	0.9

Source: General Social Survey, National Opinion Research Center, University of Chicago

Table 2.38 What Determines Performance-Based Pay, 2002

(number of working respondents aged 18 or older who are eligible for performance-based pay and percent distribution by response, 2002)

	number of respondents	percent distribution
Does the size of these performance-based payments depend on company profits or performance?		
Total eligible for performance-based pay	**613**	**100.0%**
Yes	485	79.1
No	102	16.6
Don't know	10	1.6
No answer	16	2.6
Does the size of these performance-based payments depend on work group or department performance?		
Total eligible for performance-based pay	**613**	**100.0**
Yes	343	56.0
No	244	39.8
Don't know	10	1.6
No answer	16	2.6
Does the size of these performance-based payments depend on individual performance?		
Total eligible for performance-based pay	**613**	**100.0**
Yes	380	62.0
No	206	33.6
Don't know	11	1.8
No answer	16	2.6

Source: General Social Survey, National Opinion Research Center, University of Chicago

Table 2.39 Received Performance-Based Pay, 2002

Did you receive any of these performance-based payments in the year 2001?

(number of working respondents aged 18 or older in companies with performance-based pay and percent distribution by response, 2002)

	number of respondents	percent distribution
Total in companies with performance-based pay	**613**	**100.0%**
Yes	395	64.4
No	200	32.6
Don't know	1	0.2
No answer	17	2.8

Source: General Social Survey, National Opinion Research Center, University of Chicago

Table 2.40 Value of Performance-Based Pay Received, 2002

What was the approximate total dollar value of these various payments in 2001?

(number of working respondents aged 18 or older who received performance-based pay in 2001 and percent distribution by response, 2002)

	number of respondents	percent distribution
Total who received performance-based pay	**412**	**100.0%**
Under $1,000	120	29.1
$1,000 to $2,999	97	23.5
$3,000 to $4,999	34	8.3
$5,000 to $9,999	38	9.2
$10,000 to $19,999	25	6.1
$20,000 to $29,999	5	1.2
$30,000 to $39,999	3	0.7
$40,000 to $49,999	3	0.7
$50,000 to $99,999	7	1.7
$100,000 to $499,999	4	1.0
$500,000 to $999,999	0	0.0
$1,000,000 or more	1	0.2
Other	20	4.9
Don't know	19	4.6
No answer	36	8.7

Source: General Social Survey, National Opinion Research Center, University of Chicago

Information Society

Although statistics on computers and the Internet are outdated almost as soon as they are published because of the rapid growth of computer and Internet use, it is interesting to examine the status of computer use in a particular year. The General Social Survey has done just that by asking the public about this topic in 2002. In that year, 83 percent of adults said they had a computer at home, and two-thirds said they used computers at home, at work, or at some other location. Most computer users access the Internet.

Focusing on those who access the Internet, the General Social Survey finds the biggest reason for visiting web sites is for news. In 2002, 37 percent of Internet users said they had accessed web sites for news at least five times in the past month.

Getting product information is another big factor in Internet use. Seventy-three percent of Internet users have visited web sites for product information in the past year. The 58 percent majority purchased something online. The second biggest reason for visiting web sites is to get information about a health concern, cited by 59 percent. Forty-four percent have used the Internet to look for a job.

Interpersonal communications is another big reason for computer and Internet use. Most adults maintain email contact with friends and relatives. Most of those accessing the Internet receive more emails than they send on an average day. The 62 percent majority says its ability to use the Internet is good to excellent. And the largest share (73 percent) turns to friends and family when needing advice on using computers and the Internet. Only 37 percent look in a book or manual for information when they need help, and just 11 percent pay someone to help them.

Table 2.41 Computer Use, 2002

Do you personally ever use a computer at home, at work, or at some other location?

(number of respondents aged 18 or older and percent distribution by response, 2002)

	number of respondents	percent distribution
Total	**2,765**	**100.0%**
Yes	1,835	66.4
No	913	33.0
Don't know	11	0.4
No answer	6	0.2

Source: General Social Survey, National Opinion Research Center, University of Chicago

Table 2.42 Reasons for Visiting Web Sites in Past 30 Days, 2002

In the past 30 days, how often have you visited a web site for . . .

(number of respondents aged 18 or older who access the Internet and percent distribution by response, 2002)

	total	never	one or two times	three or four times	five or more times	don't know	no answer
Number of respondents							
Financial information	1,084	473	235	111	170	1	94
School that you/your children attend	1,084	716	149	42	81	2	94
Other educational sites	1,084	456	245	126	162	1	94
Sites related to your work	1,084	426	137	89	338	1	93
News and current events	1,084	221	211	158	399	1	94
Government information	1,084	501	248	108	132	1	94
Political information	1,084	675	172	65	77	1	94
Travel	1,084	366	298	171	154	1	94
Sports	1,084	578	176	87	148	1	94
Music/concerts	1,084	520	234	114	121	1	94
Visual arts/art museums	1,084	756	161	42	30	1	94
Television or movies	1,084	574	229	98	88	1	94
Health and fitness	1,084	475	293	113	108	1	94
Religion/church related	1,084	803	117	34	35	1	94
Games you can play on your computer	1,084	600	138	87	164	1	94
Humor	1,084	604	191	93	101	1	94
Sexually explicit material	1,084	850	96	22	20	1	95
Personal home pages	1,084	742	148	38	60	2	94
Science	1,084	618	200	84	86	2	94
Hobbies and crafts	1,084	524	213	117	135	1	94
Cooking, recipes	1,084	648	183	84	74	1	94
Percent distribution							
Financial information	100.0%	43.6%	21.7%	10.2%	15.7%	0.1%	8.7%
School that you/your children attend	100.0	66.1	13.7	3.9	7.5	0.2	8.7
Other educational sites	100.0	42.1	22.6	11.6	14.9	0.1	8.7
Sites related to your work	100.0	39.3	12.6	8.2	31.2	0.1	8.6
News and current events	100.0	20.4	19.5	14.6	36.8	0.1	8.7
Government information	100.0	46.2	22.9	10.0	12.2	0.1	8.7
Political information	100.0	62.3	15.9	6.0	7.1	0.1	8.7
Travel	100.0	33.8	27.5	15.8	14.2	0.1	8.7
Sports	100.0	53.3	16.2	8.0	13.7	0.1	8.7
Music/concerts	100.0	48.0	21.6	10.5	11.2	0.1	8.7
Visual arts/art museums	100.0	69.7	14.9	3.9	2.8	0.1	8.7
Television or movies	100.0	53.0	21.1	9.0	8.1	0.1	8.7
Health and fitness	100.0	43.8	27.0	10.4	10.0	0.1	8.7
Religion/church related	100.0	74.1	10.8	3.1	3.2	0.1	8.7
Games you can play on your computer	100.0	55.4	12.7	8.0	15.1	0.1	8.7
Humor	100.0	55.7	17.6	8.6	9.3	0.1	8.7
Sexually explicit material	100.0	78.4	8.9	2.0	1.8	0.1	8.8
Personal home pages	100.0	68.5	13.7	3.5	5.5	0.2	8.7
Science	100.0	57.0	18.5	7.7	7.9	0.2	8.7
Hobbies and crafts	100.0	48.3	19.6	10.8	12.5	0.1	8.7
Cooking, recipes	100.0	59.8	16.9	7.7	6.8	0.1	8.7

Source: General Social Survey, National Opinion Research Center, University of Chicago

Table 2.43 Reasons for Visiting Web Sites in Past Year, 2002

In the past 12 months have you used the Web to do each of these things:

(number of respondents aged 18 or older who access the Internet and percent distribution by response, 2002)

	total	yes	no	don't know	no answer
Number of respondents					
Look for information you need for your work	1,084	604	385	1	94
Home finances or banking	1,084	507	482	1	94
Look for information about a product that you might want to buy	1,084	793	196	1	94
Actually buy something	1,084	623	366	1	94
Invest money in a stock or mutual fund	1,084	129	860	1	94
Tried to meet new people for social purpose.	1,084	143	846	1	94
Look up information about a health concern or medical problem.	1,084	634	355	1	94
Make an airplane or other travel reservation.	1,084	453	536	1	94
Locate someone's phone number, e-mail, or mailing address.	1,084	549	440	1	94
Play a game with someone on another computer.	1,084	187	802	1	94
Look for a new job or explore career opportunities.	1,084	471	518	1	94
Go to a chat room, news group, discussion forum, bulletin board, or similar interactive service to discuss political or social policy issues, current affairs, or political campaigns.	1,084	185	804	1	94
Go to a Web site to find information about political or social policy issues, current affairs, or political campaigns.	1,084	356	633	1	94
Percent distribution					
Look for information you need for your work	100.0%	55.7%	35.5%	0.1%	8.7%
Home finances or banking	100.0	46.8	44.5	0.1	8.7
Look for information about a product that you might want to buy	100.0	73.2	18.1	0.1	8.7
Actually buy something	100.0	57.5	33.8	0.1	8.7
Invest money in a stock or mutual fund	100.0	11.9	79.3	0.1	8.7
Tried to meet new people for social purpose.	100.0	13.2	78.0	0.1	8.7
Look up information about a health concern or medical problem.	100.0	58.5	32.7	0.1	8.7
Make an airplane or other travel reservation.	100.0	41.8	49.4	0.1	8.7
Locate someone's phone number, e-mail, or mailing address.	100.0	50.6	40.6	0.1	8.7
Play a game with someone on another computer.	100.0	17.3	74.0	0.1	8.7
Look for a new job or explore career opportunities.	100.0	43.5	47.8	0.1	8.7
Go to a chat room, news group, discussion forum, bulletin board, or similar interactive service to discuss political or social policy issues, current affairs, or political campaigns.	100.0	17.1	74.2	0.1	8.7
Go to a Web site to find information about political or social policy issues, current affairs, or political campaigns.	100.0	32.8	58.4	0.1	8.7

Source: General Social Survey, National Opinion Research Center, University of Chicago

Table 2.44 Looked for Health Information, 2002

In the past year, have you looked for information about a health concern or medical problem?

(number of respondents aged 18 or older who access the Internet and percent distribution by response, 2002)

	number of respondents	percent distribution
Total	**1,393**	**100.0%**
Not at all	724	52.0
One or two times	331	23.8
Three to five times	202	14.5
Six or more times	122	8.8
Don't know	8	0.6
No answer	6	0.4

Source: General Social Survey, National Opinion Research Center, University of Chicago

Table 2.45 Sources of Information about Health, 2002

If yes, please tell me if you tried to find such health information from:

(number of respondents aged 18 or older who had access to the Internet and looked for health information in the past year and percent distribution by response, 2002)

	total	not at all	one or more	one or two times	three to five times	six or more times	no answer
Number of respondents							
Articles in a daily newspaper	661	480	175	91	48	36	6
Articles in a general-interest magazine	661	446	209	121	57	31	6
Special health or medical magazine or newsletter	661	363	292	168	71	53	6
A doctor, nurse, or other medical professional	661	136	519	297	133	89	6
Friends or relatives	661	280	375	229	83	63	6
Radio or television programs	661	439	215	126	54	35	6
The Internet or World Wide Web	661	238	417	150	129	138	6
Percent distribution							
Articles in a daily newspaper	100.0%	72.6%	26.5%	13.8%	7.3%	5.4%	0.9%
Articles in a general-interest magazine	100.0	67.5	31.6	18.3	8.6	4.7	0.9
Special health or medical magazine or newsletter	100.0	54.9	44.2	25.4	10.7	8.0	0.9
A doctor, nurse, or other medical professional	100.0	20.6	78.5	44.9	20.1	13.5	0.9
Friends or relatives	100.0	42.4	56.7	34.6	12.6	9.5	0.9
Radio or television programs	100.0	66.4	32.5	19.1	8.2	5.3	0.9
The Internet or World Wide Web	100.0	36.0	63.1	22.7	19.5	20.9	0.9

Source: General Social Survey, National Opinion Research Center, University of Chicago

Table 2.46 Contact with Friends and Relatives, 2002

Not counting people at work or family at home, about how many other friends or relatives do you keep in contact with at least once a year?

(number of respondents aged 18 or older and percent distribution by response, 2002)

	number of respondents	percent distribution
Total	**2,765**	**100.0%**
None	32	1.2
One or two	110	4.0
Three to five	396	14.3
Six to 10	545	19.7
11 to 15	274	9.9
16 to 25	481	17.4
25 to 50	547	19.8
More than 50	326	11.8
Don't know	42	1.5
No answer	12	0.4

Source: General Social Survey, National Opinion Research Center, University of Chicago

Table 2.47 Means of Contacting Friends and Relatives, 2002

Of these friends and relatives, about how many do you stay in contact with by:

(number of respondents aged 18 or older and percent distribution by response, 2002)

	total	none	1 or 2	3 to 5	6 to 10	11 to 15	16 to 25	26 to 50	50+	don't know	no answer
Number of respondents											
Seeing them socially, face-to-face?	2,691	103	322	531	572	302	361	313	173	1	13
Talking with them on the telephone?	2,691	69	262	608	634	336	380	275	113	0	14
Exchanging cards or letters through U.S. postal mail	2,691	755	406	468	354	170	204	208	112	1	13
Seeing them at meetings or events related to church, clubs, or other groups?	2,691	982	292	384	369	174	215	153	105	4	13
Communicating through electronic mail	2,691	1,278	233	348	310	169	160	126	53	1	13
Percent distribution											
Seeing them socially, face-to-face?	100.0%	3.8%	12.0%	19.7%	21.3%	11.2%	13.4%	11.6%	6.4%	0.0%	0.5%
Talking with them on the telephone?	100.0	2.6	9.7	22.6	23.6	12.5	14.1	10.2	4.2	0.0	0.5
Exchanging cards or letters through U.S. postal mail	100.0	28.1	15.1	17.4	13.2	6.3	7.6	7.7	4.2	0.0	0.5
Seeing them at meetings or events related to church, clubs, or other groups?	100.0	36.5	10.9	14.3	13.7	6.5	8.0	5.7	3.9	0.1	0.5
Communicating through electronic mail	100.0	47.5	8.7	12.9	11.5	6.3	5.9	4.7	2.0	0.0	0.5

Source: General Social Survey, National Opinion Research Center, University of Chicago

Table 2.48 Computers in Home, 2002

Do you have one or more computers at your home (including laptops that can be used at work or home)?

(number of respondents aged 18 or older and percent distribution by response, 2002)

	number of respondents	percent distribution
Total	**1,910**	**100.0%**
Yes	1,584	82.9
No	307	16.1
No answer	19	1.0

Source: General Social Survey, National Opinion Research Center, University of Chicago

Table 2.49 Number of E-Mail Messages Sent, 2002

Thinking now about all your home, work, or other computers, about how many e-mail messages do you send from all these computers on an average day?

(number of respondents aged 18 or older who use a computer and are on the Internet at least one hour per week, and percent distribution by response, 2002)

	number of respondents	percent distribution
Total	**634**	**100.0%**
None	23	3.6
One to five	331	52.2
Six to 10	91	14.4
11 to 15	26	4.1
16 to 25	52	8.2
26 to 50	45	7.1
51 or more	18	2.8
Don't know	7	1.1
No answer	41	6.5

Source: General Social Survey, National Opinion Research Center, University of Chicago

Table 2.50 Number of E-Mail Messages Received, 2002

Thinking now about all your home, work, or other computers, about how many e-mail messages do you receive on all these computers on an average day?

(number of respondents aged 18 or older who use a computer and are on the Internet at least one hour per week, and percent distribution by response, 2002)

	number of respondents	percent distribution
Total	**634**	**100.0%**
None	15	2.4
One to five	145	22.9
Six to 10	122	19.2
11 to 15	61	9.6
16 to 25	83	13.1
26 to 50	101	15.9
51 or more	62	9.8
Don't know	4	0.6
No answer	41	6.5

Source: General Social Survey, National Opinion Research Center, University of Chicago

Table 2.51 Source of E-Mail Messages, 2002

Do any of the personal one-to-one messages you receive or send come from:

(number of respondents aged 18 or older who use a computer, are on the Internet at least one hour per week, and receive personal e-mail messages, and percent distribution by response, 2002)

	total	yes	no	don't know	no answer
Number of respondents					
People at your workplace?	598	260	296	1	41
Business or work contacts away from your workplace?	598	274	283	0	41
Family members who live with you?	598	134	423	0	41
Other family members?	598	434	123	0	41
Friends?	598	504	53	0	41
Members of your church?	598	118	439	0	41
Members of other groups or associations to which you belong?	598	272	285	0	41
Percent distribution					
People at your workplace?	100.0%	43.5%	49.5%	0.2%	6.9%
Business or work contacts away from your workplace?	100.0	45.8	47.3	0.0	6.9
Family members who live with you?	100.0	22.4	70.7	0.0	6.9
Other family members?	100.0	72.6	20.6	0.0	6.9
Friends?	100.0	84.3	8.9	0.0	6.9
Members of your church?	100.0	19.7	73.4	0.0	6.9
Members of other groups or associations to which you belong?	100.0	45.5	47.7	0.0	6.9

Source: General Social Survey, National Opinion Research Center, University of Chicago

Table 2.52 Looked for Job, 2002

In the past year, have you searched for information about a new job or career opportunities?

(number of respondents aged 18 or older who access the Internet and percent distribution by response, 2002)

	number of respondents	percent distribution
Total	**1,393**	**100.0%**
No	842	60.4
One or two times	223	16.0
Three to five times	146	10.5
Six or more times	170	12.2
Don't know	6	0.4
No answer	6	0.4

Source: General Social Survey, National Opinion Research Center, University of Chicago

Table 2.53 Sources of Information about Jobs, 2002

Please tell me how many times you tried to find such information (about jobs) from:

(number of respondents aged 18 or older who had access to the Internet and looked for job information in the past year and percent distribution by response, 2002)

	total	not at all	one or more	one or two times	three to five times	six or more times	don't know	no answer
Number of respondents								
Classified ads in a daily newspaper?	545	189	350	116	101	133	0	6
Classified ads in an industry or professional publication?	545	345	194	86	50	58	0	6
A fellow worker or human resources staff member at your work place?	545	330	209	137	44	28	0	6
Business or work contacts outside your work place?	545	216	322	186	85	51	1	6
Friends outside of work or relatives?	545	199	339	199	88	52	1	6
Any job placement or career counseling service?	545	418	119	72	27	20	2	6
Radio or television programs?	545	483	54	34	12	8	2	6
Information posted on the Internet (World Wide Web)?	545	226	311	111	71	129	2	6
Percent distribution								
Classified ads in a daily newspaper?	100.0%	34.7%	64.2%	21.3%	18.5%	24.4%	0.0%	1.1%
Classified ads in an industry or professional publication?	100.0	63.3	35.6	15.8	9.2	10.6	0.0	1.1
A fellow worker or human resources staff member at your work place?	100.0	60.6	38.3	25.1	8.1	5.1	0.0	1.1
Business or work contacts outside your work place?	100.0	39.6	59.1	34.1	15.6	9.4	0.2	1.1
Friends outside of work or relatives?	100.0	36.5	62.2	36.5	16.1	9.5	0.2	1.1
Any job placement or career counseling service?	100.0	76.7	21.8	13.2	5.0	3.7	0.4	1.1
Radio or television programs?	100.0	88.6	9.9	6.2	2.2	1.5	0.4	1.1
Information posted on the Internet (World Wide Web)?	100.0	41.5	57.1	20.4	13.0	23.7	0.4	1.1

Source: General Social Survey, National Opinion Research Center, University of Chicago

Table 2.54 When Did You Start Using E-mail, 2002

When did you first begin using e-mail?

(number of respondents aged 18 or older who access the Internet and percent distribution by response, 2002)

	number of respondents	percent distribution
Total	**1,494**	**100.0%**
This year (2002)	43	2.9
In the last year (2001)	114	7.6
One or two years ago (2000)	184	12.3
Two or three years ago (1999)	219	14.7
Three or four years ago (1998)	194	13.0
Four or five years ago (1997)	189	12.7
Five or more years ago (1990–1996)	534	35.7
Don't know	4	0.3
No answer	13	0.9

Source: General Social Survey, National Opinion Research Center, University of Chicago

Table 2.55 When Did You Start Using the Internet, 2002

When did you first begin using the World Wide Web
(for purposes other than email)?

(number of respondents aged 18 or older who access the Internet and percent distribution by response, 2002)

	number of respondents	percent distribution
Total	**1,606**	**100.0%**
This year (2002)	40	2.5
In the last year (2001)	128	8.0
One or two years ago (2000)	201	12.5
Two or three years ago (1999)	251	15.6
Three or four years ago (1998)	189	11.8
Four or five years ago (1997)	220	13.7
Five or more years ago (1990–1996)	494	30.8
Don't know	2	0.1
No answer	81	5.0

Source: General Social Survey, National Opinion Research Center, University of Chicago

Table 2.56 Ability to Use the World Wide Web, 2002

Would you rate your ability to use the World Wide Web as excellent, good, fair, poor, or very poor?

(number of respondents aged 18 or older who access the Internet and percent distribution by response, 2002)

	number of respondents	percent distribution
Total	**851**	**100.0%**
Excellent	218	25.6
Good	311	36.5
Fair	197	23.1
Poor	45	5.3
Very poor	15	1.8
No answer	65	7.6

Source: General Social Survey, National Opinion Research Center, University of Chicago

Table 2.57 Where Do You Get Advice on Using Computers and the Internet, 2002

When you want advice or assistance with surfing on the Web, finding a Web site, downloading software or some other online service, or getting your Internet connection to work, which of the following do you do (name as many as are correct)?

(number of respondents aged 18 or older who access the Internet and percent distribution by response, 2002)

	total	yes	no	don't know	no answer
Number of respondents					
Look in a printed manual or book for information?	722	266	405	3	48
Call or e-mail customer support for the product you are sending?	722	345	327	3	47
Call or e-mail technical support from your employer or school?	722	225	447	3	47
Ask someone else at your work place or school for help?	722	377	295	3	47
Ask someone else you know for help (like a friend or family member)?	722	526	146	3	47
Pay someone to help you?	722	81	591	3	47
Figure it out yourself?	722	596	76	3	47
Percent distribution					
Look in a printed manual or book for information?	100.0%	36.8%	56.1%	0.4%	6.6%
Call or email customer support for the product you are sending?	100.0	47.8	45.3	0.4	6.5
Call or email technical support from your employer or school?	100.0	31.2	61.9	0.4	6.5
Ask someone else at your work place or school for help?	100.0	52.2	40.9	0.4	6.5
Ask someone else you know for help (like a friend or family member)?	100.0	72.9	20.2	0.4	6.5
Pay someone to help you?	100.0	11.2	81.9	0.4	6.5
Figure it out yourself?	100.0	82.5	10.5	0.4	6.5

Source: General Social Survey, National Opinion Research Center, University of Chicago

Mental Health

One of the Topical Moduless of the 2002 General Social Survey probed the public's attitude toward several mental health issues such as attention deficit hyperactivity disorder, the medication of children, and relationships between doctors and patients. It found the public strongly objecting to currently popular treatments for children's mental health problems.

Eighty percent of adults agree that doctors are overmedicating children with common behavioral problems. Sixty-two percent agree that medicating children will have long-term negative effects on their development. An equally large proportion agrees that medicating children only puts off dealing with children's real problems. Among adults who know something about attention deficit hyperactivity disorder, 76 percent think it is a real disease while 20 percent do not. Eighty-four percent favor counseling for children with ADHD, while a smaller 66 percent favor medicating them.

The public is much more supportive of medications for mental health problems when children are not the focus. Eighty-five percent agree that medications can help people with mental health problems control their symptoms. But they also think medications are addictive and often have unacceptable side effects.

Americans are ambivalent about how they would try to solve their own problems. The slim majority of adults (52 percent) say they like to get advice and help from other people when they have problems. A substantial 43 percent say they prefer to solve problems on their own.

Despite the problems with health care in the United States, most Americans feel positively toward their doctor. Most think their doctor cares about them as a person, and most trust their doctor's judgment.

Table 2.58 Medicating Children, 2002

Now, I'd like to ask you for your opinions on several issues. For each question, please tell me if you strongly agree, agree somewhat, disagree somewhat, or strongly disagree with the statement.

(number of respondents aged 18 or older and percent distribution by response, 2002)

	number of respondents	percent distribution
Doctors today are over-medicating children with common behavior problems.		
Total respondents	**1,393**	**100.0%**
Strongly agree	579	41.6
Agree somewhat	529	38.0
Disagree somewhat	146	10.5
Strongly disagree	37	2.7
Don't know	90	6.5
No answer	12	0.9
Giving medications to children with behavior problems will have long-term negative effects on their development.		
Total respondents	**1,393**	**100.0**
Strongly agree	344	24.7
Agree somewhat	515	37.0
Disagree somewhat	326	23.4
Strongly disagree	89	6.4
Don't know	106	7.6
No answer	13	0.9
Giving children psychiatric medications when they are young only puts off dealing with their real problems.		
Total respondents	**1,393**	**100.0**
Strongly agree	373	26.8
Agree somewhat	484	34.7
Disagree somewhat	344	24.7
Strongly disagree	101	7.3
Don't know	76	5.5
No answer	15	1.1
Children who receive medical treatment for behavior problems are less likely to get into trouble with the law later in life.		
Total respondents	**1,393**	**100.0**
Strongly agree	112	8.0
Agree somewhat	439	31.5
Disagree somewhat	490	35.2
Strongly disagree	243	17.4
Don't know	95	6.8
No answer	14	1.0

(continued)

	number of respondents	percent distribution
In the long run, government programs that provide mental health treatment to children will save taxpayers money.		
Total respondents	**1,393**	**100.0%**
Strongly agree	209	15.0
Agree somewhat	514	36.9
Disagree somewhat	385	27.6
Strongly disagree	174	12.5
Don't know	99	7.1
No answer	12	0.9
Medications for children with behavior problems turn kids into zombies.		
Total respondents	**1,393**	**100.0**
Strongly agree	232	16.7
Agree somewhat	436	31.3
Disagree somewhat	402	28.9
Strongly disagree	223	16.0
Don't know	87	6.2
No answer	13	0.9
Medications for behavior problems just prevent families from working out problems themselves.		
Total respondents	**1,393**	**100.0**
Strongly agree	251	18.0
Agree somewhat	475	34.1
Disagree somewhat	430	30.9
Strongly disagree	161	11.6
Don't know	63	4.5
No answer	13	0.9

Source: General Social Survey, National Opinion Research Center, University of Chicago

Table 2.59 Attention Deficit/Hyperactivity Disorder (ADHD) as Real Disease, 2002

Do you think ADHD is a real disease?

(number of respondents aged 18 or older who know something about ADHD and percent distribution by response, 2002)

	number of respondents	percent distribution
Total respondents	**906**	**100.0%**
Yes	685	75.6
No	183	20.2
Don't know	37	4.1
No answer	1	0.1

Source: General Social Survey, National Opinion Research Center, University of Chicago

Table 2.60 Counseling for Children with ADHD, 2002

Should children be given counseling for ADHD?

(number of respondents aged 18 or older who know something about ADHD and percent distribution by response, 2002)

	number of respondents	percent distribution
Total respondents	**906**	**100.0%**
Yes	758	83.7
No	122	13.5
Don't know	26	2.9
No answer	0	–

Source: General Social Survey, National Opinion Research Center, University of Chicago

Table 2.61 Medication for Children with ADHD, 2002

Should children be given medication to treat ADHD?

(number of respondents aged 18 or older who know something about ADHD and percent distribution by response, 2002)

	number of respondents	percent distribution
Total respondents	**906**	**100.0%**
Yes	595	65.7
No	249	27.5
Don't know	57	6.3
No answer	5	0.6

Source: General Social Survey, National Opinion Research Center, University of Chicago

Table 2.62 Relationship with Person with Mental Health Problems, 2002

I want you to think about the person with a mental health problem with whom you have had the most contact. As a result of the mental health problem, would you say that your relationship with this person...

(number of respondents aged 18 or older who know something about ADHD and percent distribution by response, 2002)

	number of respondents	percent distribution
Total respondents	**906**	**100.0%**
Became stronger	218	24.1
Was unchanged	491	54.2
Became worse	71	7.8
Ended as a result of the problem	58	6.4
Don't know	51	5.6
No answer	17	1.9

Source: General Social Survey, National Opinion Research Center, University of Chicago

Table 2.63 Medications for People with Mental Health Problems, 2002

Please tell me how much you agree or disagree with the following statements about medicines prescribed by doctors that are intended to help people who are having problems with their emotions, nerves, or their mental health.

(number of respondents aged 18 or older and percent distribution by response, 2002)

	number of respondents	percent distribution
These medications help people control their symptoms. Do you strongly agree, agree somewhat, disagree somewhat, or strongly disagree?		
Total respondents	**1,393**	**100.0%**
Strongly agree	369	26.5
Agree somewhat	809	58.1
Disagree somewhat	103	7.4
Strongly disagree	43	3.1
Don't know	57	4.1
No answer	15	1.1
These medications are addictive.		
Total respondents	**1,393**	**100.0**
Strongly agree	472	33.9
Agree somewhat	564	40.5
Disagree somewhat	181	13.0
Strongly disagree	53	3.8
Don't know	108	7.8
No answer	15	1.1
Taking medications is a sign of weakness.		
Total respondents	**1,393**	**100.0**
Strongly agree	59	4.2
Agree somewhat	145	10.4
Disagree somewhat	437	31.4
Strongly disagree	710	51.0
Don't know	31	2.2
No answer	11	0.8
These medications often have unacceptable side effects.		
Total respondents	**1,393**	**100.0**
Strongly agree	413	29.6
Agree somewhat	646	46.4
Disagree somewhat	186	13.4
Strongly disagree	44	3.2
Don't know	92	6.6
No answer	12	0.9

Source: General Social Survey, National Opinion Research Center, University of Chicago

Table 2.64 Solve Problems on Your Own or Get Advice, 2002

When you have a problem, do you prefer to solve it on your own or do you like to talk to other people to get advice, help, or information?

(number of respondents aged 18 or older and percent distribution by response, 2002)

	number of respondents	percent distribution
Total respondents	**1,393**	**100.0%**
On own	593	42.6
Get advice	729	52.3
Something else	50	3.6
Don't know	14	1.0
No answer	7	0.5

Source: General Social Survey, National Opinion Research Center, University of Chicago

Table 2.65 Attitudes toward Medical Care, 2002

As you read each of the following statements, please think about the medical care you are now receiving. If you have not received any medical care recently, circle the answer based on what you would expect if you had to seek care today. Even if you are not entirely certain about your answers, we want to remind you that your best guess is important for each statement.

(number of respondents aged 18 or older and percent distribution by response, 2002)

	number of respondents	percent distribution
I doubt my doctor really cares about me as a person.		
Total respondents	**1,393**	**100.0%**
Strongly agree	91	6.5
Agree somewhat	190	13.6
Neither agree nor disagree	132	9.5
Disagree somewhat	378	27.1
Strongly disagree	571	41.0
Don't know	22	1.6
No answer	9	0.6
I trust my doctor's judgments about my medical care.		
Total respondents	**1,393**	**100.0**
Strongly agree	589	42.3
Agree somewhat	645	46.3
Neither agree nor disagree	51	3.7
Disagree somewhat	61	4.4
Strongly disagree	19	1.4
Don't know	20	1.4
No answer	8	0.6
I trust my doctor to put my medical needs above all other considerations when treating my medical problems.		
Total respondents	**1,393**	**100.0**
Strongly agree	597	42.9
Agree somewhat	571	41.0
Neither agree nor disagree	76	5.5
Disagree somewhat	95	6.8
Strongly disagree	25	1.8
Don't know	21	1.5
No answer	8	0.6

(continued)

My doctor is a real expert in taking care of medical problems like mine.	number of respondents	percent distribution
Total respondents	**1,393**	**100.0%**
Strongly agree	503	36.1
Agree somewhat	585	42.0
Neither agree nor disagree	149	10.7
Disagree somewhat	93	6.7
Strongly disagree	17	1.2
Don't know	35	2.5
No answer	11	0.8
I trust my doctor to tell me if a mistake was made about my treatment.		
Total respondents	**1,393**	**100.0**
Strongly agree	516	37.0
Agree somewhat	476	34.2
Neither agree nor disagree	108	7.8
Disagree somewhat	148	10.6
Strongly disagree	111	8.0
Don't know	26	1.9
No answer	8	0.6

Source: General Social Survey, National Opinion Research Center, University of Chicago

Prejudice

The General Social Survey regularly probes Americans' attitudes toward other racial and ethnic groups, doing so again in 2002. The findings show great ambivalence regarding how best to handle racial and ethnic diversity in the United States.

Ethnic group membership is important to Americans. The 58 percent majority of the public say their ethnic group membership is "very" or "moderately" important to their sense of who they are. Only 24 percent say it is "not at all important."

People are split on whether greater harmony can be achieved by ignoring ethnic group differences. Thirty-seven percent agree, 42 percent disagree, and 19 percent neither agree nor disagree. Fully 82 percent agree that society would be more harmonious if each ethnic group had the right to maintain its own traditions. But, in a seeming contradiction, 59 percent of the public also agrees that to have a smoothly functioning society, ethnic minorities must adapt to mainstream culture.

Fifty-three percent of the public thinks individuals belonging to the same ethnic group tend to be similar to one another. Sixty percent think ethnic minority groups are very distinct and different from one another.

Table 2.66 Importance of Ethnic Group Membership, 2002

When you think about yourself, how important is your ethnic group membership to your sense of who you are?

(number of respondents aged 18 or older and percent distribution by response, 2002)

	number of respondents	percent distribution
Total people	**2,765**	**100.0%**
Very important	903	32.7
Moderately important	697	25.2
Slightly important	471	17.0
Not at all important	667	24.1
Don't know	20	0.7
No answer	7	0.3

Source: General Social Survey, National Opinion Research Center, University of Chicago

Table 2.67 Ethnic Group Differences Should Be Ignored, 2002

Here are some opinions some people have expressed in connection with ethnic issues in the United States. To what extent do you agree or disagree with each one?

Harmony in the United States is best achieved by downplaying or ignoring ethnic differences.

(number of respondents aged 18 or older and percent distribution by response, 2002)

	number of respondents	percent distribution
Total people	**2,765**	**100.0%**
Strongly agree	359	13.0
Agree	667	24.1
Neither agree nor disagree	533	19.3
Disagree	814	29.4
Strongly disagree	334	12.1
Don't know	46	1.7
No answer	12	0.4

Source: General Social Survey, National Opinion Research Center, University of Chicago

Table 2.68 Ethnic Groups' Fit with Mainstream Culture, 2002

Here are some opinions some people have expressed in connection with ethnic issues in the United States. To what extent do you agree or disagree with each one?

Ethnic minority groups will never really fit in with mainstream American culture.

(number of respondents aged 18 or older and percent distribution by response, 2002)

	number of respondents	percent distribution
Total people	**2,765**	**100.0%**
Strongly agree	88	3.2
Agree	333	12.0
Neither agree nor disagree	390	14.1
Disagree	1,292	46.7
Strongly disagree	614	22.2
Don't know	37	1.3
No answer	11	0.4

Source: General Social Survey, National Opinion Research Center, University of Chicago

Table 2.69 Ethnic Groups' Right to Maintain Traditions, 2002

Here are some opinions some people have expressed in connection with ethnic issues in the United States. To what extent do you agree or disagree with each one?

If we want to help create a harmonious society, we must recognize that each ethnic group has the right to maintain its own unique traditions.

(number of respondents aged 18 or older and percent distribution by response, 2002)

	number of respondents	percent distribution
Total people	**2,765**	**100.0%**
Strongly agree	848	30.7
Agree	1,430	51.7
Neither agree nor disagree	266	9.6
Disagree	147	5.3
Strongly disagree	39	1.4
Don't know	28	1.0
No answer	7	0.3

Source: General Social Survey, National Opinion Research Center, University of Chicago

Table 2.70 Ethnic Groups' Adaptation to Mainstream Culture, 2002

Here are some opinions some people have expressed in connection with ethnic issues in the United States. To what extent do you agree or disagree with each one?

In order to have a smoothly functioning society, members of ethnic minorities must better adapt to the ways of mainstream American culture.

(number of respondents aged 18 or older and percent distribution by response, 2002)

	number of respondents	percent distribution
Total people	**2,765**	**100.0%**
Strongly agree	412	14.9
Agree	1,210	43.8
Neither agree nor disagree	546	19.7
Disagree	446	16.1
Strongly disagree	99	3.6
Don't know	42	1.5
No answer	10	0.4

Source: General Social Survey, National Opinion Research Center, University of Chicago

Table 2.71 Feelings toward Racial/Ethnic Minorities, 2002

In general, how warm or cool do you feel toward . . .?

(number of respondents aged 18 or older and percent distribution by response, 2002)

	African Americans		Asian Americans		Hispanics		Whites	
	number of respondents	percent distribution	number of respondents	percent distribution	number of respondents	percent distribution	number of respondents	percent distribution
Total	**2,765**	**100.0%**	**2,765**	**100.0%**	**2,765**	**100.0%**	**2,765**	**100.0%**
Very warm	740	26.8	562	20.3	633	22.9	953	34.5
2	318	11.5	319	11.5	349	12.6	477	17.3
3	364	13.2	379	13.7	372	13.5	361	13.1
4	264	9.5	286	10.3	290	10.5	245	8.9
5	745	26.9	784	28.4	697	25.2	522	18.9
6	105	3.8	124	4.5	121	4.4	55	2.0
7	99	3.6	107	3.9	133	4.8	53	1.9
8	35	1.3	48	1.7	43	1.6	26	0.9
Very cool	59	2.1	76	2.7	72	2.6	42	1.5
Don't know	24	0.9	69	2.5	45	1.6	21	0.8
No answer	12	0.4	11	0.4	10	0.4	10	0.4

Source: General Social Survey, National Opinion Research Center, University of Chicago

Table 2.72 Ethnic Group Member Similarities, 2002

Think about the various ethnic groups within the U.S. including Whites, African Americans, Asian Americans, Hispanics, Native Americans, and so on. To what extent do you agree with the following statement:

Individuals who belong to the same ethnic group tend to be fairly similar to one another.

(number of respondents aged 18 or older and percent distribution by response, 2002)

	number of respondents	percent distribution
Total people	**2,765**	**100.0%**
Strongly agree	272	9.8
Agree	1,201	43.4
Neither agree nor disagree	453	16.4
Disagree	645	23.3
Strongly disagree	150	5.4
Don't know	32	1.2
No answer	12	0.4

Source: General Social Survey, National Opinion Research Center, University of Chicago

Table 2.73 Ethnic Group Member Differences, 2002

Now think only about ethnic minority groups within the U.S. such as African Americans, Asian Americans, Hispanics, and Native Americans. To what extent do you agree with the following statement:

Ethnic minority groups in the U.S. are very distinct and very different from one another.

(number of respondents aged 18 or older and percent distribution by response, 2002)

	number of respondents	percent distribution
Total people	**2,765**	**100.0%**
Strongly agree	278	10.1
Agree	1,378	49.8
Neither agree nor disagree	575	20.8
Disagree	445	16.1
Strongly disagree	37	1.3
Don't know	44	1.6
No answer	8	0.3

Source: General Social Survey, National Opinion Research Center, University of Chicago

Table 2.74 White Differences from Ethnic Minorities, 2002

Think about Whites in the U.S. compared to ethnic minority groups.
To what extent do you agree with the following statement:

Whites as a group are very distinct and
different from ethnic minority groups.

(number of respondents aged 18 or older and percent distribution by response, 2002)

	number of respondents	percent distribution
Total people	**2,765**	**100.0%**
Strongly agree	258	9.3
Agree	1,108	40.1
Neither agree nor disagree	633	22.9
Disagree	652	23.6
Strongly disagree	71	2.6
Don't know	32	1.2
No answer	11	0.4

Source: General Social Survey, National Opinion Research Center, University of Chicago

Quality of Working Life

In 2002, the General Social Survey took an in-depth look at work life in the United States, examining not only working conditions but also attitudes toward work. Among all workers aged 18 or older, 80 percent say they are regular, permanent employees. Fifty-four percent have worked for their current employer for fewer than five years. The 53 percent majority of workers are paid by the hour rather than being salaried.

Job flexibility is almost the rule today. The 54 percent majority of workers say they can "often" or "sometimes" change their starting or quitting time on a daily basis. Forty-six percent say it is "not at all hard" to take time off work for personal or family matters, and another 27 percent say it is "not too hard." But more than half of workers (54 percent) say their job sometimes or often interferes with family life. A smaller 45 percent say their family often or sometimes interferes with their job.

Most workers think they have a great deal of independence on the job. The 56 percent majority says it is "very true" that they have "a lot of freedom to decide how to do my own work." Fifty-three percent say it is very true that their job security is good. But a significant 29 percent of workers say it is "not too true" or "not at all true" that their fringe benefits are good. Forty percent say their pay is "somewhat" or "much less" than they deserve. A 46 percent minority say the income from their job alone is enough to meet their family's usual monthly expenses.

Table 2.75 Work Arrangement, 2002

How would you describe your work arrangement in your main job?

(number of working respondents aged 18 or older and percent distribution by response, 2002)

	number of respondents	percent distribution
Total	**1,796**	**100.0%**
Independent contractor/consultant/ freelance worker	247	13.8
On-call, work only when called to work	41	2.3
Paid by a temporary agency	15	0.8
Work for a contractor who provides workers/services under contract	42	2.3
Regular, permanent employee	1,432	79.7
Don't know	8	0.4
No answer	11	0.6

Source: General Social Survey, National Opinion Research Center, University of Chicago

Table 2.76 Job Tenure, 2002

How long have you worked in your present job for your current employer?

(number of working respondents aged 18 or older and percent distribution by response, 2002)

	number of respondents	percent distribution
Total	**1,797**	**100.0%**
Less than one year	411	22.9
One to two years	293	16.3
Three to four years	264	14.7
Five to nine years	329	18.3
10 to 19 years	310	17.3
20 to 29 years	111	6.2
30 or more years	58	3.2
Don't know	6	0.3
No answer	15	0.8

Source: General Social Survey, National Opinion Research Center, University of Chicago

Table 2.77 Salaried or Paid by the Hour, 2002

In your main job, are you salaried, paid by the hour, or what?

(number of working respondents aged 18 or older and percent distribution by response, 2002)

	number of respondents	percent distribution
Total	**1,796**	**100.0%**
Salaried	606	33.7
Paid by the hour	957	53.3
Other	214	11.9
Don't know	7	0.4
No answer	12	0.7

Source: General Social Survey, National Opinion Research Center, University of Chicago

Table 2.78 Work Schedule, 2002

Which of the following best describes your usual work schedule?

(number of working respondents aged 18 or older and percent distribution by response, 2002)

	number of respondents	percent distribution
Total	**1,796**	**100.0%**
Day shift	1,255	69.9
Afternoon shift	78	4.3
Night shift	122	6.8
Split shift	52	2.9
Irregular shift/on-call	175	9.7
Rotating shifts	90	5.0
Don't know	10	0.6
No answer	14	0.8

Source: General Social Survey, National Opinion Research Center, University of Chicago

Table 2.79 Extra Hours of Work, 2002

How many days per month do you work extra hours beyond your usual schedule?

(number of working respondents aged 18 or older and percent distribution by response, 2002)

	number of respondents	percent distribution
Total	**1,796**	**100.0%**
None	680	37.9
One day	77	4.3
Two days	149	8.3
Three days	98	5.5
Four days	128	7.1
Five to nine days	241	13.4
10 to 19 days	186	10.4
20 or more days	200	11.1
Don't know	22	1.2
No answer	15	0.8

Source: General Social Survey, National Opinion Research Center, University of Chicago

Table 2.80 Extra Work Mandatory, 2002

When you work extra hours on your main job, is it mandatory (required by your employer)?

(number of working respondents aged 18 or older and percent distribution by response, 2002)

	number of respondents	percent distribution
Total	**1,796**	**100.0%**
Yes	461	25.7
No	1,293	72.0
Don't know	24	1.3
No answer	18	1.0

Source: General Social Survey, National Opinion Research Center, University of Chicago

Table 2.81 Flexible Starting and Quitting Times, 2002

How often are you allowed to change your starting and quitting times on a daily basis?

(number of working respondents aged 18 or older and percent distribution by response, 2002)

	number of respondents	percent distribution
Total	**1,796**	**100.0%**
Often	583	32.5
Sometimes	380	21.2
Rarely	246	13.7
Never	559	31.1
Don't know	12	0.7
No answer	16	0.9

Source: General Social Survey, National Opinion Research Center, University of Chicago

Table 2.82 Work at Home, 2002

How often do you work at home as part of your job?

(number of working respondents aged 18 or older and percent distribution by response, 2002)

	number of respondents	percent distribution
Total	**1,796**	**100.0%**
Never	1,102	61.4
A few times a year	160	8.9
About once a month	93	5.2
About once a week	108	6.0
More than once a week	215	12.0
Work mainly at home	99	5.5
Don't know	6	0.3
No answer	13	0.7

Source: General Social Survey, National Opinion Research Center, University of Chicago

Table 2.83 Why Work at Home, 2002

Asked only of those who work at home: Is it usually because you want to, you have to in order to keep up with your job, or for some other reason?

(number of respondents aged 18 or older who work at home and percent distribution by response, 2002)

	number of respondents	percent distribution
Total who work at home	**688**	**100.0%**
Want to work at home	254	36.9
Have to work at home to keep up with job	224	32.6
Other combinations and other reasons	197	28.6
No answer	13	1.9

Source: General Social Survey, National Opinion Research Center, University of Chicago

Table 2.84 Time Off Work for Family Reasons, 2002

How hard is it to take time off during your work to take care of personal or family matters?

(number of working respondents aged 18 or older and percent distribution by response, 2002)

	number of respondents	percent distribution
Total	**1,796**	**100.0%**
Not at all hard	832	46.3
Not too hard	480	26.7
Somewhat hard	270	15.0
Very hard	191	10.6
Don't know	9	0.5
No answer	14	0.8

Source: General Social Survey, National Opinion Research Center, University of Chicago

Table 2.85 Does Job Interfere with Family Life, 2002

How often do the demands of your job interfere with your family life?

(number of working respondents aged 18 or older and percent distribution by response, 2002)

	number of respondents	percent distribution
Total	**1,290**	**100.0%**
Often	231	17.9
Sometimes	471	36.5
Rarely	568	44.0
Never	506	39.2
Don't know	6	0.5
No answer	14	1.1

Source: General Social Survey, National Opinion Research Center, University of Chicago

Table 2.86 Does Family Interfere with Job, 2002

How often do the demands of your family
interfere with your work or job?

(number of working respondents aged 18 or older and percent distribution by response, 2002)

	number of respondents	percent distribution
Total	**1,186**	**100.0%**
Often	100	8.4
Sometimes	431	36.3
Rarely	635	53.5
Never	610	51.4
Don't know	6	0.5
No answer	14	1.2

Source: General Social Survey, National Opinion Research Center, University of Chicago

Table 2.87 Hours to Relax, 2002

After an average work day, about how many hours do you have to relax or pursue activities that you enjoy?

(number of working respondents aged 18 or older and percent distribution by response, 2002)

	number of respondents	percent distribution
Total	**1,796**	**100.0%**
None	114	6.3
One hour	186	10.4
Two hours	336	18.7
Three hours	251	14.0
Four hours	316	17.6
Five to nine hours	478	26.6
10 hours or more	75	4.2
Don't know	27	1.5
No answer	13	0.7

Source: General Social Survey, National Opinion Research Center, University of Chicago

Table 2.88 Second Jobs, 2002

Do you have any jobs besides your main job or do any other work for pay?

(number of working respondents aged 18 or older and percent distribution by response, 2002)

	number of respondents	percent distribution
Total	**1,796**	**100.0%**
Yes	306	17.0
No	1,471	81.9
Don't know	6	0.3
No answer	13	0.7

Source: General Social Survey, National Opinion Research Center, University of Chicago

Table 2.89 Description of Main Job, 2002

Now I'm going to read you a list of statements that might or might not describe your main job. Please tell me whether you strongly agree, agree, disagree, or strongly disagree with each of these statements.

(number of working respondents aged 18 or older and percent distribution by response, 2002)

	number of respondents	percent distribution
My job requires that I keep learning new things:		
Total	**1,796**	**100.0%**
Strongly agree	748	41.6
Agree	782	43.5
Disagree	177	9.9
Strongly disagree	70	3.9
Don't know	6	0.3
No answer	13	0.7
My job requires that I work very fast:		
Total	**1,793**	**100.0**
Strongly agree	388	21.6
Agree	716	39.9
Disagree	601	33.5
Strongly disagree	69	3.8
Don't know	9	0.5
No answer	13	0.7
I get to do a number of different things on my job:		
Total	**1,796**	**100.0**
Strongly agree	750	41.8
Agree	836	46.5
Disagree	158	8.8
Strongly disagree	32	1.8
Don't know	7	0.4
No answer	13	0.7
I have a lot of say about what happens on my job:		
Total	**1,796**	**100.0**
Strongly agree	545	30.3
Agree	741	41.3
Disagree	385	21.4
Strongly disagree	101	5.6
Don't know	11	0.6
No answer	13	0.7

(continued)

	number of respondents	percent distribution
My main satisfaction in life comes from work:		
Total	**1,796**	**100.0%**
Strongly agree	128	7.1
Agree	369	20.5
Disagree	883	49.2
Strongly disagree	389	21.7
Don't know	14	0.8
No answer	13	0.7
I have too much work to do everything well:		
Total	**1,796**	**100.0**
Strongly agree	113	6.3
Agree	367	20.4
Disagree	1,083	60.3
Strongly disagree	206	11.5
Don't know	14	0.8
No answer	13	0.7
On my job, I know exactly what is expected of me:		
Total	**1,796**	**100.0**
Strongly agree	772	43.0
Agree	890	49.6
Disagree	91	5.1
Strongly disagree	22	1.2
Don't know	8	0.4
No answer	13	0.7
My job lets me use my skills and abilities:		
Total	**1,796**	**100.0**
Strongly agree	711	39.6
Agree	879	48.9
Disagree	142	7.9
Strongly disagree	43	2.4
Don't know	7	0.4
No answer	14	0.8
At the place where I work, I am treated with respect:		
Total	**1,796**	**100.0**
Strongly agree	715	39.8
Agree	924	51.4
Disagree	105	5.8
Strongly disagree	31	1.7
Don't know	6	0.3
No answer	15	0.8

(continued)

	number of respondents	percent distribution
I trust the management at the place where I work:		
Total	**1,796**	**100.0%**
Strongly agree	548	30.5
Agree	818	45.5
Disagree	298	16.6
Strongly disagree	101	5.6
Don't know	13	0.7
No answer	18	1.0
The safety of workers is a high priority with management where I work:		
Total	**1,796**	**100.0**
Strongly agree	770	42.9
Agree	815	45.4
Disagree	136	7.6
Strongly disagree	37	2.1
Don't know	21	1.2
No answer	17	0.9
There are no significant compromises or shortcuts taken when worker safety is at stake:		
Total	**1,796**	**100.0**
Strongly agree	733	40.8
Agree	815	45.4
Disagree	157	8.7
Strongly disagree	47	2.6
Don't know	26	1.4
No answer	18	1.0
Where I work, employees and management work together to ensure the safest possible working conditions:		
Total	**1,796**	**100.0**
Strongly agree	652	36.3
Agree	900	50.1
Disagree	168	9.4
Strongly disagree	37	2.1
Don't know	23	1.3
No answer	16	0.9
The safety and health conditions where I work are good:		
Total	**1,796**	**100.0**
Strongly agree	650	36.2
Agree	969	54.0
Disagree	131	7.3
Strongly disagree	21	1.2
Don't know	10	0.6
No answer	15	0.8

(continued)

	number of respondents	percent distribution
I am proud to be working for my employer:		
Total	**1,796**	**100.0%**
Strongly agree	673	37.5
Agree	910	50.7
Disagree	150	8.4
Strongly disagree	32	1.8
Don't know	14	0.8
No answer	17	0.9
Conditions on my job allow me to be about as productive as I could be:		
Total	**1,796**	**100.0**
Strongly agree	505	28.1
Agree	971	54.1
Disagree	254	14.1
Strongly disagree	42	2.3
Don't know	9	0.5
No answer	15	0.8
The place where I work is run in a smooth and effective manner:		
Total	**1,796**	**100.0**
Strongly agree	397	22.1
Agree	925	51.5
Disagree	367	20.4
Strongly disagree	81	4.5
Don't know	11	0.6
No answer	15	0.8
Workers need strong trade unions to protect their interests:		
Total	**1,796**	**100.0**
Strongly agree	214	11.9
Agree	599	33.4
Disagree	680	37.9
Strongly disagree	211	11.7
Don't know	72	4.0
No answer	20	1.1

Source: General Social Survey, National Opinion Research Center, University of Chicago

Table 2.90 Work as Part of Team, 2002

In your job, do you normally work as part of a team, or do you mostly work on your own?

(number of working respondents aged 18 or older and percent distribution by response, 2002)

	number of respondents	percent distribution
Total	**1,796**	**100.0%**
Yes, I work as part of a team	1,015	56.5
No, I work mostly on my own	759	42.3
Don't know	8	0.4
No answer	14	0.8

Source: General Social Survey, National Opinion Research Center, University of Chicago

Table 2.91 Work with Others in Making Decisions, 2002

In your job, how often do you take part with others in making decisions that affect you?

(number of working respondents aged 18 or older and percent distribution by response, 2002)

	number of respondents	percent distribution
Total	**1,796**	**100.0%**
Often	766	42.7
Sometimes	622	34.6
Rarely	253	14.1
Never	136	7.6
Don't know	5	0.3
No answer	14	0.8

Source: General Social Survey, National Opinion Research Center, University of Chicago

Table 2.92 Work with Others in Setting the Way Things Are Done, 2002

How often do you participate with others in helping set the way things are done on your job?

(number of working respondents aged 18 or older and percent distribution by response, 2002)

	number of respondents	percent distribution
Total	**1,796**	**100.0%**
Often	819	45.6
Sometimes	616	34.3
Rarely	215	12.0
Never	126	7.0
Don't know	6	0.3
No answer	14	0.8

Source: General Social Survey, National Opinion Research Center, University of Chicago

Table 2.93 Adequate Staff to Get Work Done, 2002

How often are there not enough people or staff to get all the work done?

(number of working respondents aged 18 or older and percent distribution by response, 2002)

	number of respondents	percent distribution
Total	**1,796**	**100.0%**
Often	466	25.9
Sometimes	584	32.5
Rarely	507	28.2
Never	208	11.6
Don't know	16	0.9
No answer	15	0.8

Source: General Social Survey, National Opinion Research Center, University of Chicago

Table 2.94 More Descriptions of Main Job, 2002

Now I'm going to read you another list of statements about your main job. For each, please tell me if the statement is very true, somewhat true, not too true, or not at all true with respect to the work you do.

(number of working respondents aged 18 or older and percent distribution by response, 2002)

	number of respondents	percent distribution
The chances for promotion are good:		
Total	**1,796**	**100.0%**
Very true	364	20.3
Somewhat true	604	33.6
Not too true	401	22.3
Not at all true	375	20.9
Don't know	31	1.7
No answer	21	1.2
I have an opportunity to develop my own special abilities:		
Total	**1,796**	**100.0**
Very true	743	41.4
Somewhat true	686	38.2
Not too true	220	12.2
Not at all true	121	6.7
Don't know	11	0.6
No answer	15	0.8
I receive enough help and equipment to get the job done:		
Total	**1,796**	**100.0**
Very true	857	47.7
Somewhat true	677	37.7
Not too true	171	9.5
Not at all true	68	3.8
Don't know	9	0.5
No answer	14	0.8
I have enough information to get the job done:		
Total	**1,796**	**100.0**
Very true	1,055	58.7
Somewhat true	621	34.6
Not too true	64	3.6
Not at all true	37	2.1
Don't know	5	0.3
No answer	14	0.8
I am given a lot of freedom to decide how to do my own work:		
Total	**1,796**	**100.0**
Very true	1,011	56.3
Somewhat true	537	29.9
Not too true	148	8.2
Not at all true	79	4.4
Don't know	6	0.3
No answer	15	0.8

(continued)

	number of respondents	percent distribution
My fringe benefits are good:		
Total	**1,796**	**100.0%**
Very true	705	39.3
Somewhat true	548	30.5
Not too true	214	11.9
Not at all true	304	16.9
Don't know	10	0.6
No answer	15	0.8
My supervisor is concerned about the welfare of those under him or her:		
Total	**1,796**	**100.0**
Very true	885	49.3
Somewhat true	563	31.3
Not too true	148	8.2
Not at all true	134	7.5
Don't know	39	2.2
No answer	27	1.5
I am free from the conflicting demands that other people make of me:		
Total	**1,796**	**100.0**
Very true	479	26.7
Somewhat true	722	40.2
Not too true	350	19.5
Not at all true	184	10.2
Don't know	44	2.4
No answer	17	0.9
Promotions are handled fairly:		
Total	**1,796**	**100.0**
Very true	507	28.2
Somewhat true	622	34.6
Not too true	275	15.3
Not at all true	254	14.1
Don't know	108	6.0
No answer	30	1.7
The people I work with take a personal interest in me.		
Total	**1,796**	**100.0**
Very true	789	43.9
Somewhat true	722	40.2
Not too true	155	8.6
Not at all true	89	5.0
Don't know	20	1.1
No answer	21	1.2

(continued)

	number of respondents	percent distribution
The job security is good:		
Total	**1,796**	**100.0%**
Very true	951	53.0
Somewhat true	546	30.4
Not too true	162	9.0
Not at all true	108	6.0
Don't know	15	0.8
No answer	14	0.8
My supervisor is helpful to me in getting the job done:		
Total	**1,796**	**100.0**
Very true	867	48.3
Somewhat true	570	31.7
Not too true	155	8.6
Not at all true	132	7.3
Don't know	40	2.2
No answer	32	1.8
I have enough time to get the job done:		
Total	**1,796**	**100.0**
Very true	801	44.6
Somewhat true	665	37.0
Not too true	193	10.7
Not at all true	115	6.4
Don't know	7	0.4
No answer	15	0.8
The people I work with can be relied on when I need help:		
Total	**1,796**	**100.0**
Very true	957	53.3
Somewhat true	643	35.8
Not too true	106	5.9
Not at all true	55	3.1
Don't know	14	0.8
No answer	21	1.2
I have the training opportunities I need to perform my job safely and competently:		
Total	**1,796**	**100.0**
Very true	1,125	62.6
Somewhat true	504	28.1
Not too true	78	4.3
Not at all true	58	3.2
Don't know	15	0.8
No answer	16	0.9

Source: General Social Survey, National Opinion Research Center, University of Chicago

Table 2.95 Relationship between Management and Employees, 2002

In general, how would you describe relations in your work place between management and employees?

(number of working respondents aged 18 or older and percent distribution by response, 2002)

	number of respondents	percent distribution
Total	**1,796**	**100.0%**
Very good	646	36.0
Quite good	595	33.1
Neither good nor bad	384	21.4
Quite bad	95	5.3
Very bad	38	2.1
Don't know	20	1.1
No answer	18	1.0

Source: General Social Survey, National Opinion Research Center, University of Chicago

Table 2.96 Does Job Require Lifting, 2002

Does your job require you to do repeated lifting, pushing, or bending?

(number of working respondents aged 18 or older and percent distribution by response, 2002)

	number of respondents	percent distribution
Total	**1,796**	**100.0%**
Yes	821	45.7
No	957	53.3
Don't know	5	0.3
No answer	13	0.7

Source: General Social Survey, National Opinion Research Center, University of Chicago

Table 2.97 Does Job Require Repetitive Hand Movements, 2002

Does your job regularly require you to perform repetitive or forceful hand movements or involve awkward postures?

(number of working respondents aged 18 or older and percent distribution by response, 2002)

	number of respondents	percent distribution
Total	**1,796**	**100.0%**
Yes	906	50.4
No	871	48.5
Don't know	6	0.3
No answer	13	0.7

Source: General Social Survey, National Opinion Research Center, University of Chicago

Table 2.98 Praised for Doing Job Well, 2002

When you do your job well, are you likely to be praised by your supervisor or employer?

(number of working respondents aged 18 or older and percent distribution by response, 2002)

	number of respondents	percent distribution
Total	**1,796**	**100.0%**
Yes	954	53.1
Maybe	453	25.2
No	348	19.4
Don't know	17	0.9
No answer	24	1.3

Source: General Social Survey, National Opinion Research Center, University of Chicago

Table 2.99 Bonus for Doing Job Well, 2002

When you do your job well, are you likely to get a bonus or pay increase?

(number of working respondents aged 18 or older and percent distribution by response, 2002)

	number of respondents	percent distribution
Total	**1,796**	**100.0%**
Yes	431	24.0
Maybe	251	14.0
No	1,082	60.2
Don't know	12	0.7
No answer	20	1.1

Source: General Social Survey, National Opinion Research Center, University of Chicago

Table 2.100 Fair Pay Compared to Others, 2002

How fair is what you earn on your job in comparison to others doing the same type of work you do?

(number of working respondents aged 18 or older and percent distribution by response, 2002)

	number of respondents	percent distribution
Total	**1,796**	**100.0%**
Much less than you deserve	252	14.0
Somewhat less than you deserve	475	26.4
About as much as you deserve	874	48.7
Somewhat more than you deserve	116	6.5
Much more than you deserve	25	1.4
Don't know	37	2.1
No answer	17	0.9

Source: General Social Survey, National Opinion Research Center, University of Chicago

Table 2.101 Income from Job Meets Family's Expenses, 2002

Do you feel that the income from your job alone is enough to meet your family's usual monthly expenses and bills?

(number of working respondents aged 18 or older and percent distribution by response, 2002)

	number of respondents	percent distribution
Total	**1,796**	**100.0%**
Yes	827	46.0
No	944	52.6
Don't know	11	0.6
No answer	14	0.8

Source: General Social Survey, National Opinion Research Center, University of Chicago

Table 2.102 Laid Off in Past Year, 2002

Were you laid off your main job at any time in the last year?

(number of working respondents aged 18 or older and percent distribution by response, 2002)

	number of respondents	percent distribution
Total	**1,796**	**100.0%**
Yes	131	7.3
No	1,644	91.5
Don't know	6	0.3
No answer	15	0.8

Source: General Social Survey, National Opinion Research Center, University of Chicago

Table 2.103 Easy to Find New Job, 2002

How easy would it be for you to find a job with another employer with approximately the same income and fringe benefits as you have now?

(number of working respondents aged 18 or older and percent distribution by response, 2002)

	number of respondents	percent distribution
Total	**1,796**	**100.0%**
Very easy to find similar job	427	23.8
Somewhat easy to find similar job	626	34.9
Not easy at all to find similar job	702	39.1
Don't know	25	1.4
No answer	16	0.9

Source: General Social Survey, National Opinion Research Center, University of Chicago

Table 2.104 How Likely to Look for a New Job, 2002

Taking everything into consideration, how likely is it you will make a genuine effort to find a new job with another employer within the next year?

(number of working respondents aged 18 or older and percent distribution by response, 2002)

	number of respondents	percent distribution
Total	**1,796**	**100.0%**
Very likely	330	18.4
Somewhat likely	355	19.8
Not at all likely	1,085	60.4
Don't know	12	0.7
No answer	14	0.8

Source: General Social Survey, National Opinion Research Center, University of Chicago

Table 2.105 Age Discrimination on Job, 2002

Do you feel in any way discriminated against
on your job because of your age?

(number of working respondents aged 18 or older and percent distribution by response, 2002)

	number of respondents	percent distribution
Total	**1,796**	**100.0%**
Yes	155	8.6
No	1,620	90.2
Don't know	7	0.4
No answer	14	0.8

Source: General Social Survey, National Opinion Research Center, University of Chicago

Table 2.106 Race Discrimination on Job, 2002

Do you feel in any way discriminated against on your job because of your race or ethnic origin?

(number of working respondents aged 18 or older and percent distribution by response, 2002)

	number of respondents	percent distribution
Total	**1,796**	**100.0%**
Yes	98	5.5
No	1,676	93.3
Don't know	8	0.4
No answer	14	0.8

Source: General Social Survey, National Opinion Research Center, University of Chicago

Table 2.107 Gender Discrimination on Job, 2002

Do you feel in any way discriminated against on your job because of your race or ethnic origin?

(number of working respondents aged 18 or older and percent distribution by response, 2002)

	number of respondents	percent distribution
Total	**1,796**	**100.0%**
Yes	131	7.3
No	1,644	91.5
Don't know	7	0.4
No answer	14	0.8

Source: General Social Survey, National Opinion Research Center, University of Chicago

Table 2.108 Sexual Harassment on Job, 2002

In the last 12 months, were you sexually harassed by anyone while you were on the job?

(number of working respondents aged 18 or older and percent distribution by response, 2002)

	number of respondents	percent distribution
Total	**1,796**	**100.0%**
Yes	85	4.7
No	1,689	94.0
Don't know	6	0.3
No answer	16	0.9

Source: General Social Survey, National Opinion Research Center, University of Chicago

Table 2.109 Other Harassment on Job, 2002

In the last 12 months, were you threatened or harassed in any other way by anyone while you were on the job?

(number of working respondents aged 18 or older and percent distribution by response, 2002)

	number of respondents	percent distribution
Total	**1,796**	**100.0%**
Yes	202	11.2
No	1,572	87.5
Don't know	6	0.3
No answer	16	0.9

Source: General Social Survey, National Opinion Research Center, University of Chicago

Table 2.110 Health Status, 2002

Would you say that in general your health is excellent, very good, good, fair, or poor?

(number of respondents aged 18 or older and percent distribution by response, 2002)

	number of respondents	percent distribution
Total	**2,295**	**100.0%**
Excellent	596	26.0
Very good	640	27.9
Good	654	28.5
Fair	304	13.2
Poor	82	3.6
Don't know	9	0.4
No answer	10	0.4

Source: General Social Survey, National Opinion Research Center, University of Chicago

Table 2.111 Physical Health Not Good, 2002

Now thinking about your physical health, which includes physical illness and injury, for how many days during the past 30 days was your physical health not good?

(number of working respondents aged 18 or older and percent distribution by response, 2002)

	number of respondents	percent distribution
Total	**1,796**	**100.0%**
None	1,141	63.5
One day	105	5.8
Two days	134	7.5
Three days	69	3.8
Four days	41	2.3
Five to nine days	115	6.4
10 to 19 days	91	5.1
20 or more days	76	4.2
Don't know	9	0.5
No answer	15	0.8

Source: General Social Survey, National Opinion Research Center, University of Chicago

Table 2.112 Mental Health Not Good, 2002

Now thinking about your mental health, which includes stress, depression, and problems with emotions, for how many days during the past 30 days was your mental health not good?

(number of working respondents aged 18 or older and percent distribution by response, 2002)

	number of respondents	percent distribution
Total	**1,796**	**100.0%**
None	1,050	58.5
One day	64	3.6
Two days	117	6.5
Three days	84	4.7
Four days	44	2.4
Five to nine days	136	7.6
10 to 19 days	133	7.4
20 or more days	138	7.7
Don't know	14	0.8
No answer	16	0.9

Source: General Social Survey, National Opinion Research Center, University of Chicago

Table 2.113 Poor Health Prevented Usual Activities, 2002

During the past 30 days, for about how many days did your poor physical or mental health keep you from doing your usual activities, such as self-care, work, or recreation?

(number of working respondents aged 18 or older and percent distribution by response, 2002)

	number of respondents	percent distribution
Total	**1,796**	**100.0%**
None	1,389	77.3
One day	80	4.5
Two days	72	4.0
Three days	49	2.7
Four days	34	1.9
Five to nine days	54	3.0
10 to 19 days	51	2.8
20 or more days	45	2.5
Don't know	6	0.3
No answer	16	0.9

Source: General Social Survey, National Opinion Research Center, University of Chicago

Table 2.114 Used Up at End of Day, 2002

How often during the past month have you felt used up at the end of the day?

(number of working respondents aged 18 or older and percent distribution by response, 2002)

	number of respondents	percent distribution
Total	**1,796**	**100.0%**
Very often	333	18.5
Often	419	23.3
Sometimes	597	33.2
Rarely	301	16.8
Never	123	6.8
Don't know	7	0.4
No answer	16	0.9

Source: General Social Survey, National Opinion Research Center, University of Chicago

Table 2.115 Back Pain, 2002

In the past 12 months, have you had back pain every day for a week or more?

(number of working respondents aged 18 or older and percent distribution by response, 2002)

	number of respondents	percent distribution
Total	**1,796**	**100.0%**
Yes	506	28.2
No	1,270	70.7
Don't know	5	0.3
No answer	15	0.8

Source: General Social Survey, National Opinion Research Center, University of Chicago

Table 2.116 Hand and Arm Pain, 2002

In the past 12 months, have you had pain in the hands, wrists, arms, or shoulders every day for a week or more?

(number of working respondents aged 18 or older and percent distribution by response, 2002)

	number of respondents	percent distribution
Total	**1,796**	**100.0%**
Yes	504	28.1
No	1,271	70.8
Don't know	6	0.3
No answer	15	0.8

Source: General Social Survey, National Opinion Research Center, University of Chicago

Table 2.117 Injured on the Job, 2002

In the past 12 months, how many times have you been injured on the job?

(number of working respondents aged 18 or older and percent distribution by response, 2002)

	number of respondents	percent distribution
Total	**1,796**	**100.0%**
None	1,577	87.8
Once	128	7.1
Twice	25	1.4
Three times	17	0.9
Four times	4	0.2
Five times	6	0.3
Six times	6	0.3
Seven or more times	8	0.4
Don't know	8	0.4
No answer	17	0.9

Source: General Social Survey, National Opinion Research Center, University of Chicago

Table 2.118 Job Satisfaction, 2002

All in all, how satisfied would you say you are with your job?

(number of working respondents aged 18 or older and percent distribution by response, 2002)

	number of respondents	percent distribution
Total	**1,796**	**100.0%**
Very satisfied	872	48.6
Somewhat satisfied	707	39.4
Not too satisfied	134	7.5
Not at all satisfied	61	3.4
Don't know	6	0.3
No answer	16	0.9

Source: General Social Survey, National Opinion Research Center, University of Chicago

CHAPTER

3

International Social Survey Program 2002 Modules

The General Social Survey participates in an international effort, called the International Social Survey Program (ISSP), to probe the behavior and attitudes of national populations toward a variety of issues. The GSS usually includes ISSP topical Modules with its survey. Those same ISSP topical Modules are also included in surveys taken in dozens of other countries, allowing international comparisons of attitudes and behavior on a variety of issues.

In 2002, one of the ISSP Modules focused on social relationships, and its findings are uniquely revealing. The second ISSP topical module explored women and work, examining—among other things—how couples divide up household chores.

Social Relations and Support Systems

Contrary to the popular notion that American families are spread far and wide, in fact 57 percent of adults whose mother is alive and not living with them can get door-to-door from their house to their mother's in one hour or less. Nearly half (47 percent) can make the journey in thirty minutes or less. Most of those whose mother is alive and not living with them see their mother frequently. Nearly half (49 percent) visit her at least once a week. Seventy-one percent have other contact with their mother at least weekly, including by telephone, letters, or email.

Sixty-eight percent of Americans have close friends in their neighborhood. Among workers, 72 percent have close friends at work. Friends can come in handy. In fact, they are the single most important way people get jobs. Nineteen percent of the public got their most recent job through a close friend, a larger share than got their job by any other means including advertisements (15 percent).

Although friends are important, Americans remain wary of others. Seventy-eight percent agree with the statement, "There are only a few people I can trust completely." Sixty-nine percent agree with the statement, "If you are not careful, other people will take advantage of you." And many feel helpless to change the political process—even at the local level. The 52 percent majority say it is "not very likely" or "not at all likely" they have the ability to improve their local community.

Table 3.1 Time to Get to Mother's House, 2002

About how long would it take to get to where your mother lives?
Think about the time it usually takes door to door.

(number of respondents aged 18 or older whose mother is alive and not living with them and percent distribution by response, 2002)

	number of respondents	percent distribution
Total	**682**	**100.0%**
Less than two minutes	56	8.2
Less than 15 minutes	147	21.6
Between 15 and 30 minutes	117	17.2
Between 30 minutes and one hour	68	10.0
Between one and two hours	51	7.5
Between two and three hours	38	5.6
Between three and five hours	44	6.5
Between 5 and 12 hours	68	10.0
More than 12 hours	87	12.8
Don't know	1	0.1
No answer	5	0.7

Source: General Social Survey, National Opinion Research Center, University of Chicago

Table 3.2 Number of Adult Siblings, 2002

How many adult brothers and/or sisters—we mean brothers or sisters who are age 18 and older—do you have? (We mean brothers and sisters who are still alive. Please include step-brothers and sisters, half-brothers and sisters, and adopted brothers and sisters).

(number of respondents aged 18 or older and percent distribution by response, 2002)

	number of respondents	percent distribution
Total	**1,149**	**100.0%**
None	129	11.2
One	252	21.9
Two	259	22.5
Three	185	16.1
Four	96	8.4
Five	85	7.4
Six	48	4.2
Seven	74	6.4
Eight or more	21	1.8

Source: General Social Survey, National Opinion Research Center, University of Chicago

Table 3.3 Adult Sibling with Most Contact, 2002

Of your adult brothers and sisters, with whom do you have the most contact?

(number of respondents aged 18 or older with adult siblings and percent distribution by response, 2002)

	number of respondents	percent distribution
Respondents with adult siblings	**1,020**	**100.0%**
With a brother	414	40.6
With a sister	537	52.6
I have no contact with any adult brother or sister	58	5.7
Don't know	4	0.4
No answer	7	0.7

Source: General Social Survey, National Opinion Research Center, University of Chicago

Table 3.4 How Often See/Visit Sibling with Most Contact, 2002

How often do you see or visit this brother or sister?

(number of respondents aged 18 or older who have contact with an adult sibling and percent distribution by response, 2002)

	number of respondents	percent distribution
Respondents in contact with an adult sibling	**958**	**100.0%**
He/she lives in the same household as I do	25	2.6
Daily	67	7.0
At least several times a week	109	11.4
At least once a week	160	16.7
At least once a month	172	18.0
Several times a year	226	23.6
Less often	192	20.0
No answer	7	0.7

Source: General Social Survey, National Opinion Research Center, University of Chicago

Table 3.5 Other Contact with Sibling, 2002

And how often do you have any other contact with this brother or sister besides visiting, either by telephone, letter, fax, or e-mail?

(number of respondents aged 18 or older who have other contact with an adult sibling and percent distribution by response, 2002)

	number of respondents	percent distribution
Respondents in contact with an adult sibling	**932**	**100.0%**
Daily	110	11.8
At least several times a week	181	19.4
At least once a week	226	24.2
At least once a month	184	19.7
Several times a year	136	14.6
Less often	88	9.4
No answer	7	0.8

Source: General Social Survey, National Opinion Research Center, University of Chicago

Table 3.6 Number of Adult Children, 2002

How many children age 18 and older do you have? (We mean children who are still alive. Please include stepchildren and adopted children.)

(number of respondents aged 18 or older and percent distribution by response, 2002)

	number of respondents	percent distribution
Total	**1,149**	**100.0%**
None	691	60.1
One	99	8.6
Two	162	14.1
Three	100	8.7
Four	46	4.0
Five	18	1.6
Six or more	33	2.9

Source: General Social Survey, National Opinion Research Center, University of Chicago

Table 3.7 Adult Child in Most Contact, 2002

Of your children aged 18 and older, with whom do you have the most contact?

(number of respondents aged 18 or older with adult children and percent distribution by response, 2002)

	number of respondents	percent distribution
Respondents with adult children	**458**	**100.0%**
With a son	179	39.1
With a daughter	259	56.6
I have no contact with any of my adult children	9	2.0
Don't know	3	0.7
No answer	8	1.7

Source: General Social Survey, National Opinion Research Center, University of Chicago

Table 3.8 Frequency of Seeing/Visiting Adult Child with Most Contact, 2002

How often do you see or visit this son or daughter?

(number of respondents aged 18 or older who have contact with an adult child and percent distribution by response, 2002)

	number of respondents	percent distribution
Respondents in contact with adult child	**446**	**100.0%**
He/she lives in the same household as I do	78	17.5
Daily	64	14.3
At least several times a week	81	18.2
At least once a week	70	15.7
At least once a month	58	13.0
Several times a year	64	14.3
Less often	23	5.2
No answer	8	1.8

Source: General Social Survey, National Opinion Research Center, University of Chicago

Table 3.9 Other Contact with Adult Child, 2002

And how often do you have any other contact with this son or daughter besides visiting, either by telephone, letter, fax, or e-mail?

(number of respondents aged 18 or older not living with an adult child and percent distribution by response, 2002)

	number of respondents	percent distribution
Respondents in contact with an adult child not living with them	**368**	**100.0%**
Daily	101	27.4
At least several times a week	97	26.4
At least once a week	88	23.9
At least once a month	33	9.0
Several times a year	26	7.1
Less often	14	3.8
Don't know	1	0.3
No answer	8	2.2

Source: General Social Survey, National Opinion Research Center, University of Chicago

Table 3.10 Frequency of Seeing/Visiting Father, 2002

How often do you see or visit your father?

(number of respondents aged 18 or older and percent distribution by response, 2002)

	number of respondents	percent distribution
Total	**1,149**	**100.0%**
He lives in the same household as I do	35	3.0
Daily	40	3.5
At least several times a week	60	5.2
At least once a week	92	8.0
At least once a month	94	8.2
Several times a year	114	9.9
Less often	85	7.4
Never	55	4.8
My father is no longer alive	545	47.4
I don't know where my father lives	25	2.2
No answer	4	0.3

Source: General Social Survey, National Opinion Research Center, University of Chicago

Table 3.11 Other Contact with Father, 2002

And how often do you have any other contact with your father besides visiting, either by telephone, letter, fax, or e-mail?

(number of respondents aged 18 or older whose father is alive and not living with them and percent distribution by response, 2002)

	number of respondents	percent distribution
Respondents whose father is alive and not living with them	**544**	**100.0%**
Daily	56	10.3
At least several times a week	93	17.1
At least once a week	115	21.1
At least once a month	100	18.4
Several times a year	49	9.0
Less often	50	9.2
Never	77	14.2
No answer	4	0.7

Source: General Social Survey, National Opinion Research Center, University of Chicago

Table 3.12 Frequency of Seeing/Visiting Mother, 2002

And what about your mother? How often do you see or visit her?

(number of respondents aged 18 or older and percent distribution by response, 2002)

	number of respondents	percent distribution
Total	**1,149**	**100.0%**
She lives in the same household as I do	66	5.7
Daily	71	6.2
At least several times a week	128	11.1
At least once a week	139	12.1
At least once a month	111	9.7
Several times a year	125	10.9
Less often	85	7.4
Never	19	1.7
My mother is no longer alive	400	34.8
I don't know where my mother lives	1	0.1
No answer	4	0.3

Source: General Social Survey, National Opinion Research Center, University of Chicago

Table 3.13 Other Contact with Mother, 2002

And how often do you have any other contact with your mother besides visiting, either by telephone, letter, fax, or e-mail?

(number of respondents aged 18 or older whose mother is alive and not living with them and percent distribution by response, 2002)

	number of respondents	percent distribution
Respondents whose mother is alive and not living with them	**682**	**100.0%**
Daily	127	18.6
At least several times a week	175	25.7
At least once a week	185	27.1
At least once a month	89	13.0
Several times a year	36	5.3
Less often	28	4.1
Never	38	5.6
No answer	4	0.6

Source: General Social Survey, National Opinion Research Center, University of Chicago

Table 3.14 Contact with Other Relatives, 2002

Now some questions about your contact with other relatives. Please indicate how often you have been in contact with any of the following types of relatives in the last four weeks.

(number of respondents aged 18 or older and percent distribution by response, 2002)

	number of respondents	percent distribution
Uncles or aunts:		
Total	**1,149**	**100.0%**
More than twice in last four weeks	192	16.7
Once or twice in last four weeks	270	23.5
Not at all in last four weeks	494	43.0
I have no living relatives of this type	187	16.3
No answer	6	0.5
Cousins:		
Total	**1,149**	**100.0**
More than twice in last four weeks	225	19.6
Once or twice in last four weeks	283	24.6
Not at all in last four weeks	580	50.5
I have no living relatives of this type	54	4.7
Don't know	2	0.2
No answer	5	0.4
Parents-in-law:		
Total	**1,149**	**100.0**
More than twice in last four weeks	223	19.4
Once or twice in last four weeks	141	12.3
Not at all in last four weeks	221	19.2
I have no living relatives of this type	555	48.3
Don't know	2	0.2
No answer	7	0.6
Brothers- or sisters-in-law:		
Total	**1,149**	**100.0**
More than twice in last four weeks	313	27.2
Once or twice in last four weeks	278	24.2
Not at all in last four weeks	307	26.7
I have no living relatives of this type	242	21.1
Don't know	3	0.3
No answer	6	0.5

(continued)

	number of respondents	percent distribution
Nieces and nephews:		
Total	**1,149**	**100.0%**
More than twice in last four weeks	359	31.2
Once or twice in last four weeks	270	23.5
Not at all in last four weeks	354	30.8
I have no living relatives of this type	157	13.7
Don't know	4	0.3
No answer	5	0.4
Godparents:		
Total	**1,149**	**100.0**
More than twice in last four weeks	39	3.4
Once or twice in last four weeks	55	4.8
Not at all in last four weeks	291	25.3
I have no living relatives of this type	749	65.2
Don't know	5	0.4
No answer	10	0.9

Source: General Social Survey, National Opinion Research Center, University of Chicago

Table 3.15 Friends at Work, 2002

Now we would like to ask you about people you know, other than your family and relatives. The first question is about people at your work place. Thinking about people at your work place, how many of them are close friends of yours?

(number of working respondents aged 18 or older and percent distribution by response, 2002)

	number of respondents	percent distribution
Total	**763**	**100.0%**
No close friends	206	27.0
One	121	15.9
Two	146	19.1
Three	84	11.0
Four	57	7.5
Five to nine	97	12.7
10 to 19	36	4.7
20 or more	9	1.2
Don't know	1	0.1
No answer	6	0.8

Source: General Social Survey, National Opinion Research Center, University of Chicago

Table 3.16 Friends in Neighborhood, 2002

Thinking now of people who live near you—in your neighborhood or district: How many of these people are close friends of yours?

(number of respondents aged 18 or older and percent distribution by response, 2002)

	number of respondents	percent distribution
Total	**1,149**	**100.0%**
No close friends	356	31.0
One	122	10.6
Two	200	17.4
Three	110	9.6
Four	96	8.4
Five to nine	168	14.6
10 to 19	63	5.5
20 or more	27	2.3
Don't know	1	0.1
No answer	6	0.5

Source: General Social Survey, National Opinion Research Center, University of Chicago

Table 3.17 Best Friend, 2002

Now think about your best friend, the friend you feel closest to (but not your partner). Is this best friend:

(number of respondents aged 18 or older and percent distribution by response, 2002)

	number of respondents	percent distribution
Total	**1,149**	**100.0%**
A male relative	151	13.1
A female relative	186	16.2
A man who is not a relative	328	28.5
A woman who is not a relative	419	36.5
I don't have a close friend	56	4.9
Don't know	2	0.2
No answer	7	0.6

Source: General Social Survey, National Opinion Research Center, University of Chicago

Table 3.18 Frequency of Seeing/Visiting Best Friend, 2002

And how often do you see or visit your friend
(the friend you feel closest to)?

(number of respondents aged 18 or older with a close friend and percent distribution by response, 2002)

	number of respondents	percent distribution
Respondents with a close friend	**1,091**	**100.0%**
He/she lives in the same household as I do	26	2.4
Daily	118	10.8
At least several times a week	221	20.3
At least once a week	254	23.3
At least once a month	185	17.0
Several times a year	173	15.9
Less often	94	8.6
Never	12	1.1
Don't know	1	0.1
No answer	7	0.6

Source: General Social Survey, National Opinion Research Center, University of Chicago

Table 3.19 Other Contact with Best Friend, 2002

And how often do you have any other contact with this friend besides visiting, either by telephone, letter, fax, or e-mail?

(number of respondents aged 18 or older with a close friend not living with them and percent distribution by response, 2002)

	number of respondents	percent distribution
Respondents with a close friend not living with them	**1,064**	**100.0%**
Daily	192	18.0
At least several times a week	282	26.5
At least once a week	241	22.7
At least once a month	169	15.9
Several times a year	80	7.5
Less often	50	4.7
Never	43	4.0
No answer	7	0.7

Source: General Social Survey, National Opinion Research Center, University of Chicago

Table 3.20 Participation in Groups and Associations, 2002

People sometimes belong to different kinds of groups or associations. The next few questions contain different types of groups. For each type of group, please select a response to say whether you have participated in the activities of this group in the past 12 months.

(number of respondents aged 18 or older and percent distribution by response, 2002)

	number of respondents	percent distribution
A political party, club, or association:		
Total	**1,149**	**100.0%**
I have participated more than twice	113	9.8
I have participated once or twice	100	8.7
I belong to such a group but never participate	75	6.5
I do not belong to such a group	853	74.2
Don't know	1	0.1
No answer	7	0.6
A trade union or professional association:		
Total	**1,149**	**100.0**
I have participated more than twice	101	8.8
I have participated once or twice	86	7.5
I belong to such a group but never participate	90	7.8
I do not belong to such a group	864	75.2
Don't know	1	0.1
No answer	7	0.6
A church or other religious organization:		
Total	**1,149**	**100.0**
I have participated more than twice	422	36.7
I have participated once or twice	184	16.0
I belong to such a group but never participate	116	10.1
I do not belong to such a group	420	36.6
No answer	7	0.6
A sports group, hobby, or leisure club:		
Total	**1,149**	**100.0**
I have participated more than twice	303	26.4
I have participated once or twice	117	10.2
I belong to such a group but never participate	25	2.2
I do not belong to such a group	697	60.7
No answer	7	0.6

(continued)

	number of respondents	percent distribution
A charitable organization or group:		
Total	**1,149**	**100.0%**
I have participated more than twice	190	16.5
I have participated once or twice	151	13.1
I belong to such a group but never participate	46	4.0
I do not belong to such a group	754	65.6
No answer	8	0.7
A neighborhood group or association:		
Total	**1,149**	**100.0**
I have participated more than twice	82	7.1
I have participated once or twice	103	9.0
I belong to such a group but never participate	46	4.0
I do not belong to such a group	911	79.3
No answer	7	0.6
Other associations or groups:		
Total	**1,149**	**100.0**
I have participated more than twice	160	13.9
I have participated once or twice	125	10.9
I belong to such a group but never participate	50	4.4
I do not belong to such a group	807	70.2
No answer	7	0.6

Source: General Social Survey, National Opinion Research Center, University of Chicago

Table 3.21 If You Had the Flu, Who Would You Turn to First for Help, 2002

Now we would like to ask you how you would get help in situations that anyone could find herself or himself in. First, suppose you had the flu and had to stay in bed for a few days and needed help around the house, with shopping, and so on. Who would you turn to first for help?

(number of respondents aged 18 or older and percent distribution by response, 2002)

	number of respondents	percent distribution
Total	**1,149**	**100.0%**
Husband, wife, partner	547	47.6
Mother	137	11.9
Father	26	2.3
Daughter	98	8.5
Daughter-in-law	7	0.6
Son	33	2.9
Son-in-law	0	0.0
Sister	51	4.4
Brother	27	2.3
Other blood relative	17	1.5
Other in-law relative	7	0.6
Close friend	113	9.8
Neighbor	25	2.2
Someone you work with	6	0.5
Someone at a social services agency	3	0.3
Someone you pay to help	2	0.2
Other	14	1.2
No one	29	2.5
Don't know	1	0.1
No answer	6	0.5

Source: General Social Survey, National Opinion Research Center, University of Chicago

Table 3.22 If You Had the Flu, Who Would You Turn to Second for Help, 2002

And who would you turn to second if you had the flu and needed help around the house?

(number of respondents aged 18 or older and percent distribution by response, 2002)

	number of respondents	percent distribution
Total	**1,149**	**100.0%**
Husband, wife, partner	84	7.3
Mother	165	14.4
Father	54	4.7
Daughter	169	14.7
Daughter-in-law	9	0.8
Son	95	8.3
Son-in-law	6	0.5
Sister	86	7.5
Brother	41	3.6
Other blood relative	44	3.8
Other in-law relative	44	3.8
Close friend	182	15.8
Neighbor	48	4.2
Someone you work with	24	2.1
Someone at a social services agency	4	0.3
Someone you pay to help	5	0.4
Other	16	1.4
No one	57	5.0
Don't know	2	0.2
No answer	14	1.2

Source: General Social Survey, National Opinion Research Center, University of Chicago

Table 3.23 If You Needed Money, Who Would You Turn to First for Help, 2002

Now, suppose you needed to borrow a large sum of money.
Who would you turn to first for help?

(number of respondents aged 18 or older and percent distribution by response, 2002)

	number of respondents	percent distribution
Total	**1,149**	**100.0%**
Husband, wife, partner	144	12.5
Mother	186	16.2
Father	164	14.3
Daughter	32	2.8
Son	33	2.9
Sister	56	4.9
Brother	64	5.6
Other blood relative	36	3.1
Other in-law relative	36	3.1
Godparent	0	0.0
Close friend	61	5.3
Neighbor	0	0.0
Someone you work with	8	0.7
Employer	2	0.2
Government or social worker	6	0.5
Bank or credit union	88	7.7
Private money lender	5	0.4
Someone else	75	6.5
No one	134	11.7
Don't know	6	0.5
No answer	13	1.1

Source: General Social Survey, National Opinion Research Center, University of Chicago

Table 3.24 If You Needed Money, Who Would You Turn to Second for Help, 2002

And who would you turn to second if you needed to borrow a large sum of money?

(number of respondents aged 18 or older and percent distribution by response, 2002)

	number of respondents	percent distribution
Total	**1,149**	**100.0%**
Husband, wife, partner	42	3.7
Mother	123	10.7
Father	124	10.8
Daughter	30	2.6
Son	32	2.8
Sister	78	6.8
Brother	79	6.9
Other blood relative	63	5.5
Other in-law relative	70	6.1
Godparent	0	0.0
Close friend	96	8.4
Neighbor	3	0.3
Someone you work with	7	0.6
Employer	7	0.6
Government or social worker	5	0.4
Bank or credit union	33	2.9
Private money lender	17	1.5
Someone else	86	7.5
No one	235	20.5
Don't know	9	0.8
No answer	10	0.9

Source: General Social Survey, National Opinion Research Center, University of Chicago

Table 3.25 If You Were Depressed, Who Would You Turn to First for Help, 2002

Now suppose you felt just a bit down or depressed, and you wanted to talk about it. Who would you turn to first for help?

(number of respondents aged 18 or older and percent distribution by response, 2002)

	number of respondents	percent distribution
Total	**1,149**	**100.0%**
Husband, wife, partner	363	31.6
Mother	102	8.9
Father	21	1.8
Daughter	55	4.8
Son	14	1.2
Sister	70	6.1
Brother	32	2.8
Other blood relative	11	1.0
Other in-law relative	13	1.1
Close friend	348	30.3
Neighbor	5	0.4
Someone you work with	8	0.7
Priest or member of the clergy	3	0.3
Family doctor	7	0.6
A psychologist	11	1.0
Self-help group	0	0.0
Someone else	32	2.8
No one	44	3.8
Don't know	3	0.3
No answer	7	0.6

Source: General Social Survey, National Opinion Research Center, University of Chicago

Table 3.26 If You Were Depressed, Who Would You Turn to Second for Help, 2002

And who would you turn to second if you felt a bit down or depressed and wanted to talk about it?

(number of respondents aged 18 or older and percent distribution by response, 2002)

	number of respondents	percent distribution
Total	**1,149**	**100.0%**
Husband, wife, partner	125	10.9
Mother	135	11.7
Father	42	3.7
Daughter	89	7.7
Son	36	3.1
Sister	110	9.6
Brother	62	5.4
Other blood relative	35	3.0
Other in-law relative	37	3.2
Close friend	281	24.5
Neighbor	13	1.1
Someone you work with	32	2.8
Priest or member of the clergy	2	0.2
Family doctor	9	0.8
A psychologist	5	0.4
Self-help group	0	0.0
Someone else	38	3.3
No one	86	7.5
Don't know	5	0.4
No answer	7	0.6

Source: General Social Survey, National Opinion Research Center, University of Chicago

Table 3.27 Doing Things for Others, 2002

During the past 12 months, how often have you done any of the following things for people you know personally, such as relatives, friends, neighbors, or other acquaintances?

(number of respondents aged 18 or older and percent distribution by response, 2002)

	number of respondents	percent distribution
Helped someone outside of your household with housework or shopping:		
Total	**1,149**	**100.0%**
More than once a week	135	11.7
Once a week	98	8.5
Once a month	196	17.1
At least two or three times in the past year	340	29.6
Once in the past year	121	10.5
Not at all in the past year	250	21.8
Don't know	1	0.1
No answer	8	0.7
Lent quite a bit of money to another person:		
Total	**1,149**	**100.0**
More than once a week	11	1.0
Once a week	23	2.0
Once a month	61	5.3
At least two or three times in the past year	201	17.5
Once in the past year	235	20.5
Not at all in the past year	610	53.1
No answer	8	0.7
Spent time talking with someone who was a bit down or depressed:		
Total	**1,149**	**100.0**
More than once a week	200	17.4
Once a week	172	15.0
Once a month	256	22.3
At least two or three times in the past year	338	29.4
Once in the past year	90	7.8
Not at all in the past year	86	7.5
No answer	7	0.6
Helped somebody to find a job:		
Total	**1,149**	**100.0**
More than once a week	26	2.3
Once a week	26	2.3
Once a month	75	6.5
At least two or three times in the past year	295	25.7
Once in the past year	222	19.3
Not at all in the past year	497	43.3
No answer	8	0.7

Source: General Social Survey, National Opinion Research Center, University of Chicago

Table 3.28 How Did You Find Out about Current Job, 2002

There are many ways people hear about jobs—from other people, from advertisements or employment agencies, and so on. Please indicate how you first found out about work at your present employer. If you are not currently working for pay, please answer this question for your last job.

(number of respondents aged 18 or older and percent distribution by response, 2002)

	number of respondents	percent distribution
Total	**1,149**	**100.0%**
I have never worked for pay	18	1.6
From parents, brothers, or sisters	58	5.0
From other relatives	56	4.9
From a close friend	218	19.0
From an acquaintance	145	12.6
From a public employment agency or service	62	5.4
From a private employment agency	24	2.1
From a school or university placement office	55	4.8
From an advertisement or sign	177	15.4
The employer contacted me about the job	103	9.0
I just called them or went there to ask for work	179	15.6
Don't know	29	2.5
No answer	25	2.2

Source: General Social Survey, National Opinion Research Center, University of Chicago

Table 3.29 Important Qualities in a Close Friend, 2002

People look for various things in a close friend and can differ on how important or not some things are for them. Please select a response to say how important or not it is for close friends of yours to be each of the following:

(number of respondents aged 18 or older and percent distribution by response, 2002)

	number of respondents	percent distribution
Someone who is intelligent and makes me think:		
Total	**1,149**	**100.0%**
Extremely important	262	22.8
Very important	418	36.4
Fairly important	304	26.5
Not too important	114	9.9
Not at all important	39	3.4
Don't know	4	0.3
No answer	8	0.7
Someone who helps me get things done:		
Total	**1,149**	**100.0**
Extremely important	190	16.5
Very important	327	28.5
Fairly important	347	30.2
Not too important	232	20.2
Not at all important	43	3.7
Don't know	3	0.3
No answer	7	0.6
Someone who really understands me:		
Total	**1,149**	**100.0**
Extremely important	411	35.8
Very important	446	38.8
Fairly important	206	17.9
Not too important	57	5.0
Not at all important	19	1.7
Don't know	2	0.2
No answer	8	0.7
Someone who is enjoyable company:		
Total	**1,149**	**100.0**
Extremely important	548	47.7
Very important	467	40.6
Fairly important	109	9.5
Not too important	12	1.0
Not at all important	5	0.4
Don't know	5	0.4
No answer	8	0.7

Source: General Social Survey, National Opinion Research Center, University of Chicago

Table 3.30 Attitudes toward Helping Others, 2002

Please select a response to indicate how much you agree or disagree with each of the following statements.

(number of respondents aged 18 or older and percent distribution by response, 2002)

	number of respondents	percent distribution
Adult children have a duty to look after their elderly parents:		
Total	**1,156**	**100.0%**
Agree strongly	406	35.1
Agree	417	36.1
Neither agree nor disagree	198	17.1
Disagree	79	6.8
Disagree strongly	25	2.2
Can't choose	17	1.5
No answer	7	0.6
You should take care of yourself and your family first, before helping other people:		
Total	**1,158**	**100.0**
Agree strongly	494	42.7
Agree	455	39.3
Neither agree nor disagree	146	12.6
Disagree	41	3.5
Disagree strongly	3	0.3
Can't choose	1	0.1
No answer	9	0.8
People who are better off should help friends who are less well off:		
Total	**1,158**	**100.0**
Agree strongly	188	16.2
Agree	470	40.6
Neither agree nor disagree	360	31.1
Disagree	91	7.9
Disagree strongly	7	0.6
Can't choose	24	2.1
No answer	9	0.8
It is all right to develop friendships with people just because you know they can be of use to you:		
Total	**1,149**	**100.0**
Agree strongly	24	2.1
Agree	109	9.5
Neither agree nor disagree	211	18.4
Disagree	475	41.3
Disagree strongly	308	26.8
Can't choose	13	1.1
No answer	9	0.8

Source: General Social Survey, National Opinion Research Center, University of Chicago

Table 3.31 Child Care as Government Responsibility, 2002

On the whole, do you think it should or should not be the government's responsibility to provide child care for everyone who wants it?

(number of respondents aged 18 or older and percent distribution by response, 2002)

	number of respondents	percent distribution
Total	**1,160**	**100.0%**
Definitely should be	145	12.5
Probably should be	268	23.1
Probably should not be	310	26.7
Definitely should not be	320	27.6
Can't choose	95	8.2
No answer	11	0.9

Source: General Social Survey, National Opinion Research Center, University of Chicago

Table 3.32 Number of Close Friends, 2002

How many other close friends do you have—apart from those at work, in your neighborhood, or family members? Think, for instance, of friends at clubs, church, or the like.

(number of respondents aged 18 or older and percent distribution by response, 2002)

	number of respondents	percent distribution
Total	**1,149**	**100.0%**
No other close friends	180	15.7
One	57	5.0
Two	99	8.6
Three	138	12.0
Four	88	7.7
Five to nine	251	21.8
10 to 19	191	16.6
20 or more	131	11.4
Don't know	4	0.3
No answer	10	0.9

Source: General Social Survey, National Opinion Research Center, University of Chicago

Table 3.33 Family and Friends Make Too Many Demands, 2002

Do you feel that your family, relatives, and/or friends make too many demands on you?

(number of respondents aged 18 or older and percent distribution by response, 2002)

	number of respondents	percent distribution
Total	**1,149**	**100.0%**
No, never	504	43.9
Yes, but seldom	282	24.5
Yes, sometimes	269	23.4
Yes, often	54	4.7
Yes, very often	27	2.3
Don't know	3	0.3
No answer	10	0.9

Source: General Social Survey, National Opinion Research Center, University of Chicago

Table 3.34 Trust in Others, 2002

To what extent do you agree or disagree with the following statements?

(number of respondents aged 18 or older and percent distribution by response, 2002)

	number of respondents	percent distribution
There are only a few people I can trust completely:		
Total	**1,149**	**100.0%**
Agree strongly	445	38.7
Agree	455	39.6
Neither agree nor disagree	106	9.2
Disagree	107	9.3
Strongly disagree	18	1.6
Can't choose	8	0.7
No answer	10	0.9
Most of the time you can be sure other people want the best for you:		
Total	**1,149**	**100.0**
Agree strongly	158	13.8
Agree	542	47.2
Neither agree nor disagree	268	23.3
Disagree	131	11.4
Strongly disagree	25	2.2
Can't choose	14	1.2
No answer	11	1.0
If you are not careful, other people will take advantage of you:		
Total	**1,149**	**100.0**
Agree strongly	280	24.4
Agree	514	44.7
Neither agree nor disagree	180	15.7
Disagree	143	12.4
Strongly disagree	12	1.0
Can't choose	9	0.8
No answer	11	1.0

Source: General Social Survey, National Opinion Research Center, University of Chicago

Table 3.35 Length of Time in Community, 2002

How long have you lived in the city, town, or local community where you live now?

(number of respondents aged 18 or older and percent distribution by response, 2002)

	number of respondents	percent distribution
Total	**1,149**	**100.0%**
Since before 1920	5	0.4
Since 1920–29	20	1.7
Since 1930–39	24	2.1
Since 1940–49	43	3.7
Since 1950–59	91	7.9
Since 1960–69	118	10.3
Since 1970–79	171	14.9
Since 1980–89	199	17.3
Since 1990–99	307	26.7
Since 2000 or later	152	13.2
Don't know	5	0.4
No answer	14	1.2

Source: General Social Survey, National Opinion Research Center, University of Chicago

Table 3.36 Ability to Improve Local Community, 2002

Suppose you wanted the local government to bring about some improvement in your local community. How likely is it that you would be able to do something about it?

(number of respondents aged 18 or older and percent distribution by response, 2002)

	number of respondents	percent distribution
Total	**1,149**	**100.0%**
Very likely	101	8.8
Somewhat likely	364	31.7
Not very likely	409	35.6
Not at all likely	186	16.2
Don't know	78	6.8
No answer	11	1.0

Source: General Social Survey, National Opinion Research Center, University of Chicago

International Social Survey Program 2002 Modules:

Women and Work

Another International Social Survey Program topical module included in the 2002 General Social Survey focused on women and work. Many other countries included the same topical module in their social surveys, allowing researchers to compare responses cross-nationally. Survey results for the United States show that Americans are overwhelmingly supportive of working women—not a surprising finding since working women are now the norm.

The majority of the public disagrees with the statement, "A man's job is to earn money; a woman's job is to look after the home and family." Fifty-seven percent of the public thinks both husband and wife should contribute to household income. Eighty-four percent agree that women should receive paid maternity leave when they have a baby. The 55 percent majority think families should receive financial benefits for childcare if both parents work.

The 63 percent majority of respondents to the General Social Survey think men ought to do a larger share of housework. Seventy-one percent think men should do more childcare. Forty percent of respondents say they do their fair share of household work, while 39 percent say they do more than their fair share and 17 percent admit to doing less. More than two-thirds of married respondents rarely or never argue about household chores.

Sixty-seven percent of the public "strongly agree" they have too much to do at home. Interestingly, a much smaller 41 percent strongly agree they have too much to do at work.

Table 3.37 Men's and Women's Roles, 1994 and 2002

Do you agree or disagree:

A man's job is to earn money; a woman's job is to look after the home and family.

(number of respondents aged 18 or older and percent distribution by response, 1994 and 2002)

	number of respondents	percent distribution
2002		
Total respondents	**1,171**	**100.0%**
Strongly agree	101	8.6
Agree	172	14.7
Neither agree nor disagree	276	23.6
Disagree/strongly disagree	608	51.9
Can't choose	13	1.1
No answer	1	0.1
1994		
Total respondents	**1,447**	**100.0**
Strongly agree	76	5.3
Agree	227	15.7
Neither agree nor disagree	271	18.7
Disagree/strongly disagree	840	58.1
Can't choose	8	0.6
No answer	25	1.7

Source: General Social Surveys, National Opinion Research Center, University of Chicago

Table 3.38 Men Concentrate Too Much on Work, 1994 to 2002

Do you agree or disagree:

Family life often suffers because men concentrate too much on their work.

(number of respondents aged 18 or older and percent distribution by response, 1994–2002)

	number of respondents	percent distribution
2002		
Total respondents	**908**	**100.0%**
Strongly agree	99	10.9
Agree	415	45.7
Neither agree nor disagree	108	11.9
Disagree	264	29.1
Strongly disagree	16	1.8
Can't choose	6	0.7
No answer	0	0.0
2000		
Total respondents	**1,877**	**100.0**
Strongly agree	209	11.1
Agree	877	46.7
Neither agree nor disagree	331	17.6
Disagree	361	19.2
Strongly disagree	34	1.8
Can't choose	43	2.3
No answer	22	1.2
1996		
Total respondents	**1,460**	**100.0**
Strongly agree	230	15.8
Agree	825	56.5
Neither agree nor disagree	169	11.6
Disagree	198	13.6
Strongly disagree	21	1.4
Can't choose	16	1.1
No answer	1	0.1
1994		
Total respondents	**1,447**	**100.0**
Strongly agree	122	8.4
Agree	695	48.0
Neither agree nor disagree	286	19.8
Disagree	243	16.8
Strongly disagree	41	2.8
Can't choose	33	2.3
No answer	27	1.9

Source: General Social Surveys, National Opinion Research Center, University of Chicago

Table 3.39 Single-Parent vs. Two-Parent Families, 1994 and 2002

Do you agree or disagree:
One parent can bring up a child
as well as two parents together.

(number of respondents aged 18 or older and percent distribution by response, 1994 and 2002)

	number of respondents	percent distribution
2002		
Total respondents	**1,171**	**100.0%**
Strongly agree	198	16.9
Agree	292	24.9
Neither agree nor disagree	143	12.2
Disagree	344	29.4
Strongly disagree	181	15.5
Can't choose	12	1.0
No answer	1	0.1
1994		
Total respondents	**1,447**	**100.0**
Strongly agree	124	8.6
Agree	387	26.7
Neither agree nor disagree	203	14.0
Disagree	542	37.5
Strongly disagree	159	11.0
Can't choose	10	0.7
No answer	22	1.5

Source: General Social Surveys, National Opinion Research Center, University of Chicago

Table 3.40 Living Together Outside of Marriage Is OK, 1994 to 2002

Do you agree or disagree:
It is all right for a couple to live together without intending to get married.

(number of respondents aged 18 or older and percent distribution by response, 1994–2002)

	number of respondents	percent distribution
2002		
Total respondents	**1,171**	**100.0%**
Strongly agree	188	16.1
Agree	348	29.7
Neither agree nor disagree	199	17.0
Disagree	217	18.5
Strongly disagree	201	17.2
Can't choose	17	1.5
No answer	1	0.1
1998		
Total respondents	**1,284**	**88.7**
Strongly agree	213	14.7
Agree	329	22.7
Neither agree nor disagree	258	17.8
Disagree	201	13.9
Strongly disagree	230	15.9
Can't choose	29	2.0
No answer	24	1.7
1994		
Total respondents	**1,447**	**100.0**
Strongly agree	140	9.7
Agree	447	30.9
Neither agree nor disagree	232	16.0
Disagree	357	24.7
Strongly disagree	228	15.8
Can't choose	18	1.2
No answer	25	1.7

Source: General Social Surveys, National Opinion Research Center, University of Chicago

Table 3.41 Couples Should Live Together before Marriage, 1994 to 2002

Do you agree or disagree:
It is all right for a couple to live together without intending to get married.

(number of respondents aged 18 or older and percent distribution by response, 1994–2002)

	number of respondents	percent distribution
2002		
Total respondents	**1,171**	**100.0%**
Strongly agree	240	20.5
Agree	312	26.6
Neither agree nor disagree	227	19.4
Disagree	215	18.4
Strongly disagree	159	13.6
Can't choose	17	1.5
No answer	1	0.1
1998		
Total respondents	**1,284**	**88.7**
Strongly agree	188	13.0
Agree	299	20.7
Neither agree nor disagree	329	22.7
Disagree	211	14.6
Strongly disagree	199	13.8
Can't choose	31	2.1
No answer	27	1.9
1994		
Total respondents	**1,447**	**100.0**
Strongly agree	141	9.7
Agree	330	22.8
Neither agree nor disagree	332	22.9
Disagree	383	26.5
Strongly disagree	213	14.7
Can't choose	25	1.7
No answer	23	1.6

Source: General Social Surveys, National Opinion Research Center, University of Chicago

Table 3.42 Divorce Is Best for Couples with Problems, 1994 and 2002

Do you agree or disagree:

Divorce is usually the best solution when a couple can't seem to work out their marriage problems.

(number of respondents aged 18 or older and percent distribution by response, 1994 and 2002)

	number of respondents	percent distribution
2002		
Total respondents	**1,171**	**100.0%**
Strongly agree	156	13.3
Agree	338	28.9
Neither agree nor disagree	233	19.9
Disagree	302	25.8
Strongly disagree	120	10.2
Can't choose	21	1.8
No answer	1	0.1
1994		
Total respondents	**1,447**	**100.0**
Strongly agree	126	8.7
Agree	548	37.9
Neither agree nor disagree	272	18.8
Disagree	334	23.1
Strongly disagree	112	7.7
Can't choose	33	2.3
No answer	22	1.5

Source: General Social Surveys, National Opinion Research Center, University of Chicago

Table 3.43 Paid Maternity Leave, 1994 and 2002

Do you agree or disagree:

Working women should receive paid maternity leave when they have a baby.

(number of respondents aged 18 or older and percent distribution by response, 1994 and 2002)

	number of respondents	percent distribution
2002		
Total respondents	**1,171**	**100.0%**
Strongly agree	571	48.8
Agree	411	35.1
Neither agree nor disagree	98	8.4
Disagree	56	4.8
Strongly disagree	19	1.6
Can't choose	15	1.3
No answer	1	0.1
1994		
Total respondents	**1,447**	**100.0**
Strongly agree	384	26.5
Agree	633	43.7
Neither agree nor disagree	148	10.2
Disagree	150	10.4
Strongly disagree	26	1.8
Can't choose	26	1.8
No answer	80	5.5

Source: General Social Surveys, National Opinion Research Center, University of Chicago

Table 3.44 Financial Benefits for Child Care, 1994 and 2002

Do you agree or disagree:
Families should receive financial benefits for child care when both parents work.

(number of respondents aged 18 or older and percent distribution by response, 1994 and 2002)

	number of respondents	percent distribution
2002		
Total respondents	**1,171**	**100.0%**
Strongly agree	333	28.4
Agree	312	26.6
Neither agree nor disagree	206	17.6
Disagree	216	18.4
Strongly disagree	74	6.3
Can't choose	29	2.5
No answer	1	0.1
1994		
Total respondents	**1,447**	**100.0**
Strongly agree	204	14.1
Agree	407	28.1
Neither agree nor disagree	261	18.0
Disagree	389	26.9
Strongly disagree	71	4.9
Can't choose	35	2.4
No answer	80	5.5

Source: General Social Surveys, National Opinion Research Center, University of Chicago

Table 3.45 How Couples Manage Money, 1994 and 2002

How do you and your spouse/partner organize the income that one or both of you receive? Please choose the option that comes closest.

(number of married or living-as-married respondents aged 18 or older and percent distribution by response, 1994 and 2002)

	number of respondents	percent distribution
2002		
Total respondents	**715**	**100.0%**
I manage all the money and give my partner his/her share	82	11.5
My partner manages all the money and gives me my share.	83	11.6
We pool all the money and each take out what we need.	366	51.2
We pool some of the money and keep the rest separate.	69	9.7
We each keep our own money separate.	86	12.0
Don't know	8	1.1
No answer	21	2.9
1994		
Total respondents	**835**	**100.0**
I manage all the money and give my partner his/her share	95	11.4
My partner manages all the money and gives me my share.	62	7.4
We pool all the money and each take out what we need.	483	57.8
We pool some of the money and keep the rest separate.	80	9.6
We each keep our own money separate.	76	9.1
Don't know	1	0.1
No answer	38	4.6

Source: General Social Surveys, National Opinion Research Center, University of Chicago

Table 3.46 Men Should Do More Housework, 2002

To what extent do you agree or disagree:

Men ought to do a larger share of household work than they do now.

(number of respondents aged 18 or older and percent distribution by response, 2002)

	number of respondents	percent distribution
Total respondents	**1,171**	**100.0%**
Strongly agree	250	21.3
Agree	482	41.2
Neither agree nor disagree	311	26.6
Disagree/strongly disagree	105	9.0
Can't choose	22	1.9
No answer	1	0.1

Source: General Social Survey, National Opinion Research Center, University of Chicago

Table 3.47 Men Should Do More Child Care, 2002

To what extent do you agree or disagree:

Men ought to do a larger share of child care than they do now.

(number of respondents aged 18 or older and percent distribution by response, 2002)

	number of respondents	percent distribution
Total respondents	**1,171**	**100.0%**
Strongly agree	294	25.1
Agree	534	45.6
Neither agree nor disagree	251	21.4
Disagree/Strongly disagree	74	6.3
Can't choose	17	1.5
No answer	1	0.1

Source: General Social Survey, National Opinion Research Center, University of Chicago

Table 3.48 Who Does the Household Chores, 2002

In your household who does the following things?

(number of married or living-as-married respondents aged 18 or older and percent distribution by response, 2002)

	number of respondents	percent distribution
Does the laundry:		
Total respondents	**707**	**100.0%**
Always me	170	24.0
Usually me	140	19.8
About equal or both together	187	26.4
Usually my spouse/partner	151	21.4
Always my spouse/partner	22	3.1
Is done by a third person	10	1.4
Can't choose	6	0.8
No answer	21	3.0
Makes small repairs around the house:		
Total respondents	**707**	**100.0**
Always me	142	20.1
Usually me	147	20.8
About equal or both together	129	18.2
Usually my spouse/partner	219	31.0
Always my spouse/partner	15	2.1
Is done by a third person	30	4.2
Can't choose	3	0.4
No answer	22	3.1
Cares for sick family members:		
Total respondents	**707**	**100.0**
Always me	129	18.2
Usually me	127	18.0
About equal or both together	292	41.3
Usually my spouse/partner	93	13.2
Always my spouse/partner	5	0.7
Is done by a third person	6	0.8
Can't choose	32	4.5
No answer	23	3.3

(continued)

	number of respondents	percent distribution
Shops for groceries:		
Total respondents	**707**	**100.0%**
Always me	138	19.5
Usually me	119	16.8
About equal or both together	290	41.0
Usually my spouse/partner	131	18.5
Always my spouse/partner	5	0.7
Is done by a third person	1	0.1
Can't choose	1	0.1
No answer	22	3.1
Does the household cleaning:		
Total respondents	**707**	**100.0**
Always me	128	18.1
Usually me	151	21.4
About equal or both together	243	34.4
Usually my spouse/partner	121	17.1
Always my spouse/partner	7	1.0
Is done by a third person	30	4.2
Can't choose	5	0.7
No answer	22	3.1
Prepares the meals:		
Total respondents	**707**	**100.0**
Always me	155	21.9
Usually me	152	21.5
About equal or both together	207	29.3
Usually my spouse/partner	157	22.2
Always my spouse/partner	9	1.3
Is done by a third person	3	0.4
Can't choose	2	0.3
No answer	22	3.1

Source: General Social Survey, National Opinion Research Center, University of Chicago

Table 3.49 How Much Time Spent on Household Work, 2002

On average, how many hours a week do you personally spend on household work, not including child care and leisure time activities?

(number of married or living-as-married respondents aged 18 or older and percent distribution by response, 2002)

	number of respondents	percent distribution
Total respondents	**707**	**100.0%**
Fewer than 10	380	53.7
10 to 19	185	26.2
20 to 29	63	8.9
30 to 39	28	4.0
40 to 49	15	2.1
50 to 59	7	1.0
60 to 69	3	0.4
70 to 79	1	0.1
80 or more hours	1	0.1
Don't know	2	0.3
No answer	22	3.1

Source: General Social Survey, National Opinion Research Center, University of Chicago

Table 3.50 How Much Time Spouse Spends on Household Work, 2002

And what about your spouse/partner? On average, how many hours a week does he/she spend on household work, not including child care and leisure time activities?

(number of married or living-as-married respondents aged 18 or older and percent distribution by response, 2002)

	number of respondents	percent distribution
Total respondents	**707**	**100.0%**
Fewer than 10	427	60.4
10 to 19	148	20.9
20 to 29	61	8.6
30 to 39	21	3.0
40 to 49	14	2.0
50 to 59	2	0.3
60 to 69	2	0.3
70 to 79	1	0.1
80 or more hours	2	0.3
Don't know	4	0.6
No answer	25	3.5

Source: General Social Survey, National Opinion Research Center, University of Chicago

Table 3.51 Sharing of Household Work, 2002

Which of the following best applies to the sharing of household work between you and your spouse / partner?

(number of married or living-as-married respondents aged 18 or older and percent distribution by response, 2002)

	number of respondents	percent distribution
Total respondents	**707**	**100.0%**
I do much more than my fair share of the household work	139	19.7
I do a bit more than my fair share of the household work	136	19.2
I do roughly my fair share of the household work	283	40.0
I do a bit less than my fair share of the household work	87	12.3
I do much less than my fair share of the household work	35	5.0
Don't know	3	0.4
No answer	24	3.4

Source: General Social Survey, National Opinion Research Center, University of Chicago

Table 3.52 Disagreement about Household Work, 2002

How often do you and your spouse/partner disagree about the sharing of household work?

(number of married or living-as-married respondents aged 18 or older and percent distribution by response, 2002)

	number of respondents	percent distribution
Total respondents	**707**	**100.0%**
Several times a week	47	6.6
Several times a month	75	10.6
Several times a year	61	8.6
Less often/rarely	268	37.9
Never	211	29.8
Can't choose	22	3.1
No answer	23	3.3

Source: General Social Survey, National Opinion Research Center, University of Chicago

Table 3.53 Decisions about Childrearing, 2002

Who usually makes / made the decisions about how to bring up your children?

(number of married or living-as-married respondents aged 18 or older and percent distribution by response, 2002)

	number of respondents	percent distribution
Total respondents	**707**	**100.0%**
Mostly me	81	11.5
Mostly my spouse/partner	44	6.2
Sometimes me/sometimes my spouse/partner	102	14.4
We decide together	305	43.1
Someone else	6	0.8
Does not apply	145	20.5
No answer	24	3.4

Source: General Social Survey, National Opinion Research Center, University of Chicago

Table 3.54 Who Makes Household Decisions, 2002

When you and your spouse / partner make decisions about the following, who has the final say?

(number of married or living-as-married respondents aged 18 or older and percent distribution by response, 2002)

	number of respondents	percent distribution
Choosing shared weekend activities:		
Total respondents	**707**	**100.0%**
Mostly me	99	14.0
Mostly my spouse/partner	69	9.8
Sometimes me/sometimes my spouse/partner	207	29.3
We decide together	302	42.7
Someone else	4	0.6
Don't know	1	0.1
No answer	25	3.5
Buying major things for the home:		
Total respondents	**707**	**100.0**
Mostly me	116	16.4
Mostly my spouse/partner	92	13.0
Sometimes me/sometimes my spouse/partner	120	17.0
We decide together	350	49.5
Someone else	4	0.6
Don't know	2	0.3
No answer	23	3.3

Source: General Social Survey, National Opinion Research Center, University of Chicago

Table 3.55 Too Much to Do at Home, 2002

To what extent do you agree or disagree:
There are so many things to do at home, I often run out of time before I get them all done.

(number of respondents aged 18 or older and percent distribution by response, 2002)

	number of respondents	percent distribution
Total respondents	**1,171**	**100.0%**
Strongly agree	384	32.8
Agree	399	34.1
Neither agree nor disagree	170	14.5
Disagree	153	13.1
Strongly disagree	46	3.9
Can't choose	16	1.4
No answer	3	0.3

Source: General Social Survey, National Opinion Research Center, University of Chicago

Table 3.56 Stress of Home Life, 2002

To what extent do you agree or disagree:

My life at home is rarely stressful.

(number of respondents aged 18 or older and percent distribution by response, 2002)

	number of respondents	percent distribution
Total	**1,171**	**100.0%**
Strongly agree	175	14.9
Agree	383	32.7
Neither agree nor disagree	174	14.9
Disagree	309	26.4
Strongly disagree	114	9.7
Can't choose	14	1.2
No answer	2	0.2

Source: General Social Survey, National Opinion Research Center, University of Chicago

Table 3.57 Too Much to Do at Work, 2002

To what extent do you agree or disagree:

There are so many things to do at work, I often run out of time before I get them all done.

(number of respondents aged 18 or older and percent distribution by response, 2002)

	number of respondents	percent distribution
Total	**1,171**	**100.0%**
Strongly agree	203	17.3
Agree	274	23.4
Neither agree nor disagree	213	18.2
Disagree	252	21.5
Strongly disagree	60	5.1
Can't choose	159	13.6
No answer	10	0.9

Source: General Social Survey, National Opinion Research Center, University of Chicago

Table 3.58 Stress of Work Life, 2002

To what extent do you agree or disagree:

My job is rarely stressful.

(number of respondents aged 18 or older and percent distribution by response, 2002)

	number of respondents	percent distribution
Total respondents	**1,171**	**100.0%**
Strongly agree	73	6.2
Agree	249	21.3
Neither agree nor disagree	198	16.9
Disagree	329	28.1
Strongly disagree	151	12.9
Can't choose	160	13.7
No answer	11	0.9

Source: General Social Survey, National Opinion Research Center, University of Chicago

Table 3.59 Work/Family Stresses in Past Three Months, 2002

How often has each of the following happened to you during the past three months?

(number of respondents aged 18 or older and percent distribution by response, 2002)

	number of respondents	percent distribution
I have come home from work too tired to do the chores which need to be done:		
Total respondents	**1,171**	**100.0%**
Several times a week	253	21.6
Several times a month	216	18.4
Once or twice	302	25.8
Never	109	9.3
Doesn't apply/no job	277	23.7
Don't know	7	0.6
No answer	7	0.6
It has been difficult for me to fulfill my family responsibilities because of the amount of time I spent on my job:		
Total respondents	**1,171**	**100.0**
Several times a week	94	8.0
Several times a month	134	11.4
Once or twice	261	22.3
Never	353	30.1
Doesn't apply/no job	313	26.7
Don't know	6	0.5
No answer	10	0.9
I have arrived at work too tired to function well because of the household work I had done:		
Total respondents	**1,171**	**100.0**
Several times a week	27	2.3
Several times a month	48	4.1
Once or twice	244	20.8
Never	524	44.7
Doesn't apply/no job	318	27.2
Don't know	4	0.3
No answer	6	0.5
I have found it difficult to concentrate at work because of my family responsibilities.		
Total respondents	**1,171**	**100.0**
Several times a week	31	2.6
Several times a month	60	5.1
Once or twice	279	23.8
Never	464	39.6
Doesn't apply/no job	328	28.0
Don't know	4	0.3
No answer	5	0.4

Source: General Social Survey, National Opinion Research Center, University of Chicago

Table 3.60 How Happy Are You, 2002

If you were to consider your life in general, how happy or unhappy would you say you are, on the whole?

(number of respondents aged 18 or older and percent distribution by response, 2002)

	number of respondents	percent distribution
Total respondents	**1,171**	**100.0%**
Completely happy	141	12.0
Very happy	510	43.6
Fairly happy	391	33.4
Neither happy nor unhappy	69	5.9
Fairly unhappy	32	2.7
Very unhappy	16	1.4
Completely unhappy	1	0.1
Can't choose	7	0.6
No answer	4	0.3

Source: General Social Survey, National Opinion Research Center, University of Chicago

Table 3.61 Satisfaction with Job, 2002

All things considered, how satisfied are you with your (main) job?

(number of working respondents aged 18 or older and percent distribution by response, 2002)

	number of respondents	percent distribution
Total workers	**874**	**100.0%**
Completely satisfied	127	14.5
Very satisfied	289	33.1
Fairly satisfied	264	30.2
Neither satisfied nor dissatisfied	53	6.1
Fairly dissatisfied	47	5.4
Very dissatisfied	29	3.3
Completely dissatisfied	11	1.3
Can't choose	45	5.1
No answer	9	1.0

Source: General Social Survey, National Opinion Research Center, University of Chicago

Table 3.62 Satisfaction with Family Life, 2002

All things considered, how satisfied are you with your family life?

(number of respondents aged 18 or older and percent distribution by response, 2002)

	number of respondents	percent distribution
Total respondents	**1,171**	**100.0%**
Completely satisfied	265	22.6
Very satisfied	467	39.9
Fairly satisfied	286	24.4
Neither satisfied nor dissatisfied	70	6.0
Fairly dissatisfied	31	2.6
Very dissatisfied	20	1.7
Completely dissatisfied	9	0.8
Can't choose	19	1.6
No answer	4	0.3

Source: General Social Survey, National Opinion Research Center, University of Chicago

Table 3.63 Should Wives Work Before Having Children, 2002

Do you think that women should work outside the home full-time, part-time, or not at all, when a couple has not yet had a child?

(number of respondents aged 18 or older and percent distribution by response, 2002)

	number of respondents	percent distribution
Total respondents	**1,171**	**100.0%**
Work full-time	841	71.8
Work part-time	97	8.3
Stay at home	22	1.9
Can't choose	206	17.6
No answer	5	0.4

Source: General Social Survey, National Opinion Research Center, University of Chicago

Table 3.64 Both Husband and Wife Should Contribute to Household Income, 2002

Do you agree or disagree:
Both the husband and the wife should contribute to the household income?

(number of respondents aged 18 or older and percent distribution by response, 2002)

	number of respondents	percent distribution
Total respondents	**1,171**	**100.0%**
Strongly agree	341	29.1
Agree	327	27.9
Neither agree nor disagree	369	31.5
Disagree/strongly disagree	109	9.3
Can't choose	23	2.0
No answer	2	0.2

Source: General Social Survey, National Opinion Research Center, University of Chicago

Table 3.65 Which Spouse Has Higher Income, 2002

Considering all sources of income, between you and your spouse / partner, who has the higher income?

(number of married or living-as-married respondents aged 18 or older and percent distribution by response, 2002)

	number of respondents	percent distribution
Total respondents	**707**	**100.0%**
My spouse/partner has no income	65	9.2
I have a much higher income	127	18.0
I have a higher income	100	14.1
We have about the same income	75	10.6
My spouse/partner has a higher income	198	28.0
My spouse/partner has a much higher income	70	9.9
I have no income	29	4.1
Don't know	18	2.5
No answer	25	3.5

Source: General Social Survey, National Opinion Research Center, University of Chicago

General Social Survey Methodology and Contact Information

Sample Type

National area probability sample of noninstitutionalized adults. Black oversamples in 1982 and 1987. In 1993, there was a split-frame experiment in which half the cases were drawn from NORC's 1980 sampling frame and half from the new 1990 sampling frame.

Sample Size

About 1,500 for the first 19 surveys, increased to 3,000 when the survey became biennial in 1994.

Data Collection Method

In-person interview.

Average Length of Interview

About 90 minutes.

Response Rates

1975—76 percent	1983—79 percent	1989—78 percent	1994—78 percent
1976—75 percent	1984—79 percent	1990—74 percent	1996—76 percent
1977—77 percent	1985—79 percent	1991—78 percent	1998—76 percent
1978—74 percent	1986—76 percent	1992*	2000—70 percent
1980—76 percent	1987—75 percent	1993—82 percent	2002—70 percent
1982—78 percent	1988—77 percent		

*While there was no 1992 GSS, there was a special survey in which respondents to the 1991 GSS were re-contacted by mail or telephone, with a response rate of 84 percent.

Key Findings

As a trend study, the GSS does not have "findings" as such because the data collection is ongoing and the purpose of the data analysis is to study ongoing social trends. Certain important trends the GSS has noted have been a dramatic increase over the past thirty years in support for racial equality and integration, and a steady increase in support for civil liberties.

Please Send Us Your Research

We would greatly appreciate it if you would send us references to and, if possible, copies of your research using the GSS. We are interested in books, articles, conference papers, and reports. Also, we would like to hear about research by students. We want to include master's theses and dissertations.

Contact Information

Tom W. Smith, General Social Survey, National Opinion Research Center, 1155 East 60th St. Chicago, IL 60637; e-mail: smitht@norcmail.uchicago.edu

Index